Truth Revealed

Truth Revealed

The Message of the Gospel
of John—Then And Now

Robert P. Vande Kappelle

WIPF & STOCK · Eugene, Oregon

TRUTH REVEALED
The Message of the Gospel of John—Then And Now

Copyright © 2014 Robert P. Vande Kappelle. All rights reserved. Except for brief quotations in critical publications or reviews, no part of this book may be reproduced in any manner without prior written permission from the publisher. Write: Permissions. Wipf and Stock Publishers, 199 W. 8th Ave., Suite 3, Eugene, OR 97401.

Wipf and Stock
An Imprint of Wipf and Stock Publishers
199 W. 8th Ave., Suite 3
Eugene, OR 97401

www.wipfandstock.com

ISBN 13: 978-1-4982-0220-6

Manufactured in the U.S.A.   10/09/2014

Unless otherwise noted, Bible quotations are from the *New Revised Standard Version of the Bible*, copyright © 1989 by the Division of Christian Education of the National Council of the Churches of Christ in the United States of America. Used by permission.

In Memoriam

Dedicated to Bruce Manning Metzger
(1914–2007)

mentor, friend, and biblical scholar par excellence

Jesus said to Pilate:

"For this I was born, and for this I came into the world, to testify to the truth."

—JOHN 18:37

Pilate asked: "What is truth?"

—JOHN 18:38

Jesus said: "I am the way, and the truth, and the life."

—JOHN 14:6

Jesus prayed for his disciples:

"Sanctify them in the truth; your word is truth."

—JOHN 17:17

Jesus said: "If you continue in my word, you are truly my disciples; and you will know the truth, and the truth will set you free."

—JOHN 8:32

Contents

Preface | ix
Acknowledgments | xvii

Introduction | 1

Part I – Beginnings

CHAPTER 1: John's Prologue (John 1:1–18) | 25

    Essay 1: The Cultural, Religious, and Intellectual Background of John's Gospel | 41

Part II – The Public Ministry of Jesus, Phase One

CHAPTER 2: The Initial Revelation of Jesus: The First Witnesses (John 1:19–51) | 47

    Essay 2: John's Jesus–Then and Now | 54

CHAPTER 3: Belief and Disbelief: The Early Signs and Discourses (John 2:1—4:54) | 63

    Essay 3: John's Dualistic Imagery | 84

Part III – The Public Ministry of Jesus, Phase Two

CHAPTER 4: Jesus, the Sabbath, and Exodus Imagery (John 5:1—6:71) | 91

    Essay 4: Jesus and "the Jews" in John's Gospel | 108

CHAPTER 5: Jesus and Jewish Festivals: Part One (John 7:1—8:59) | 112

    Essay 5: The Johannine "I Am" Sayings | 124

CHAPTER 6:   Jesus and Jewish Festivals: Part Two (John 9:1—10:42) | 128

        Essay 6:   The Paradoxical Nature of Faith | 141

CHAPTER 7:   Scenes Preparatory to the Glorification of Jesus (John 11:1—12:50) | 147

        Essay 7:   John's Realized Eschatology | 159

Part IV – The Private Ministry of Jesus

CHAPTER 8:   Jesus' Farewell: Part One (John 13:1—14:31) | 165

        Essay 8:   John's Sacramental Language | 183

CHAPTER 9:   Jesus' Farewell: Part Two (John 15:1—17:26) | 187

        Essay 9:   John's Use of Misunderstanding and Irony as Literary Techniques | 203

Part V – The Glorification of Jesus

CHAPTER 10:   Jesus' Passion (John 18:1—19:42) | 213

        Essay 10:   John's Perspective on the Passion of Jesus | 234

CHAPTER 11:   Jesus' Resurrection (John 20:1–31) | 239

        Essay 11:   Women as Witnesses in John's Gospel | 251

Part VI – New Beginnings

CHAPTER 12:   John's Epilogue (John 21:1–25) | 259

        Essay 12:   John's Ecclesiology: Leadership Models in John's Gospel | 266

Epilogue | 273
Appendix: The Relation of John's Gospel to the Epistles and to Revelation | 279

Bibliography | 289
Subject/Name Index | 293

Preface

CHRISTIANITY, THE PREDOMINANT, MOST accessible, and most diffuse of the world's religions, has arguably inspired the world's greatest art, music, and architecture. It has also inspired its most memorable speeches, sermons, and lectures; its most elevated theology and philosophy; and its most elegant rhetoric and prose. At the heart of this movement that has captured the imagination of people around the globe is its scripture, known as the Holy Bible, a library of books divided into Testaments, one Jewish and the other Christian. The latter comprises twenty-seven books, consisting of four gospels, one history, thirteen letters attributed to Paul of Tarsus, eight additional writings known as General Epistles, and an apocalyptic work called Revelation.

The Bible, the all-time best-selling book, is the most read, best known, most published, and most widely disseminated book in the world. Its value is inestimable, for it has single-handedly changed the course of world history, guiding empires, influencing legal systems, and impacting the lives of untold millions around the globe. Columbus took a copy to the New World, Charles Lindbergh stowed a copy in the cramped quarters of the Spirit of St. Louis on his epic trans-Atlantic flight, and astronaut James Irwin, who carried a copy on his moon walk, became the first person to quote from the Bible while on the moon: "I will lift up my eyes unto the hills, from whence cometh my help" (Ps. 121:1, KJV).

If the New Testament represents the crown jewels of Christianity, the Gospel of John is its "pearl of great price," the most beloved, most read, most memorized, most quoted, most distinctive, most memorable, most debated book in its canon. It contains the most familiar verse in the Bible (John 3:16), the shortest verse ("Jesus wept," 11:34, RSV), the most elegant description of Jesus, the most intriguing discourses of Jesus, the most compelling of his miracles, the loftiest theology, the most moving prayer of Jesus, the most dramatic account of his trial, the most poignant account of his crucifixion, and the most memorable account of his resurrection. While it includes no Sermon on the Mount, it does contain memorable farewell discourses, including passages read at Christian funerals, such as the familiar line: "In my Father's house are many mansions" (14:2, KJV). The Fourth Gospel presents unforgettable characters that dot the landscape of the Christian imagination: Lazarus, who was raised from the dead; Nicodemus, the ruler of the Jews who comes to Jesus by night; the Samaritan woman, a person of questionable reputation to whom Jesus gave "living water"; Thomas, the doubting disciple who confesses Jesus to be God; Mary Magdalene, the first witness to the resurrection; the man born blind, whose heroic confession leads to his expulsion by the Jewish authorities; and the unnamed Beloved Disciple, an enigmatic figure who reclines next to Jesus at the Last Supper and claims to be the author of John's Gospel.

Had the Beloved Disciple been an eyewitness of Jesus and one of his most intimate friends, then surely John's Gospel becomes the most accurate and reliable of the gospels. Yet when the members of the scholarly think tank known as the Jesus Seminar presented their findings regarding the authenticity of the words of Jesus recorded in the four gospels, they concluded that less than 20 percent of the words attributed to Jesus in the entire gospel tradition were actually spoken by him, meaning that more than 80 percent were not. Of words attributed to Jesus by John, only one line was deemed authentic: the statement in 4:44 about a prophet having no honor in his own country, a parenthetical editorial remark. By this standard, the Fourth Evangelist is not credited with having recorded a single authentic saying of Jesus. Despite the extremity of this judgment, modern readers can take comfort in the words of Bishop John Shelby Spong, himself a member of the Jesus Seminar, who describes John as being "the least literal, but the most profoundly true of the four canonical gospel writers," noting that this Gospel "captures the essence of the Jesus experience more profoundly than any other part of the New Testament."[1]

The product of a marginal community, the Gospel of John presents a perspective of Jesus that fueled heresies and spawned some of the fiercest doctrinal conflicts in Christian history. Yet if the Christian scriptures were to be reduced to a single text, the Gospel of John would sufficiently provide its theology, anthropology, Christology, soteriology, and

---

1. Spong, *Re-Claiming the Bible*, 385.

eschatology. The Fourth Gospel promises the sky—abundant life, eternal life, truth—and it delivers!

The notion of truth is foundational to John's Gospel, as it is to Western civilization. The cultural ancestors of Western thought, the Greeks, esteemed truth above all else. The holy grail of their philosophical pursuit was the True, the Good, and the Beautiful. Modern Americans also prize truth, for truth represents core values such as dependability and reliability, the bedrock of America's system of justice and jurisprudence. Few sayings attributed to Jesus are better known or more widely quoted than the words "You shall know the truth, and the truth shall make you free" (8:32). Those memorable words are prominently incised on the U.S. Supreme Court building in Washington, DC. Though cherished in Western culture, they come not from a Greek philosopher but from a Jewish sage, whose mission was not rooted in the Hellenism of Greece and Rome but in the Hebraic worldview of Jewish Torah, much closer in spirit to Moses than Socrates. In the context of John 8, truth is not an abstract concept but a relational one, rooted in discipleship, as 8:31 makes clear: "If you continue in my word, you are truly my disciples; and you will know the truth . . ."

The concept of truth is central to John, as a survey of the Gospel makes clear:[2]

1. In 1:14, perhaps John's most distinctive teaching—the incarnation of the eternal Word (Logos) in human flesh —we discover that Jesus, the eternal Word, is "full of grace and truth." In 1:17, Jesus is described as bringer of truth;

2. In 3:21, "those who do what is true" refers to those who live by God's standards, as revealed in the Torah and now through Jesus Christ;

3. In 14:6, the sixth of the "I Am" sayings in John, Jesus speaks of himself as "the truth" and therefore as the only way to God the Father;

4. In 16:13, Jesus refers to the Holy Spirit as the "Spirit of truth," for the Spirit's work will guide the community "into all the truth," a reference to the Spirit's continuing work of revelation initiated by Jesus (16:14–16);

---

2. Scholars regularly refer to the Gospel of John simply as "John," a practice I follow frequently. This usage, however, conveys no implication concerning the identity of the author.

5. In Jesus' prayer on behalf of his disciples, he requests their consecration: "Sanctify them in the truth; your word is truth" (17:17). This sanctification accompanies adherence to truth (17:19);

6. At his trial, in his conversation with Pilate, Jesus declares that his purpose in life is to witness to the truth: "For this I was born, and for this I came into the world, to testify to the truth. Everyone who belongs to the truth listens to my voice" (18:37). Pilate responds with the Gospel's most memorable question: "What is truth?," a question found only in John's Gospel. And strangely, Jesus does not provide Pilate an answer. The reason is obvious to readers of the Fourth Gospel, for the answer has already been provided in the "farewell discourses," when Jesus declared: "I am the way, and the truth, and the life; no one comes to the Father except through me" (14:6). This threefold perspective, how Jesus can simultaneously be "way," "truth," and "life," is central to John's purpose. Truth, for Christians in the Johannine community and for Christians ever since, is not an abstraction but a person—Jesus Christ—who embodies a way of living, thinking, and believing that enables believers to live life abundantly as children of God. That is the meaning and the message of the Gospel of John—then and now.

The central theme of the New Testament is a person, Jesus of Nazareth, a wandering preacher of the first century who has changed the course of history. Whether Christian or not, all who live in the Western world have been influenced by the teachings and life of this individual. Early disciples envisioned Jesus as the climactic historical figure, the Messiah who brought the long-awaited messianic Kingdom of God, a rule that by ending evil and suffering would usher in an age of bliss. Later followers would view Jesus' role as pivotal, representing the midpoint of history. This view is maintained by Ernst Renan, famous nineteenth-century scholar, who wrote: "All history is incomprehensible without Christ"; by Napoleon, who confessed toward the end of his life: "This man, Jesus, vanished for eighteen hundred years, still holds the character of men as in a vise"; and by H. G. Wells, who once declared: "I am an historian. I am not a believer. But I must confess, as an historian, that this penniless preacher from Galilee is irresistibly the center of history."

The Gospel of John, the best-known and most beloved of gospels, has been the source of delight and inspiration but also of great vexation to the world's biblical scholars, who disagree more sharply over the background and interpretation of this Gospel than over almost any other biblical subject. John is at once the simplest of the gospels and yet the most difficult to interpret. On account of its simplicity and its profundity, the Fourth Gospel has been likened to a pool shallow enough for a wading child yet deep enough for a swimming elephant, its message clear as a mountain stream yet murky as the ocean depths.

The Fourth Gospel, named for its place of order in the New Testament as well as for its traditional date of publication, arrived last among the canonical gospels, at least in its final literary form. Dubbed by the second-century theologian Clement of Alexandria the "spiritual gospel," John was highly valued in ancient times and was perhaps the single most influential New Testament book in fashioning early Christian dogma. Because its depiction of Jesus, its doctrinal peculiarities, and its unique point of view are so different from the first three gospels, called Synoptic on account of their similarities, John's Gospel was, until recently, largely overlooked by critical scholars. The first half of the twentieth century brought a renewed interest in the Fourth Gospel, generated by controversy over the Gospel's authorship, place of origin, theological affirmations, and historical value. Since then numerous biblical scholars, ranging across the theological and critical spectrum, have devoted their entire scholarly career to the study of John's Gospel, specializing in topics such as Johannine theology and literary style.

My experience as biblical scholar and professor of religious studies at an undergraduate liberal arts college has made it difficult to specialize in this manner, for such institutions value instruction over research and generalists over specialists. However, despite this emphasis on breadth of teaching, my schedule has allowed me to offer at least one survey course in biblical studies each semester, in addition to courses on Romans, Revelation, and biblical Wisdom literature during the January Intersession. My academic career has led me finally to the study of the Fourth Gospel, the central volume in the Johannine corpus (comprising also the epistles of John and the book of Revelation), a literary collection produced by an assortment of Christian congregations during the late first century known as the Johannine community.[3]

Focus on the Gospel of John brings me full-circle, for it was during my formative years as the son of missionary parents in Costa Rica that I

---

3. For additional information on the Johannine corpus and the historical development of the Johannine community, see the Appendix: "The Relation of John's Gospel to the Epistles and to Revelation."

was introduced to this Gospel, with its dual emphasis on a loving God who desires the salvation of the world and its unique presentation of Jesus as fully God and fully man. The Latin America Mission, the missionary organization with whom my parents served for thirty-three years in the mid-twentieth century, emphasized biblical literacy, creating a publishing house to distribute literature that promoted its evangelistic endeavors. When free correspondence courses were created to disseminate biblical perspectives, the Fourth Gospel had a prominent role. I was encouraged to take those courses, and I did so willingly, for my love affair with scripture began at an early age. That encounter with the Gospel of John contributed to my religious identity, including my understanding of God, the cosmos, and the Christian life, as well as my destiny as a child of God.

Because of its intuitively accessible symbolism, often presented simplistically through contrasting ways of knowing, living, and believing, the Fourth Gospel, of all the New Testament writings, admirably serves evangelistic, didactic, apologetic, and polemical purposes. However, the Gospel serves a greater purpose, aligned more closely with that of early Christians. Whereas Christians today often approach the gospels for facts about God, Jesus, and the early church, facts that indicate *what* we should believe, early Christians developed the gospels to figure out *how* they should live in their particular Christian community, to understand God's counter-cultural "rule" (traditionally called the Kingdom of God)[4] from their particular community's perspective, and to interpret the significance of Jesus as he was to be understood in their own community. Communities produced the gospels to help them train their own and future generations in a particular way of living. In this way, the writing process itself became a formative process, and the gospels became formative documents. Early on, therefore, the emphasis was less on the details of Jesus' life and ministry and more on their significance for daily life. And that's how one should read and study John, because this Gospel raises the formative process to a higher level than do the Synoptic Gospels.

---

4. The Greek word *basileus*, normally translated as "kingdom," is more accurately translated as "realm." A kingdom is a place, but a realm is more of an experience or a level of consciousness and hence communicates more closely what the Fourth Evangelist is attempting to portray.

Distinctive Features

My goal in writing this book is to produce a commentary on the Gospel of John that addresses the interests and needs of a general Christian audience, providing guidelines for understanding the message of this ancient work and its application to twenty-first century readers. *Truth Revealed* is not an exegetical commentary, for it does not offer verse-by-verse analysis of the text. Neither is it a textual study, in which a scholar makes a case for a preferred reading. Instead it offers perspective on specific topics that arise as one follows the narrative, always with an eye on the big picture, namely, guidance for daily living.

This study divides the Gospel of John into twelve units, each discussed as a whole, providing biblical, literary, theological, historical, and textual comments where appropriate. My goal is to proceed from text to understanding and from understanding to application. To that end, each chapter includes the following features:

1. overview of the passage;
2. key verse(s) of the passage;
3. central theme of the passage;
4. important symbol(s) in the passage;
5. learning objectives for the passage;
6. outline of the passage;
7. analysis of the passage;
8. an essay related to the passage, and
9. questions to ponder.

Acknowledgements

THIS BOOK IS THE eighth of my scholarly career, a number that in the Bible is said to represent new beginnings, the day of resurrection (the eighth day), and Jesus the Christ, the central figure in God's new covenant with humanity. This study on John, a keystone of the Bible and a cornerstone of biblical theology, marks my transition from academia to retirement.

Writing *Truth Revealed*, like *Hope Revealed* (my commentary on the book of Revelation), has renewed my love for scripture, challenged previous conclusions and interpretations, and convinced me that the Gospel of John, properly understood, speaks as profoundly to the present as it did to the past.

My textual analysis relied on commentaries written by C. K. Barrett, Raymond E. Brown, Rudolph Bultmann, D. A. Carson, C. H. Dodd, Edwyn C. Hoskyns, Leon Morris, and N. T. Wright. I acknowledge particular indebtedness to R. Alan Culpepper, Gail R. O'Day, and Ben Witherington, resonating most with the latter's perspective in *John's Wisdom*, indispensable for scholars, preachers, and students alike. My literary and theological analysis, particularly material in the essays found at the end of each chapter, is indebted to seminal Johannine studies written by Paul N. Anderson, John Ashton, R. Alan Culpepper, Demetrius Dumm, A. E. Harvey, Craig R. Koester, Robert Kysar, Carol J. Miller, Gerard S. Sloyan, and D. Moody Smith.[1]

Finally, this commentary could not have been written without the editorial assistance of Mary Ann Johnson and the ongoing encouragement and support of my wife Susan and of my colleagues at Washington & Jefferson College: Dan Stinson, David Novitsky, and Walt Weaver. I dedicate this book to the memory of Bruce M. Metzger, mentor, friend, and biblical scholar par excellence.

---

1. Their works are listed in the bibliography.

Introduction

DURING THE SECOND CENTURY the books that comprise the New Testament began to impact the emerging Christian community as a whole. From among a broad range of sources including letters, gospels, collections of saying of Jesus, acts of various apostles, manuals, homilies, and apocalypses, Christian leaders began to decide which were canonical, meaning which were essential for Christians to read and revere. Four gospels were selected (Matthew, Mark, Luke, and John) as well as letters attributed to Paul, James, Peter, John and other early Christian leaders; the book of Acts (a historical perspective on the early church associated with Luke); and the book of Revelation.[1] These writings were produced by Christians in different social, cultural, and geographical settings, representing diverse expressions of Christian living, ethical values, social organization, perspectives of Christ, sacramental practices, and leadership styles. It might come as a surprise to think of such diversity in early Christianity, but scholars agree that diversity was greater in early Christianity than in contemporary Christianity. While it is customary to assume that Christianity began as something unified and cohesive, that is not the case. Diversity in Christianity preceded the uniformity of later generations.

In the early days of the church, before there was a New Testament or even gospels, people learned about Jesus and God's alternative kingdom from wandering prophets and teachers who moved from village to village spreading the good news. Some of these evangelists might have had a direct encounter with Jesus, numbering among his actual disciples and therefore valued as apostolic eyewitnesses. Others might have known Jesus indirectly, perhaps having had limited contact with him,

---

1. The canonical process is considered to have been finalized in the year 367, at least in the East, when the list of the twenty-seven books of the New Testament appeared in an Easter letter sent by Bishop Athanasius of Alexandria.

while the majority probably had only a visionary experience of Jesus that fueled their passion. Most of the early believers were probably (1) *visionary Christians*. Before there were written gospels, people relied upon orally communicated information for their knowledge of Jesus and the Christian life. Certainly some of the tradition concerning Jesus, including words spoken in his name, were authentic, but many deeds and words attributed to Jesus actually came from local leaders and wandering prophets, who spoke in Jesus' name and with his authority because they were believed to have Jesus' Spirit within them. Their words came directly from Jesus but in a different way, not from the historical figure, but from the divine inspiration begun by his presence and maintained charismatically. Ultimately it was believed that all the teachings came from God, through Jesus, through the Spirit, to the believers, and to the world.

Not everyone heard in the same manner the story about Jesus and God's rule, however. Some, like the Thessalonians to whom Paul wrote or like the Asian Christians to whom John of Patmos wrote the book of Revelation, assumed they were living in the end-times, when Jesus would return from the sky and bring judgment to the world. These (2) *apocalyptic Christians* eagerly awaited the final apocalypse that would cause evil to end and bring God's Kingdom into physical reality.

Others, perhaps more philosophically or ethically inclined, may have expected a new wisdom from above, through a sage carrying God's wisdom for a new age. These (3) *wisdom Christians*, building on the Israelite Wisdom tradition found in Proverbs and in deuterocanonical works such as Sirach or the Wisdom of Solomon, were particularly attracted to the parables and discourses of Jesus and of later Christian sages who interpreted Jesus as the Wisdom of God. In this pre-gospel period, some participants had a school-like concern, focusing on the wisdom sayings of Jesus and elaborating them with accounts that were applicable to different circumstances. These pedagogical Christians valued the process of elaborating sayings as instrumental in educating the young as well as in making converts and perpetuating tradition.

Yet another group was attracted to Jesus and the Christian movement through the filter of healing. In an age when medicine was expensive and unreliable, people interpreted miraculous healing as a sign of God's presence, or, at least, as sign of an intervening divine power. Common people in particular were persuaded by healing miracles. The Jewish lens correlated healing with the prophetic tradition. Likewise, Greeks and Romans had traditions about the god Asclepius who could heal the sick, so when people heard the stories of miracles by Jesus and his followers, some became (4) *healing Christians*, interpreting miracles within their own cultural frame.

Interestingly, all four approaches, emphasizing charismatic/prophetic, apocalyptic, wisdom, and healing traditions, can be found in the gospels, though each gospel community favors one over the others. Like these early Christians, each Evangelist (gospel writer) saw in the tradition a new way to live, organized around a different way of understanding Jesus as representative of God's new world order. Mark wrote first, from Rome around the volatile year 70, when Romans were destroying Jerusalem and Christians were beginning to separate from Judaism, establishing the pattern for the gospels to follow. Matthew's Gospel probably came next, written around 80 from Antioch in Syria, when the Jewish world was in turmoil. The temple had been destroyed, and the Jewish religious rites that centered on the temple could no longer be performed. Luke's Gospel, the first volume of a two-book project that included Acts of the Apostles, was written around 85 for a Greco-Roman audience, possibly from Asia Minor. John's Gospel was clearly written last. Its composition history is complex, as it was probably written in stages and at different locations before it was completed, edited, and published no earlier than 90 or 95, in all likelihood in Ephesus, a port city in Asia Minor and one of the leading cities in the Roman Empire.

By the beginning of the second century two organizational models predominated in conventional Christian orthodoxy: (1) apostolic authority, representing the Pauline/Petrine tradition and supported by the Synoptic tradition and the book of Acts, and (2) charismatic authority, represented by the Johannine literature, which refers back to the earlier mode of church organization and revelation, with diverse leaders and modes of revelation, while retaining some of the Synoptic tradition. The two traditions, divergent in many ways, would eventually coalesce, as evidenced by their presence in the Christian canon. However, one cannot read John's Gospel contextually without noting that it represents a late first-century renewal movement that retains a different model of Christian origins than the apostolic tradition and a different understanding of Christian life.[2]

The Gospel of John is arguably the most influential book of the New Testament. One has only to think of the doctrine of the Trinity to see the

---

2. Valantasis, *Gospels and Christian Life*, 23.

importance of John's Gospel for Christian thought. The relationship of Jesus to God as Son to Father emerges fully here, as does the dual nature of Jesus as human and divine. And John has more to say about the Holy Spirit than does any other book in the New Testament.

The central focus of John is clearly the figure of Jesus, and the narrative leads the reader into a profound exploration of Jesus' identity and the significance of his life. Unlike Mark's Gospel, where Jesus keeps his identity secret from potential followers, and where even those closest to him discover who he really is only at or after his death and resurrection, in John Jesus tells everyone who he is. From the very first chapter, both Jesus and others use the loftiest titles of the church to describe his identity. Perhaps for that reason John is the gospel most frequently translated into other languages and the first gospel recommended for reading to non-Christians.

The Problems of John's Gospel

In an endlessly fascinating way, the Fourth Gospel poses challenges to its readers, who never doubt that John is the work of an early Christian theologian and writer without peer. Among its challenges, modern commentators have identified the following, which comprise some of the greatest challenges in New Testament studies:

1. authorship and place of composition;
2. unity and composition;
3. audience and destination;
4. final date of publication;
5. underlying tradition and religious influences;
6. historical value, as well as its relationship to the Jesus of history;
7. symbolic language and dualistic imagery;
8. relation to the Johannine epistles and the book of Revelation;
9. ecclesiology; and
10. double eschatology, which concentrates on the fulfillment of Israel's hopes in the coming of Jesus while allowing for future fulfillment.

Ongoing areas of debate in Johannine gospel scholarship include:

1. relation to the Synoptic tradition;

INTRODUCTION

2. stylistic peculiarities;
3. theological peculiarities;
4. sacramental language;
5. literary qualities;
6. outline; and
7. purpose.

These problems will be addressed in due course, beginning with the Fourth Gospel's methodology, authorship, dating, destination, and relation to the Synoptic Gospels.

Authorship, Compositional History, and Destination of the Fourth Gospel

Most of us know how to read different kinds of writing. We know what to expect of a newspaper's editorial pages or its comics and how these differ from the news sections or the crossword puzzle. We know the differences between poetry and prose, and between a novel and a textbook. The Bible also contains different types of literature. Some books are narratives, some are poetry, and others are letters. Some draw on more than one genre or type of writing. Knowing what to expect from each type of literature helps us understand how to read each book with deeper insight.

What Kind of Book Is John?

To get our bearings, we need to consider the background of John, where this writing came from, and what it was intended to do. We start with the obvious: John is a gospel. But what exactly is a gospel? The most common answer is that it is one of four books in the New Testament that tell the story of Jesus, focusing on his life and teaching. Although these gospels were written anonymously, two to three generations after the death and resurrection of Jesus (about forty years later in the case of Mark's Gospel and about sixty-five years later in the case of John's Gospel), in the second century they came to be attributed to early followers of Jesus named Matthew, Mark, Luke, and John. These four, transmitted and regarded as canonical, were not the only gospels to be written, but the rest perished or were relegated to secondary (apocryphal) status by the church because they lacked the literary power and spiritual reliability associated with the canonical gospels.

Until recently, it was believed that the gospels had no literary ancestors, being a unique genre of literature peculiar to Christianity, unwittingly invented by the first compiler of the gospel tradition, an early Christian named Mark. As a unique invention, combining history, theology, and literature, the gospel told the story of the Son of God, focusing on the good news of God's redemptive plan for humanity as seen through the birth, ministry, passion, and triumphant resurrection from the dead. While many New Testament scholars still hold the view that the gospels are unique, their genre being developed out of primitive Christian preaching and teaching and determined by the needs of evolving Christian communities, the gospel genre has now been found to be analogous to certain types of biographical and dramatic writings in antiquity.

Ancient biographies, for example, were often written by devoted disciples whose intent was to produce an instructive story of a model person's life. Frequently these biographies included extended teachings of the individual's philosophy, in addition to emphasizing the particular lifestyle the person modeled. The biographies related the particularities of the person's birth, emphasizing the presence of divine forces and agents attending the birth and the death of the person. The point of such biographies was not so much to inform as to model a way of life through the narrative, including social relationships for those choosing the holy person's way of life, connections to cultic centers and religious leaders, and even attitudes toward the emperor and Roman society. In other words, "the holy person became an exemplar of a whole set of social relationships consistent with the holy person's way of life."[3] The gospels, like ancient biographies, were not simply written to inform audiences but were designed to evoke a response from the listener.

If the gospel is related to the ancient biographical genre, as commonly held, a feature of all such ancient documents was a prologue or introduction, generally separate from the portrayal of the central character. In *What Are the Gospels?* Richard Burridge lists six features common to ancient biographies, including (1) a prologue, (2) focus on a particular individual, (3) the use of chronological, geographical, and topical categories to arrange the material, (4) the recording of deeds and words used to reveal a person's character, (5) a length of no more than 24,000 words (John's Gospel

---

3. Valantasis, *The Gospels and Christian Life*, 37. For a detailed comparison between the gospels and other ancient biographies, see Burridge, *What Are the Gospels?*

contains 15,416 words), and (6) a tone that is respectful or even reverential for the subject. John's Gospel conforms fully to this pattern.

In addition to its reliance on certain features common to ancient biographies, the Fourth Gospel also displays affinities to ancient drama, particularly ancient tragedy. While more a matter of mode of presentation than of genre in John—too many features of ancient drama are missing for the work to be viewed simply as a play—the Evangelist seems to have ancient tragic drama in mind. The story of Jesus seems to be presented here in a dramatic mode, drawing on certain familiar elements and techniques from the theater such as (1) the initial hymn of homage; (2) the use of irony throughout (saying something on one level while referring to something on a different plane); (3) the stress on the stupendousness of Jesus' miracles and other actions in the story; (4) the playing up of dualisms; (5) the use of the crescendo effect, including the crescendo of the miraculous, of confessions of Jesus, and of opposition to Jesus; (6) the self-contained nature of certain scenes, like scenes in a play; (7) the use of rhetoric at key junctures for the sake of persuasion; (8) adherence of the rule in Greco-Roman drama of having no more than three figures speak in any one scene (see John 3, 4, 9); and (9) the emphasis on surprising revelations that come to Jesus and dictate the action, meant to show the central figure's dependence on God, and thus his heroic and positive character.

In these and other ways the Evangelist has drawn on Greco-Roman literary conventions.

The Relationship of John to the Synoptic Gospels

An examination of the four canonical gospels reveals that three—Matthew, Mark, and Luke—have much in common and, in general, present the life and teachings of Jesus from the same point of view. The presentation of the words, deeds, and even of the person of Jesus is strikingly different in John's Gospel, so much so that it seems to represent an independent tradition. Unlike the Synoptics, where Jesus speaks in parables, in John Jesus speaks no parables but rather offers long discourses. The subject of these discourses is always the same—the identity of Jesus. The subject of the parables in the Synoptics, by contrast, is consistently the Kingdom of God; unlike the Synoptic Jesus, who speaks regularly of God's Kingdom, John's Jesus speaks rarely of kingdom but often of eternal life. Another difference is that the Synoptics record only one trip to Jerusalem and one celebration of the Passover, portraying Jesus' ministry in Galilee. John, however, focuses almost entirely on Jesus' work in Jerusalem, recording at least three Passovers and other visits to Jerusalem to celebrate major festivals. The Jewish festivals in Jerusalem are of central importance to John, structurally and thematically.

The Fourth Gospel differs substantially from the Synoptics in theological emphases. Instead of beginning with the genealogy of Jesus or with the birth of Jesus, John starts with the preexistence of the Logos, the Word of God, who became incarnate in Jesus Christ. While there is no Virgin Birth in John, no other Gospel places the incarnation at the center of its theological world in this manner. John's Jesus does not simply speak God's words and do God's works; rather, he does those things because he is God's word and work in the world.

The Synoptics record many miracles performed by Jesus, often as reward for faith, whereas John records only eight wondrous works and distinctively refers to these as signs, designed to elicit faith. Foremost among the miracles attributed to Jesus in the Synoptics, particularly in Mark, is the exorcism. In John only Jesus is said to have a demon (8:48); John's Jesus never exorcises demons. John also fails to mention the healing of lepers, another commonality in the Synoptics. Despite the paucity of wondrous works of Jesus in John, their quality is heightened over those claimed by the Synoptics. The illnesses cured are longer (see 9:1), and in cases where Jesus works marvelously with nature, the claims are more startling. Examples include the transformation of water into wine (2:1–10), unique to John, and the extraordinary catch of fish (21:11; cf. Luke 5:6).

Noteworthy as well are important events in the Synoptic life of Jesus missing from John: Jesus' baptism by John the Baptist; the temptation in the wilderness (John's Jesus seems far above temptation); the confession at Caesarea Philippi where Peter declares Jesus to be the Messiah; the transfiguration; the agony of Jesus in the garden of Gethsemane (cf.12:27); the institution of the Last Supper (cf. 6:51–56); and the cry of dereliction from the cross, "My God, my God, why have you forsaken me?" found in Mark 15:34 and Matthew 27:46.

There was a time when scholars believed that John wrote with knowledge of the Synoptics, either to correct misapprehensions that might arise from them or to supplement them. More recently, that view has been called into question. While it appears that John may have made some use of Mark, and to a lesser extent of Luke, there is an increasing consensus that

John is independent of the Synoptic writers.[4] The most convincing explanation for the similarities is the view that the Fourth Evangelist had access to an independent tradition (most likely oral) that was associated with the Synoptic traditions. As the dynamic oral transmission of Jesus' words and deeds developed following the crucifixion, that transmission took several different forms (as the differences among the Synoptics themselves also suggest). One form of the tradition was utilized by the Fourth Evangelist, which by this time differed significantly from that which was incorporated into the Synoptic Gospels. This development resulted from the needs and practical interests of the primitive Christian community, as well as from the preaching ministry of the church, which proclaimed the Jesus' story in such a way as to evoke faith in the hearers. It was also the result of faith that Jesus was still alive and active in the church, speaking through Christian prophets and teachers. Hence the Jesus' material was not fixed by the memory of eyewitnesses but was dynamic and growing, still rich and active when the Evangelists wrote.

Other explanations account for the differences between John and the Synoptics, as between the Synoptic writers themselves, including (a) the limitation in knowledge based on what each Evangelist had available from his/her individual tradition or source; (b) the specific needs and interests of the audience for whom a Gospel was written; (c) the theology of the author or of the target community, including the portrait of Jesus that each Evangelist wished to depict; and finally (d) the role played by geography in accounting for the divergent traditions underlying the gospels. While the streams of tradition had a common source, there could also have been interaction between them. The Fourth Evangelist, like the other Gospel writers, was "not unlike a good Christian theologian (or preacher) of our own day who tries faithfully to articulate the heritage of her or his religion in response to the burning questions of the day."[5]

---

4. There are numerous places in John's Gospel where its narrative runs close to the Synoptics. The first and briefest is the encounter with John the Baptist (especially 1:24–24); the second is the account of the feeding of the crowds and Jesus' walking on the water in chapter 6; the last and longest is the passion narrative (chapters 18—19). The strongest recent argument for dependence is that of Barrett, who bases his case on the agreement in order of numerous passages in Mark and John and on some striking verbal resemblances. Upon closer examination, however, the arguments are not really persuasive, since they can be explained more convincingly through dependence upon oral tradition.

5. Kysar, *Maverick Gospel*, 19.

Who Wrote the Fourth Gospel?

Can we know the identity of the Fourth Evangelist and of the Johannine community, and can we know the place and time of the Gospel's composition? The answers to these questions are much debated by biblical scholars.

Like all other gospels, John is anonymously written; its traditional title, "The Gospel According to John," first appeared as the heading of late second-century manuscripts. By this time the Gospel had become widely accepted as authoritative, due in part to its association with the disciple of Jesus, John the son of Zebedee, thus according the Gospel apostolic authority. However, that tradition is viewed with considerable skepticism today.

The closest the Gospel comes to identifying its author is in the epilogue (John 21), where he is called "the disciple whom Jesus loved," commonly known as the Beloved Disciple (21:7, 20, 24). The epilogue testifies to an extended process of composition of the Gospel within the Johannine community. The closing chapter raises a host of questions that points to various individuals and groups in the compositional process, particularly 21:24: "This is the disciple who is testifying to these things and has written them, and we know that his testimony is true." For instance, who is the disciple writing "these things," and who are the "we" affirming the text's truthfulness? And why does this disciple wish to remain anonymous, yet call himself "the disciple whom Jesus loved"? If modesty is what led this eyewitness not to refer to himself by name, why would he constantly call attention to Jesus' special love for him?

At a minimum, scholars generally distinguish between this disciple, whom they identify as the Evangelist, and an editor who wrote at least the final two verses or possibly all of chapter 21, since the Gospel seems to reach a natural conclusion at 20:30–31. The similarity between 21:24 and 19:35 suggests that the editor may have added these verses and perhaps other references to the Beloved Disciple scattered throughout the second half of the Gospel. Six passages mention the disciple whom Jesus loved: (1) 13:23–26, where he leans against Jesus during the Last Supper and Peter signals him to ask Jesus about the betrayer; (2) 19: 25–27, where he stands near the cross and Jesus gives Mary to him as his mother; (3) 20:2–10, where he appears with Peter after Mary finds the tomb empty; (4) 21:7, where he is in a fishing boat with Peter and six other disciples, being the first to recognize Jesus; (5) 21:20–23, where Peter turns and asks Jesus about him, and Jesus' reply leads us to conclude that the disciple is no longer alive when the Gospel was published in its final form; and (6) 21:24, where the Beloved Disciple is said to be the source of the narration.

Modern scholars propose various theories to explain the identity of the Beloved Disciple.[6] Some suggest figurative designations, ranging from the ideal Christian disciple, to members of the Johannine community, to the Jewish branch of early Christians, and even to the Hellenistic branch of early Christians. The majority prefer a solution that associates the Beloved Disciple with a particular follower of Jesus, whether (a) *Lazarus* (whom Jesus raised from the dead; cf. 21:23), repeatedly designated by the Evangelist to be one whom Jesus loves (11:3, 36); (b) *Thomas*, one of the Twelve given prominence in the Gospel, both at the midpoint (11:16) where he is ready to give his life, and at the end, where he sees the risen Christ and declares Jesus to be his "God" (20:28); (c) *John Mark*, an associate of Peter (Col. 4:10), as was the Beloved Disciple, whose home was in Jerusalem, the focal point of Jesus' ministry in the Fourth Gospel, and who might well have been known to the high priest, since Mark's cousin Barnabas was a Levite (Acts 4:36; cf. 18:15–18, where an unknown disciple is present with Peter at the home of Caiaphas); and (d) *John the son of Zebedee*, the natural candidate since the late second century, when Bishop Irenaeus, the leading advocate of the four-gospel tradition, identified John, the son of Zebedee, with the "disciple whom Jesus loved," thereby declaring the Fourth Gospel apostolic.

The earliest attribution of the Gospel to the apostle John seems to have come from Gnostics, unorthodox Christians who wrote the first commentaries on John. John's popularity among the Gnostics, together with its differences from the Synoptics, may explain why it was slow in being accepted by the church. Strangely, church fathers during the early part of the second century who mention the apostle John are silent regarding the Fourth Gospel.[7] The claims of apostolic authorship surfaced around the time the Gospel was beginning to be cited by orthodox Christians, no earlier than Irenaeus in the late second century and then by Eusebius in the fourth century; in all likelihood the argument that the Fourth Gospel was written by the apostle John was important in securing its acceptance by the church.

---

6. See the full discussion in Brown, *John*, 1:xcii–xcviii.

7. These include Ignatius, who wrote to the Ephesians ca. AD 110; Papias, who wrote 120 to 140; Polycarp, who wrote a letter to the Philippians; and Justin Martyr, who lived in Ephesus and then Rome. Irenaeus, a late second-century writer, is the first to connect John with Ephesus.

The merits of the traditional view on authorship, which connects the Fourth Gospel with John the son of Zebedee, should not be easily dismissed. These include (1) the eyewitness nature of the account, including firsthand references to persons, time, and place; (2) the author's knowledge of Jewish customs, perspectives, and situations; (3) insights into the disciples as well as into Jesus' intentions; (4) archaeological and topographical details demonstrating firsthand familiarity with Judea and Jerusalem; (5) the issue of anonymity regarding the Beloved Disciple, which in itself need not be viewed as an anomaly, since anonymity seems to be a regular feature in John's narrative, including the mother of Jesus (2:1–12; 6:42; 19:25–27) and various other disciples of Jesus (1:35, 37; 18:16; 20:2–8).

In recent years numerous arguments have been raised against the traditional view of authorship, including that (1) the apostle John is a Galilean, whereas most of the Gospel deals with Jesus' ministry in Judea; (2) John, as a Galilean fisherman, would have been uneducated and unable to read or write (see Acts 4:13); (3) in the Synoptics, John is part of the inner core of three disciples who are present at key events in the life of Jesus, including the transfiguration and at the Garden of Gethsemane, whereas in John there is no record of these events, nor are the inner three singled out as a group; and (4) the Beloved Disciple is at the cross in John, but the Synoptics note that all the male disciples (the Twelve) fled (Mark 14:50). Individually, none of these arguments may be convincing, but together they pose formidable difficulties.

Despite many proposed solutions, the identity of the Beloved Disciple remains inconclusive. What seems apparent is that he was an eyewitness, at least of the end of Jesus' ministry in Jerusalem, that he has died by the time the Gospel is finalized, that the Gospel attributes to him a place equal to that of Peter, and that he seems to be a source of John's distinctive memory of Jesus.[8]

Composition Theories of the Fourth Gospel

Without doubt, the landmark account of the origin and nature of John's Gospel is Rudolph Bultmann's commentary, which in a highly novel manner addressed perplexing literary, historical, and theological features of the Johannine text. Assuming that the Evangelist was a disciple

---

8. Anderson, *Riddles*, 89.

of John the Baptist, Bultmann argued that the Fourth Evangelist was a master literary craftsman (hence not an unsophisticated Galilean fisherman such as John of Zebedee) who drew together three major sources in composing the Gospel: a passion source, a revelation source, and a signs source. Given his rejection of the Evangelist as a firsthand witness to the ministry of Jesus, based in part on the difference between the Johannine and the Synoptic passion narrative, it is clear why Bultmann inferred the existence of an independent passion source. The second source, understood to consist of discourse material, was Bultmann's most controversial proposal, for it posited a gnostic revelation-redeemer myth underlying John's Christology, particularly in the prologue. Bultmann posited that John took this myth about a cosmic redeemer and rewrote it by making Jesus the redeemer-revealer.

Bultmann's third source, a signs source said to underlie John's distinctive miracles, has received wider acceptance. For Bultmann, the function of this hypothetical source, which depicted Jesus doing miracles in ways reminiscent of the Hebrew prophets, targeted Jewish audiences in hopes of convincing them that Jesus was the Jewish Messiah.

The merits of a signs source hypothesis, including its uniqueness to John, have been questioned by numerous scholars since Bultmann. When one examines the signs in John, including the changing of the water into wine (2:1–11); the healing of the royal official's son (4:46–54); the healing of a lame man (5:1–18); the feeding of the five thousand (6:1–14); the walking on the sea (6:16–21); the healing of the blind man (9:1–41); the raising of Lazarus (11:1–44), and the miraculous catch of fish (21:1–14), one notices that with the exception of the wine miracle at the Cana wedding, each of these miracles has some counterpart in the Synoptic tradition. It seems more credible to postulate common oral traditions about Jesus as the source of these stories than a formal signs source. A number of eminent scholars continue to argue for a signs source, but their proposals are generally more expansive than Bultmann's, to include discourse material and even biographical material concerning Jesus.

To explain perceived differences in writing style as well as numerous literary inconsistencies, repetitive passages, transitional difficulties, and other irregularities (called literary seams or *aporias*) in the text of John,[9] Bultmann posited an ecclesiastical editor (redactor) responsible for the final form of the Gospel. To this editor he attributed the incorrect

---

9. For examples see Bart Ehrman's text, *Brief Introduction*, 116–18.

reordering of chapters 4 through 7 (originally said to be 4, 6, 5, and 7), and dozens of additional textual anomalies, which Bultmann restored to the "original" textual order. He also attributed to the redactor numerous ecclesiastical changes, including the Eucharistic section in 6:51–58, his own material emphasizing futuristic eschatology, and the restoration of Peter in the epilogue (21:15–19). While the task Bultmann assigned to a redactor is considered excessive, the thesis of a final editor or editors of the Gospel is shared by numerous scholars.

Among additional composition theories suggested by scholars, the most influential has been Raymond Brown's. While he revised his theory in later years, his original proposal consists of five distinct stages in the composition of John, two pre-literary and three literary.[10] They are: (1) a collection of traditional materials containing the words and works of Jesus, independent in origin from the Synoptic tradition(s); (2) the oral teaching and preaching of the Johannine community over several decades, a development stage that shaped the tradition characteristically; (3) the organization of this material into the first edition of the Gospel (containing both signs and discourses), the work of a master teacher and theologian we call the Evangelist; (4) a second edition (and possibly others) by the Evangelist, to account for engagements by the Johannine community with groups like followers of John the Baptist, incorporated Samaritans who held anti-Judean biases, believers in Jesus associated with the synagogue, secret Jewish followers of Jesus, leaders among Asia Minor synagogues, believers with gnostic tendencies, and members of "the larger church" (the apostolic/Petrine tradition); and (5) a final redaction by someone other than the Evangelist. Unlike Bultmann's redactor, whose ecclesiastical and sacramental views were thought to be quite different from those of the Evangelist, Brown's editor was a disciple or close associate of the Evangelist. The sections that Brown attributes to the redactor, in addition to chapter 21, include the prologue, the Eucharistic words of Jesus at the supper in 6:51–58; 3:31–36; 12:44–50; John 15—17, with 16:4–33 a variant duplicate of chapter 15; and John 11—12.

Tradition holds that the Beloved Disciple was John, the son of Zebedee, and Brown agrees. He believes that the "other disciple" in the Johannine narrative (18:15, 16; 20:2–10; cf. 1:35–40; 13:23–25; 19:26, 27, 35; 21:7, 20–23) is this person's self-designation, while claiming that his status as the beloved of Jesus is the work of his own followers. The redactor,

---

10. Brown, *John*, 1:xxxiv–xxxix.

an admirer and co-worker of the apostle, used additional material developed within the Johannine school, possibly shortly after the death of the Evangelist. If such is the case, the death of this apostolic authority would have precipitated, if not a crisis, at least a new stage in the life of the community. John's affirmations regarding the continuing role of the Paraclete (the Holy Spirit) in teaching the community (14:26), Jesus' promise not to leave the disciples orphans (14:18), and Jesus' prayer for those who would come after the disciples (17:20–26) all take on new meaning when read in light of the evidence that the Gospel, at least in its finished form, addressed a second or third generation of Christians. Brown did not find the redactor(s) to be overly concerned with displacements, awkward literary seams, and inconsistencies in the text, so long as, in some fashion, the important information was included. The Gospel reflects, therefore, not only the Evangelist's theological and literary genius but also the history of the community in which it was shaped.

A third compositional perspective is offered by Randel Helms in his volume, *Who Wrote the Gospels?* In that brief book he suggests that the Gospel of John underwent three stages of development over a fifty-year period, each stage the product of a different author.

1. *The "Signs Gospel"*: the first stage is the period of the "Signs Gospel," attributed to a Greek-speaking Christian of the mid-first-century who was familiar with the Greek Septuagint version of the Hebrew Bible and who regarded Jesus as a new Moses. This author wrote from Alexandria, Egypt, where he was heavily influenced by the Septuagint account of Moses's miracles: Moses "performed the signs before the people. And the people believed" (Exod. 4:30–31 LXX). The author of the Signs Gospel borrowed from this passage in telling of the story of Jesus at Cana in Galilee, where Jesus "performed the first of the signs, and his disciples believed" (John 2:11; cf. 20:30–31). In order to demonstrate that Jesus is indeed the new Moses and therefore the promised Messiah, the Signs Gospel presents seven miracle stories as "signs" to elicit faith in Jesus as Messiah. According to Helms, the author of the Signs Gospel expected an imminent *parousia* (Second Coming) of Christ, meaning that it was written prior to the Roman destruction of the temple and the city of Jerusalem in AD 70.

2. *"John"*: the second stage is attributed to a person who wrote during the 90s, presumably also from Alexandria, Egypt, at a time when the delay of the *parousia* had become an embarrassment to the church (or was no longer expected by many Christians), and when the destruction

of Jerusalem was no longer linked to the expected apocalypse. An unknown author ("John") came to the conclusion that the long-awaited eschatological event had indeed occurred, in two stages: it had happened (a) in the person of Jesus himself (see John 3:13), and (b) in the coming of the Paraclete (the Holy Spirit), bestowed by Jesus in fulfillment of the "Second Coming" promise (14:15–21, 23–26; 16:19–20). For "John," the eschatological hope of the coming spiritual Kingdom of God had already been fulfilled, a view known as "realized eschatology" (see 3:36). According to Helms, this edition of the Gospel downplayed the sacraments of baptism and the Eucharist, presented a docetic view of Jesus (that Jesus only appeared to be human, but his flesh was not real), and replaced the traditional role of Peter with a figure called the Beloved Disciple (13:21–26; 18:15–17; 20:2–9).

3. *"John 2"*: this second edition was not accepted by mainstream Christians until it was revised by an unknown redactor ("John 2") in Ephesus, but it became attractive to gnostic Christians in Alexandria (an allusion to their perspective appears in 3:6–8, where "born of the Spirit" trumps "born of the flesh"). Evidence of a third viewpoint is seen in chapter 21, where by using the term "we" (21:24), the redactor informs his audience that he is not the author of the rest of the Gospel. Not knowing the author of the original Gospel, "John 2" refers to him as "the disciple whom Jesus loved" (the Beloved Disciple). "John 2" is a traditionalist who replaced the realized eschatology of the earlier "John" with traditional eschatology, adding the futurist statement about the dead rising from their graves on the last day (6:40). Unlike "John," the redactor emphasized the sacraments, adding "water and" to 3:5 (but neglected to add the phrase in 3:8, causing confusion) and also added Eucharistic literalism at 6:51, 53–56 while neglecting to remove the phrase that "the flesh is useless" in 6:63. "John 2" also added that Jesus himself is baptizing in 3:22, while keeping "John's" earlier statement that it was only the disciples, not Jesus (4:2), who were baptizing. According to Helms, the phrase "And the Word became flesh" (1:14) was added to the prologue at this stage. In his revision, "John 2" worked to restore Peter and the other disciples (who represent mainstream Christianity) to the center, making Peter the spokesman for the true faith (6:67–69). This effort culminated in chapter 21, with Peter fully restored as leader of the church (21:15–17).

Whatever one thinks of these reconstructions, the Gospel of John should be understood as the result of a rather long process of composition, stretching over several decades and including the tradition received from the Beloved Disciple, the work of the Evangelist, and the revisions of the redactor.

When and Where Was the Fourth Gospel Written?

While it is not possible to date the various editions and redactions of the Gospel, we can be fairly certain in dating the Gospel in its present form between 80 and 110 from Ephesus, in Asia Minor. Among the canonical gospels, it came last. The oldest fragment of the New Testament in existence, an Egyptian papyrus fragment that dates from AD 130, contains a few words from John 18, suggesting that the Gospel was known in Egypt during the early second century. John was clearly in wide circulation by the middle of that century.

A Journey into Three Worlds

People read the Bible, or specific books or passages within the Bible, for all sorts of reasons. As we proceed to the exegetical study of John's Gospel, it helps to clarify that the presentation will examine three worlds of the Bible: the historical, the literary, and the contemporary. (1) By *historical* I mean the background and context of the Gospel, its relation to the first-century Middle-Eastern milieu, and its place within the Jewish and Greco-Roman world at the time it was written, including the needs and concerns of its original audience. In examining that context, one must also examine (2) the Gospel as a *literary creation*, including the author's theological and symbolic intentions. (3) The final context of our study requires that we address the role of John for *modern readers* and its practical application in their lives. The interests, needs, and concerns that readers bring, whether as secular students or as persons of faith, must be central to our interpretation.

Though some interpret the Bible narrowly as a work of ancient history or as a revelatory word of God, none of us live exclusively in one world; therefore the Bible, as read by contemporary reader, cannot be confined to one dimension. Our lives—culturally, intellectually, and spiritually—are informed by the heritage of the past, the needs of the present, and the hopes of the future. As you read *Truth Revealed*, you too will journey into these three worlds.

Outline of the Gospel of John

Although the pattern I follow divides the Gospel into six parts, subdivided into twelve chapters, the outline below is the simplest and best-known:[11]

I. The Prologue (1:1–18): An early Christian hymn, probably stemming from Johannine circles, adapted to serve as an overture to the Gospel narrative of the career of the incarnate Word.

II. The Book of Signs (1:19—12:50): The public ministry of Jesus, where in sign and word he shows himself to his own people as the revelation of his Father, only to experience rejection.

III. The Book of Glory (13:1—20:31): To those who accept him, Jesus shows his glory by returning to the Father in "the hour" of his crucifixion, resurrection, and ascension. Fully glorified, he communicates the Spirit of life.

IV. The Epilogue (21:1–25): An added series of post-resurrection appearances in Galilee.

Guiding Principles of This Study

The following principles guide this study:

1. Keep in mind the centrality of the historical context. To understand John's Gospel, we must recognize that it was not written to us. While its compositional history is complex—the Gospel appears to have been written in stages to meet new needs and ongoing concerns—the final canonical version, like earlier editions, contains a particular message to a particular situation. While an enduring message may be found within the text, modern readers must filter that message through the hopes and expectations of the original readers and their situation.

2. Look beyond the literal approach. Whereas traditional Christians read the Gospel of John as factual and therefore as historically accurate, modern scholarship approaches the Evangelists as creative theologians, each targeting or representing specific audiences with distinctive theological perspectives that helped to shape individual and communal images and self-understandings. In John, history and metaphor are symbiotic, so tightly intertwined that one can rarely ascertain where history ends and metaphor begins.

---

11. Brown, *John*, 1:cxxxviii.

3. Be aware of the Gospel's literary nature. While the Fourth Gospel has traditionally been read as scripture and therefore as a repository of revealed doctrine, only recently has it been appreciated for its literary value, including its rich use of irony, misunderstanding, symbolism, and dualistic imagery.[12] Its symbolism transcends core images such as light, bread, water, life, and vine to include characters, actions, narrative, narrative time, narrator and point of view, plot, implicit commentary, and implied reader. The Fourth Evangelist views the natural world, created by the Logos, as containing a storehouse of symbols, many pointing to Jesus, himself a symbolic revelation of God.

4. Read John canonically. As scripture, John's Gospel must be read in its biblical context and therefore primarily against the background of biblical (first-century Jewish and early Christian) hopes and expectations. While the Bible is a "library of books," with a variety of theologies and conflicting points of view, it contains a unified story. The following headings adequately describe the biblical plot: Creation, Covenant, Christ, Church, and Consummation. The Fourth Evangelist certainly viewed history as unfolding according to divine plan.

5. Look for practical application. Examine John's Gospel for its wisdom and hopeful message, embracing positive, broadly ecumenical possibilities over narrow polemical exclusivism. In reading John, individuals should recognize that they are being invited into the realm of experience, not imitative experience, whether of a specific community or even to replicate the experience of the founder, but to experience the founder, who is "the way, and the truth, and the life" (14:6), and through that experience to a transformative encounter with the love of God, revealed in the mission and message of Jesus. Readers should take into account the centrality of the metaphor "Life" in John, described in 10:10 as life in abundance and elsewhere as "eternal life" (3:16). John 14:6, centrally placed at the heart of the Fourth Gospel, is its lodestar. The concept of Jesus as Life is found throughout the Gospel, affirmed at the start (1:4) and also at the close (20:13), where experiencing Jesus Christ (described as "believing ... in his name") brings Life.

6. Remain open to scholarly insight. While lay readers of John should avoid getting sidetracked by technical debates or problems in the text, they should build upon the results of biblical scholarship and willingly engage in the critical process. The Bible should be approached

---

12. The best explorations of John's literary techniques are those by Culpepper, *Anatomy*, and Koester, *Symbolism*.

holistically, equally valuing three essential human ways of knowing: (a) *faith*, a deep and intuitive sense of the sacred dimension of life that embraces uncertainty, takes risks, and is guided by deep appreciation of mystery; (b) *reason*, an approach that values facts, logic, science, analysis, and experimentation and remains open to newness and discovery; and (c) *imagination*, a deeply personal and often interpersonal way that values experience, creativity, and thinking "outside the box," discovering reality through dialogue and reflection and expressing truth artistically, through poetry and creative narrative.

While these three dimensions of life have been valued throughout history, the modern period (1650–1950) has placed them on a collision course, treating them as irreconcilable. We are said to be living today in a postmodern age, characterized by epistemological relativity and cosmological indeterminacy. In this current climate, perhaps it is possible once again to synthesize faith and reason. If faith characterized the premodern period and reason the modern period, can imagination, a postmodern quality, function as the catalyst that unites reality for us today?

Initial Assignment

The Gospel of John should be approached as a work of art. In seeking to appreciate a symphony, for example, one must listen to the entire work in order to grasp the full impact of its total composition—its musical forms, motifs, tonal colors, and relationships. Only after listening to the work as a whole can one analyze the elements and details of its composition and study the techniques of its composer. Likewise, John can be fully appreciated only when analyzed in its entirety, because each episode in the life and ministry of Jesus and every symbol takes its import in relation to the overall literary and theological perspective.

I recommend that you read John in its entirety, remembering the central claim found in 10:10: "I came that they may have life, and have it abundantly." Everything John tells us about the ministry and mission of Jesus leads to and follows from this affirmation. The promise of newness of life in the present—of eternal life as a present reality—runs like a refreshing mountain stream through this Gospel, renewing John's readers and sustaining them throughout their lives. As you read the Fourth Gospel, focus on the images of the second birth, the living water, the bread of life, the light of the world, the good shepherd, the gate, and the true vine, pondering the truth they reveal. Hold these images and their promises as you conclude your reading. Following your initial reading, keep a copy of John handy, or better yet, several different English versions, for you will need to consult the text regularly as you read this commentary.

Questions to Ponder

1. Having read John, what seems to be its primary message?
2. Is there an underlying message in John's Gospel that has practical value in your present circumstances?
3. Of the six guiding principles listed above, which do you find most helpful? Why?
4. In your estimation, how reliable is the Fourth Gospel in its presentation of Jesus? Should one read John primarily as history, literature, scripture, or as all three?
5. In your estimation, what is the identity of the Beloved Disciple, and why do you believe the author chose to create such an anonymous character?
6. What does John's Gospel tell you about God and God's nature?
7. What does John's Gospel tell you about the role of Jesus as Revealer of God's Truth?

PART I ——————————————

Beginnings

(JOHN 1:1–18)

CHAPTER 1

John's Prologue
(John 1:1–18)

Summary: The prologue provides readers with initial, reliable exposition of the identity of Jesus. We are told that Jesus is the Word, the true light, the Word that became flesh, and the only Son from the Father. Verses 9–13 summarize the plot: the true light comes into the world, but the world does not recognize him; he comes to his own people, but his own do not receive him; nevertheless, those who believe in his name are empowered to become "children of God." As the story unfolds, Jesus' identity as God's Revealer is attested by a host of witnesses, beginning with John the Baptist.

Assignment: Read John 1:1–18

Key Passage: John 1:14

Central Theme: Jesus is God's Word

Key Symbols/Concepts: Word (Logos), life, light, darkness, the world, belief, children of God, flesh, glory, grace, truth

Learning Objectives
Participants will examine:

1. The nature and mission of Jesus in relation to God, the world, and his followers
2. The themes in the passage and their relation to the rest of the Gospel

3. The literary nature of this passage
4. The relation of this passage to other Christological passages in the New Testament
5. The Jewish background of John's Gospel
6. Ways to interpret John's symbolic and technical language
7. The Logos Christology of John

Outline to John 1:1–18
I. The Word and God 1:1–2
II. The Word and Creation 1:3–5 The Word and John 1:6–8
III. The Word and the World 1:9–13
IV. The Word and the Community 1:14–18

The Purpose of John's Gospel

The central theme of John, as of the New Testament, is Jesus of Nazareth, a wandering preacher of the first century who changed the course of history. It is he who personifies "truth," who answers the question "what is truth?" by pointing to himself as "the way, the truth, and the life" (14:6). For Christians in the Johannine community and for Christians ever since, "truth" is not an abstract concept but a person: Jesus the Christ, who embodies a way of living, thinking, and believing that enables believers to live life abundantly as children of God. To know Jesus in that way is to know the truth (8:32).

Truth, for John as for the rest of the Bible, is neither an abstract concept nor a body of knowledge that can be known in one's head. It can only be known in relationship. The concept of knowing, for John as for the rest of scripture, is less about certainty and more about intimacy. In Genesis 4:1 we read that Adam "knew his wife Eve," a form of knowing that includes the deepest level of relationship, including emotional, spiritual, and physical intimacy. In John's Gospel, knowing the truth pertains to the process whereby humans may:

1. Know (experience) God (1:18), not in the sense of comprehending God's essence, but recognizing God's benevolent intention toward humanity and all nature as Creator. When humans speak of "knowing" God, they are primarily speaking of experiencing God's love, for love is the only kind of union between persons of which they have any possible experience;

2. Know (experience) Jesus (20:31), not in the sense of comprehending Trinitarian essence, but recognizing Christ's benevolent intention as bringer of Life; and

3. Know (experience) the power and possibilities incumbent in their status as children of God (1:12), described as "having [abundant] life" (10:10; 20:31) or as "having eternal life" (3:16).

The ways of the world may be partial truths, lesser understandings of what is true, but Jesus, the "true light," sheds light on human darkness. With the coming of Jesus, what is real, eternal, and good becomes fully knowable. This Light is the only true light; it is the light that "enlightens everyone." For John there is no other truth.

John's Gospel is written as a mystery or detective story, with cryptic clues strategically located for readers to follow. The author sets up a series of pointers for his audience, using the word *sēmeia* ("signs") for clues to guide and move readers through the narrative. The signs, taken together, point to the climax of the story, confirming what Jesus had promised he would do for his followers when, early in the narrative, he indicates to a fledgling disciple (Nathanael, whose name means "gift of God," represents the ideal seeker) that he would see heaven opened (1:51), an experience likened to that of Jacob, who saw the angels of God ascending and descending at the intersection of heaven and earth, and which, for the Church, is the place where truth is revealed, it being the place where Jesus is. Like Nathanael, people of faith are told they will experience moments "when heaven is opened, when the transforming power of God's love bursts in to the present world."[1] That promise, as John explains in 20:31, is why he is writing this Gospel.

At first glance, John's explicit statement of purpose in 20:31 appears "the clearest statement of literary intentionality anywhere in the Bible,"[2] until we examine the grammatical form of the verb "believe." While the

---

1. Wright, *John*, 1:21.
2. Anderson, *Riddles*, 85.

goal is clear (that believers might have life in Jesus' name), the meaning of "belief" is problematic. Some ancient manuscripts contain a verbal form (aorist subjunctive) best translated "may come to believe" (*pisteusēte*), while other manuscripts have a form (present subjunctive) that should be translated "may continue to believe" (*pisteuēte*). The difference between the two Greek words is slight, only a single letter, but the difference in meaning is significant. The first suggests that the Gospel was written with an evangelistic (apologetic) purpose, to bring people to faith for the first time, whereas the second reading suggests an edificatory (pastoral) purpose, associated with faithfulness, in which case the primary purpose of the Gospel would be to sustain current believers, that they might abide and remain in Jesus as a matter of faithfulness, not abandoning the community as the schismatics of the epistles appear to have done. Both meanings can be found throughout John.

Those who see an evangelistic intent in John appeal to three factors: (1) the many *witnesses* presented in the Gospel—John the Baptist, the Samaritan woman, the man born blind, the Father, the Paraclete, Jesus' works, Moses, the Beloved Disciple, even Jesus' followers—whose primary role is to testify that Jesus is the Christ, the Son of God; (2) the so-called *signs* of Jesus, given to evoke faith, as 20:20–21 suggests; and (3) numerous references to *scripture* being fulfilled in Jesus, introduced to confirm the authenticity of Jesus' mission and to demonstrate that he is the Christ (1:23 = Isa. 40:3; 1:45 = Deut. 18:15; 2:17 = Ps. 69:9; 3:14–15 = Numb. 21:9; 6:45 = Isa. 54:13; 12:13 = Ps. 118:25–26; 12:13–16 = Zech. 9:9; 12:38 = Isa. 53:1; 12:39–41 = Isa. 6:10; 19:24 = Ps. 22:18; 19:28–29 = Ps. 69:21; 19:31–36 = Exod. 12:10, 46; 19:34–37 = Zech. 12:10; cf. 2:22; 20:9, and Hebrew scripture in general).[3]

Parts of John, however, leave the impression that they are intended for Johannine believers, calling them to stay in solidarity with the community. For example, Jesus admonishes his followers to abide (remain) in him as he abides in them: by eating and drinking his flesh and blood (6:56); by remaining connected to the vine (15:4–10); by the indwelling of the Spirit of truth (14:17). A passage such as the healing of the blind man in chapter 9, which in the original signs source may have contained a missionary function, in its Johannine setting points beyond the healing to the ensuing story, which highlights the faithfulness to Jesus of the one who was healed, despite concerns by the man's parents and threats by

---

3. Additional examples are listed in Anderson, *Riddles*, 85–86.

the ruling authorities (9:22–34). The account skips from the historical Jesus to the ongoing experience of the Johannine community, seemingly describing "the general state of the whole Christian movement toward the end of the first century."[4]

Might there be two main purposes of the Johannine Gospel instead of one, particularly if the earlier edition was expanded by the addition of passages such as 1:1–18; chapters 6, 15—17, and 21; and 19:34–35? The intention of earlier and later editions of John may indeed have been different. If the first edition was primarily apologetic in nature—intended to lead Jews to belief in Jesus as the Jewish Messiah—the later material had a primarily pastoral function, calling Christians (Jewish and Gentile alike) into solidarity with Jesus and his community in the face of later hardship.

Part of John's goal in writing a book for Jewish Christians and proselytes is to make the notion of a crucified Messiah coherent. While he cannot remove the intrinsic offence of the cross, he is aware how big a "stumbling-block" the cross is to Jews (see 1 Cor. 1:23). What he must do is demonstrate that the cross was a factor from the beginning of Jesus' ministry (Jesus is early announced in John as the Lamb of God, 1:29) and that the cross was God's own plan, God's means to bring cleansing (note the centrality of the foot-washing episode at the Last Supper, 13:1–20) and life to his people and glory to himself. If Jesus is the Lamb of God, the cross is the victory of the Lamb of God and the triumph of the obedient Son, who in consequence of his obedience bequeaths his life, peace, joy, and his Spirit. The purpose of John can be summarized in two words: Christology and discipleship, for Jesus represents "truth in person" and discipleship represents "truth in practice."

Overture

John's prologue has been likened to a musical overture, which sets the mood and describes its themes. The Gospel of John, a theological odyssey, covers the gamut of time—from preexistent time to the end of time. The prologue transports readers to time immemorial, depicted poetically: "In the beginning was the Word."

Scientists, in describing the primal reality said to underlie the cosmic Big Bang, speak of singularity, of a presence of staggering density, incalculable potential, and unimaginable size, a singularity so small that

---

4. Kysar, *Maverick Gospel*, 26.

if it were enlarged a trillion trillion times, the world's most powerful microscope wouldn't be able to reveal it. In other words, there was a time when the universe was smaller than a single atom. And this singularity, which John describes as Logos, this indispensable principle of reality, was with God, and was God.

John's singularity, a revelatory incarnation of cosmic grandeur called Logos, became human. This singular Word, born in time and space as Jesus, is John's version of the cosmic Big Bang. This Person of infinite love, released on behalf of a World of darkness and disbelief, this conception as original as the universe itself, this Being of Life and Light, came to transform ordinary humans into children of God. The Good News of this Gospel distinguishes Christianity from all other religions, philosophies, and cultural perspectives. Its portrayal of Christ's death on a cross—vicarious, victorious, and glorious—epitomizes John's understanding of God's character, as revealed in Jesus Christ. The telling of this amazing story, attributed to a man named John, is the subject of our study.

John's prologue, constructed by the Fourth Evangelist out of earlier materials, joins two strands of early Christian tradition, (a) a hymn that celebrated the cosmic origins and preexistence of Wisdom and (b) John the Baptist material, viewed as the traditional starting point for the account of Jesus' ministry. One focuses on the beginning beyond time and the other on time and history. For the writer of John, the two belong together.

Biblical scholar Morna Hooker has argued that the entire Gospel of John must be read in light of this prologue. She maintains there is a "messianic secret" in John, namely that Jesus is the Logos, the one who has come from above and returns to the Father. In John, understanding Jesus depends on knowing where he has come from and where he is going. This "secret," known to the reader, is hidden from the characters in the narrative. Thus the opening hymn becomes the Christological basis for John's argument throughout the Gospel. If that is so, the whole of the Fourth Gospel is dependent on the Wisdom hymn in the prologue, for it sets the stage for the story about the One who comes from and returns to the Father. If one thinks of the Son in terms of descending and ascending Wisdom, it affirms that the first half of the Gospel (John 2—12) is about the descent and engagement of God's Wisdom/Son into and with the world, while the second half (comprising the Farewell Discourse and the passion material in John 13—20) is about Wisdom's rejection and consequent death and exaltation.[5] One might go farther than Hooker in arguing that the whole of John must be read in light of the very first verse, for it means that the deeds and words of Jesus are the deeds and words of the eternal Logos, who existed prior to all of creation.

As noted above, in his prologue John ties Jesus (as yet unnamed) to the God of the Old Testament, to the creation of all matter, and to the creation of life. The Word of God *is* God, and God is the Creator of everything. The Evangelist does not begin with a particular event in time, like Jesus' birth or the start of Jesus' ministry, as the Synoptics do. Rather, the beginning is outside the normal calculations of time, in the cosmic preexistence of the Word with God. This beginning focuses the reader's attention on the meaning of what follows: the Gospel story is about the very character of God, as known to the world through the life and death of Jesus.

Analysis of John 1:1–18

Literary Analysis

By any standard John's prologue is one of the most profound passages in the Bible. As simple as the language and phrases are, the prologue's description of Jesus as the Logos has exerted a lasting influence on Christian theology. Like John, each Synoptic Gospel begins with a prologue. Mark's prologue, brief and succinct, is limited to one verse (1:1) yet is important in that it offers a summary of the gospel: Jesus is the Christ and the Son of God. Matthew begins with a genealogy of Jesus, the son of David, the son of Abraham (1:1). This introduction is followed by an account of Jesus' birth and infancy, his identity as the Messianic Son whose name means "God with us" (Matt. 1:18, 23), and his fulfillment of the Moses typology (Matt. 2:1–23). The beginning of Matthew thereby emphasizes Jesus' Jewish origin. Luke also offers an account of Jesus' birth and infancy, adding to that account the birth of John the Baptist. Like Matthew, he includes a genealogy, inserting it later in the account. The genealogy augments Matthew's account in that it extends Jesus' lineage back to Adam, the "son of God." Throughout his infancy narrative Luke demonstrates Jesus' superiority to John the Baptist, a theme that the Fourth Gospel develops as well.

---

5. Witherington, *John's Wisdom*, 54.

Each prologue educates or prepares the reader for the remainder of the Gospel. Important themes are signaled, and the identity of Jesus is established at the start by means of Christological titles, divine portents, or the manner of Jesus' birth. While all the prologues contain Christological affirmations, John's is the only one to speak of Jesus' preexistence as the Logos and the only Gospel to include a poetic prologue.

Earlier we noted that in ancient biographies it was common to begin with a prologue and in Roman drama to sing a hymn to the emperor prior to the dramatic presentation. John seems to follow suit, whether in adopting this custom or because it provides a key for the hearer or reader to understand the drama of Jesus' life. Throughout the Gospel, knowing where the Son of God came from and where he is going is the key to understanding his identity, and thus is also a key to understanding why so many misunderstand and reject him.

Because there is an obvious poetic quality to the prologue, the question arises as to its origin. Did the Evangelist compose it? Was it an earlier Christian hymn adapted to this Gospel? Or is it a Christian adaptation of a hymn to Wisdom? While no one can answer these questions definitively, the best solution lies in viewing the original poem as a hymn composed in the Johannine church. Whereas the first five verses are poetic, the hand of the Evangelist or redactor is evident in verses 6–9, 13, 15 and 17. Some scholars find a continuation of the original hymn in verses 10–12b. If verses 14, 16, and 18 were part of the hymn, then it had already been adapted for Christian use. The pattern of John's hymnic material bears similarities to hymns in Philippians 2:6–11, Colossians 1:15–20, and in Hebrews 1:2–4. These passages have had more impact on Christian thinking about Jesus Christ's divine being than have any other New Testament passages.

It has been suggested that the Gospel of John originally began with verses 6–8 and 15. These verses lead directly into verse 19, and if they once formed the start of the Fourth Gospel, then that Gospel originally began much like Mark, with John the Baptist's testimony to Jesus. These passages also reflect a polemic against false understandings of the role of John the Baptist and Moses, and explain the identity of the true children of God. In the Fourth Gospel, the Baptist is presented primarily as a witness to Jesus (1:19–34; 3:26–30; 10:41). As the Gospel unfolds, the opposition between followers of Jesus and followers of Moses increases, and Jesus is presented as the "prophet like Moses" in fulfillment of Deuteronomy 18:18–19. He is like Moses, only superior (1:16–17; 6:32). In the end, those who respond to Jesus are the true children of God (1:12), while those who oppose Jesus are exposed as children of the devil (8:44).

Four beautifully crafted poetic stanzas can be found in John's prologue. Modern readers need to know that Hebrew poetry does not rhyme in sound but rather in thought. For example, ancient Hebrew poetry used couplets with various kinds of parallelism between the two lines: *synonymous* parallelism, where the second line of a pair restates the ideas of the first line, utilizing new words and images; *antithetical* parallelism, where the second line presents a set of opposite ideas, contrasting those of the first line; and a third type, known as *ascending* parallelism, where the second line completes the thought of the first, often in a stairstep progression of thought, whereby the second noun in each line becomes the first noun in the next line.

An example of stairstep parallelism is found in 1:1–2:

In the beginning (A) was the Word (B),
And the Word (B) was with God (C),
And what God (C) was, the Word (B′) was.
This one (B′) was with God in the beginning (A′).[6]

The letters in parentheses indicate a further pattern as well, a structure called a chiasm, where the pattern doubles back on itself. This V-pattern in chiastic structures is typical of hymns in Jewish Wisdom literature. The bottom line in a chiasm, represented in John 1:1–2 by the letter "C," is the central element in the poem. The chiastic structure of the opening lines of the prologue indicates that we might find a chiastic structure in the prologue as a whole. Alan Culpepper detects seven chiastic parallels in the prologue, locating the pivot (the central element) in verse 12b, where believers in Jesus are conferred the status "children of God." In debates with non-Christians, "such a designation may have had a particular importance for the Johannine community. It defined their status and identity as the true community of the children of God."[7]

While the chiastic structure of the opening lines is striking, as the prologue progresses, its poetic structure becomes less clear. The following outline, tentative at best, informs the literary analysis.

First Strophe: The Word and God (1:1–2)

---

6. This discussion on Hebrew poetry is adapted from Culpepper, *Gospel and Letters*, 111–12, as is the translation of John 1:1–2.

7. Ibid., 116.

Second Strophe: The Word and Creation (1:3–5)

Interpolation: The Word and John (1:6–9, 15)

Third Strophe: The Word and the World (1:10–12b)

Interpolation: How One Becomes a Child of God (1:12c–13)

Fourth Strophe: The Word and the Community (1:14)

Editorial Conclusion: The Word and the Community Continued (1:16–18).

Some scholars view verses 16–18 as a fifth strophe, but these appear to be more editorial than poetic.

Roughly speaking, the hymn can be broken down into five major themes: (1) the preexistent Word (1:1–2); (2) the Word and creation (1:3–5); (3) the response of those created: rejection and reception (1:10–12b); (4) the incarnation and revelation (1:14a); and (5) the response of the faithful community ("we have seen his glory"; 1:14b).

The poetic material seems to have been taken from an independent hymn, for some of the key terms here are found nowhere else in the Gospel. These include *logos* (1:1, 14)," "fullness" (1:16), "grace" (1:14, 16, 17), "came into being" (1:3, 10), the idea of the Word tabernacling or setting up his tent in our midst (translated in 1:14 as "lived among us"), and the central theme of the prologue, that Jesus is the Word made flesh (1:14). These are linked more closely to 1 John than to John's Gospel, so the determination of the relation of the Gospel to the epistles of John might help clarify when the prologue was added to the Gospel. In addition, there are major differences in the poetic, almost hymnic style of the prologue and the simple Greek style found throughout the rest of the Gospel.

Some aspects of the prologue, however, seem germane to the rest of the narrative, including (a) distinctive terms in the prologue such as "light" (1:4, 5, 7, 8, 9), "darkness" (1:5), "glory" (1:14), and "truth" (1:14, 17), which reverberate throughout John's narrative; (b) the announcement in the prologue that those who believe in the name of Jesus Christ are welcomed into the family of God (1: 12), which matches the announced purpose of the Gospel in 20:31; (c) the use of the first-person plural language "we" in the prologue (1:14, 16), found in the final words of the editor in the epilogue (21:24) and ninety times in the Johannine epistles; (d) the parenthetical remarks concerning the ministry of John the Baptist in the prologue (1:6–8, 15), further developed in chapters 1 and 3 of the Gospel; and (e) finally, to the prologue and to the Gospel as a whole, the centrality of the theme that Jesus is the Word made flesh

(1:14). While the precise Logos terminology may not have been repeated in the Gospel, it can be argued to have been foundational to John. If fleshly existence was irrelevant to the Evangelist, why write a *gospel*, an account of a real historical human?

Ben Witherington identifies three sources for John 1:1–18 and for other New Testament Christological hymns such as Philippians 2:6–11 and Colossians 1:15–20: (1) previous Jewish discussions about personified Wisdom; (2) the earliest Christian preaching about Jesus, particularly about his death and vindication beyond death, and (3) the Christological use of the psalms, especially Psalm 110. It appears in general that the incarnational language of Christological hymns draws on the Jewish Wisdom tradition; the soteriological language (about Jesus' death or sacrifice) draws on the passion material and early Christian preaching; and the references to Jesus' exaltation and vindication draw on material from the psalms. The V-narrative pattern of these hymns, addressing in turn the pretemporal, temporal, and post temporal life of Christ, reflects earlier Jewish sapiential speculation on the career of personified Wisdom, who is said to be preexistent with God and to have been involved in the work of creation (Prov. 3:19–20 and 8:22–31), who is described as having come down and dwelt in the midst of God's people (Sir. 24:8–12), and who is said to have been rejected by people on earth and so returned to dwell in heaven with God (1 Enoch 42). Early Christological imagery also draws on the Wisdom of Solomon, a Jewish sapiential work written late in the first century BC, mere decades before the Christological hymns. There one finds hymns praising Wisdom and also soteriological language associated with Wisdom: "Who has learned your counsel, unless you have given wisdom and sent your holy spirit from on high? And thus the paths of those on earth were set right, and people were taught what pleases you, and *were saved by wisdom*" (Wis. 9:17–18). Christ's career, envisioned as having both heavenly and earthly scope, "led early Jewish Christians to draw on the most exalted language they could find—Jewish wisdom speculation, coupled to some degree with messianic interpretation of the psalms and soteriological reflections on Christ's death."[8]

While John's prologue also draws on material from Genesis 1, the influence is indirect, for the Genesis account does not personify divine attributes or introduce agents assisting God in creation. Rather it is the use of the Genesis material in hymnic material about Wisdom, both in

---

8. Witherington, *John's Wisdom*, 51.

the Old Testament and in later Jewish sapiential writings, which provides the font of ideas and forms used in creating this hymn. For example, Proverbs 3 and 8 indicate the presence of personified Wisdom at creation, but also Wisdom's call of God's people back to the right paths with offers of life and favor from God (Prov. 8:35). These are the very things said of the Word in John's prologue. By the third century BC, this sort of Wisdom reflection included speculation about Torah, God's written word, at which time Torah and Wisdom were viewed as interrelated, the former being the consummate expression of the latter (Sir. 24:23).

John's description of the Logos echoes the story of the coming of Torah to Israel, especially as told in Sirach 24, where Torah is identified with Wisdom. In John's prologue the author identifies Torah/Wisdom with Christ, who is seen as eclipsing the Law of Moses (1:17), thereby fulfilling the earlier institutions of Judaism.

Textual Analysis

The description of the Word with God before creation is remarkably brief; there is no interest in metaphysical speculation here, as in the Gospel generally. The emphasis in John is on God's relation to humanity, rather than on God's essence or self. "In the beginning was the Word" (1:1); this *logos* or Word was present with God before the space-time continuum or universe began. Not only so, this Word is said to be God. The key phrase, "and the Word was God," does not mean "the Word was a god." The text does not say: "the Word was *the* God," for that would then mean that the Word was all there was to the Godhead, and that is an idea the Evangelist does not wish to convey.

The first three words of the prologue are the same words that open the book of Genesis. John makes this connection intentionally, for it suits his intention and creates a bridge for his audience. Notice the parallels: in Genesis God creates by speaking; in the Gospel God creates through the Word. In Genesis God's first creative act results in the emergence of light from the darkness; in the Gospel the Word is associated with light that shines in the darkness. In both cases the light is distinguished from darkness. Many of John's first-century contemporaries, whether pagan, Jewish, or Christian, considered matter to be evil. Genesis makes clear that light is good; through the connection to Genesis, John reminds us that everything God makes is good. John's hymn, then, emphasizes the goodness of creation—both God and the Word are involved with it, and both are involved with its redemption as well. Thus, however dark and fallen the creation may have become, it must be remembered that our author is not supporting the views of second-century Gnostics that matter was inherently evil and spirit inherently good. The Fourth Evangelist does not envision a permanent, irreconcilable dualism in the universe of good versus evil or spirit versus matter.

The prologue does not move *to* Jesus but *from* him. The prologue is not so much a preface to the Gospel as a summary of it, for what John means by the Word, what he means by the architecture of his prologue, he makes known in the body of his work. From the beginning, the Evangelist makes clear that the words of Jesus are meaningless apart from their relation to their essential underlying meaning in the Word, much as the apostles are insignificant apart from their relation to Jesus, and that Jesus profits little unless he be the incarnate Word of God. But this Word is not an abstraction. It is related to this world, incarnated in flesh—infinity to time, eternity to history. The world is where the Word of God is recognized, believed, and known. Because this Word is beyond time and space, it is timeless and spaceless and hence belongs to every epoch in time and to every race on earth. The Word neither grows old nor becomes new. As the Word of God, it both represents meaning and provides meaning to the entire cosmos, which is created through the agency of the Word (1:3). With the words "came into being," readers are brought to the sphere of creation. The cosmos is intimately related to the Word, for it was created through the Word but also in him. The same emphasis is found in the hymn of Colossians 1:16: "all things have been created through him and for him." In John, the Word came forth from God, a going forth that carried, however, no diminution. The Word remains the Life and Light and Glory of God. The Word is the Life of humans and of all things. When this Life is recognized and accepted, it is Light, for Light is the manifestation of Life (1:4).

Writing for a Christian audience, whether Jewish or Gentile, John's choice of a summarizing title for Jesus in the prologue—Word—is brilliant. "Word" is one way to translate the original Greek term *logos*, though it is certainly not the only possible translation, for the term is practically untranslatable. Part of the difficulty comes from the intellectual environment. It is important to remember that during the first century the boundaries between religions, philosophies, and cultures were fluid. One cannot draw a sharp line between Hellenism and Judaism, for example, because the two were in constant contact in the eastern Mediterranean world. In that world, the term *logos* appeared in a variety of settings with which Jews and early Christians, including the writer of John, would have been familiar.

In early Stoicism *logos* figures prominently as a term for the rational principle of the universe, and while the cosmological sense of *logos* is evident in John's prologue, it is more likely that the Johannine community's use of the term was influenced more by Jewish and early Christian interpretations of Wisdom in Judaism, perhaps by someone steeped in Hellenistic culture.

For the Johannine community, the meanings of *logos* are rich and revealing. They include, in addition to personified Wisdom, relational concepts such as "conversation," "discourse," "telling a story," "dramatic narrative," and even "a rationale for a way of living." This association, favored by scholars who stress the prophetic and charismatic nature of the Johannine community, views members of the community as being engaged (by means of the Holy Spirit) in a wide variety of conversations with the risen Christ. Building on the well-known Matthean declaration that "where two or three are gathered in my name, I am there among them" (Matt. 18:20), this approach comprehends John's Gospel as the conversation (*logos*) of people with Jesus. Richard Valantasis, a proponent of this reading of John, suggests that John 1:1 be translated to read: "In the beginning was the conversation, and the conversation was in God's presence, and the conversation was God." Early Christians, in this instance members of the Johannine community, enter a way of living through discourse with the living and speaking Jesus that confirms their status as "children of God" (1:12). In this setting, *logos* represents "the divine utterance within the midst of all conversations and debates."[9] For Valantasis, the Beloved Disciple represents the ideal disciple, any person in the flock of Jesus who recognizes the voice of the Shepherd and follows him without question, no matter how challenging the circumstances or the message.

While the prologue states that the Word "enlightens everyone" (1:9), John's narrative will show that many were scandalized by Jesus' claims, meaning they were not brought to the light of faith. The term "enlighten," however, can mean bringing someone's true character to light (cf. 1 Cor. 4:5), meaning that all who encounter Jesus will be exposed under the

---

9. Valantasis, *Gospels and Christian Life*, 254.

searching light of truth. The good news is that as long as the light shines, the possibility of being drawn from unbelief to faith remains (see 12:46). Recognizing that light may generate blindness as well as sight, John's Gospel emphasizes that Jesus' proper work is to bring people to the light of life that comes from knowing God. Whenever Jesus is portrayed as light, he is the light of the world, which means light for the world (1:5, 9; 8:12; 9:4; 11:9; 12:46).

The third strophe of the original hymn (1:10–12b) seems to deal with the earthly ministry of Jesus. Some scholars find in these verses a reference to the Word's activity in the world or in Israel during the pre-Christian period, but if that were so, it would mean that the editor of the prologue misunderstood the hymn by inserting the reference to John the Baptist before verse 10. The conclusive argument that 1:10–12 refers to the ministry of Jesus is found in verse 12. It does not seem possible that in a hymn coming out of Johannine circles the ability to become a child of God would be explained in another way than in terms of having been begotten from above by the Spirit of Jesus (3:5). The hymn of Philippians 2:6–11 also passes from Jesus in the form of God directly to Jesus in his human ministry as a servant.

The incarnation represents the core paradox of the prologue (1:14), for the divine "glory" (*doxa*)—a reference to the majestic splendor, power, and overwhelming weightiness of the divine presence—can be seen in "flesh" (*sarx*), the worldly realm in general and the human sphere in particular. In using terms such as "glory" and "glorify," which figure prominently in the Fourth Gospel, John picks up the Hebraic sense of "glory" as the manifest presence of God whose presence is now visible in Jesus. As John's narrative unfolds, it becomes clear that for the Evangelist, the fullest expression of Jesus' glory is found in his death, resurrection, and ascension (7:39; 12:16, 23, 28; 13:31).

The use of Old Testament language and imagery intensifies as the focus of the prologue turns from the eternal Word to the incarnation, and then to its impact on the believing community. And this Word "lived among us," making his dwelling with humanity. This expression is rich with Old Testament associations, because it recalls God's promise to dwell with God's people (Ezek. 37:27). It comes from the same root as the noun for "tabernacle" or "tent," the place where God spoke to Moses and where God's glory was seen (Exod. 33:9; 40:34). God's "tenting" with humanity is the first in a series of images recalling Israel's Sinai experience that figure in the concluding verses of the prologue ("glory," 1:14; "law," 1:17, and "Moses," 1:17). "The Father's only Son" (1:18) is a Johannine way of speaking of the relationship between God and Jesus. It emphasizes Jesus' unique relationship with God. "Full of grace and truth" (1:14, 17) echoes the Hebrew word pair *hesed* and *'emeth* ("steadfast love and "faithfulness"; Exod. 34:6). "Truth" here and throughout the Gospel, refers not only to accurate information but to Life-giving truth that enlightens and saves. The grace and truth of the Word become the "grace upon grace" (1:16) of the community's life. The double use of "grace" underscores the abundance of gifts available to believers through the incarnate Word. John establishes the theme here and illustrates it throughout the Gospel without naming it[10] ("grace" occurs four times in this Gospel, all in the prologue).

Verse 17 does not disparage Torah, the gift of God through Moses, but points to the gift now available through Jesus Christ as something wondrously new. In this verse Jesus Christ is named in the Gospel for the first time. The ending of the prologue recalls the hymn in Philippians where Jesus also is not named until the end of the hymn (2:10–11). Verse 18 concludes the prologue, but also states explicitly John's understanding of Jesus' ministry: to make God known. The verb "to make known" indicates that Jesus comes as God's interpreter. This bold assertion is supported by three phrases that establish the uniqueness of the revelation of God in Jesus. First, John reminds the reader of a well-known assumption in Judaism: no one has ever seen God. Then he identifies Jesus as "God the only Son." This verse does not claim that the Son is a second God (some manuscripts substitute "Son" for "God" to temper the claim of this phrase; note the variants in the NRSV footnotes), for that would threaten the monotheistic basis of Judaism and Christianity, but rather that the only Son shares in the fullness of God. This is the same claim made in 1:1, "and the Word was God." Third, 1:18 speaks of the intimate relationship between Father and Son, recalling "the Word was with God" in 1:1. In this last verse of the prologue the Evangelist returns to earlier themes, but restates them in the concrete language of the Son and the Father instead of the Word and God. The reader has moved from the eternal Word to the grace and truth of Jesus Christ, the incarnate Word, and is now ready to engage the Gospel narrative.

The introduction of a person named John in 1:6–8 and 15 further underscores that the story has moved from the eternal and preexistent to a specific time and place. John is never called "the Baptist" in the Gospel

---

10. O'Day, *John*, 522–23.

because his role is to witness to Jesus. Witnessing is an important vocation in John because through witness the world comes to know the presence of God in Jesus; this is what the Evangelist means when he refers to believing "in his name" (1:12, 20:31)—that one sees and knows God through Jesus the Word. Those who believe in his name receive new life and existence as children of God.

In an important sense the opening of the Gospel is as much about the origins of the believing community to which it is addressed as it is about the origins of Jesus. In 1:4–5 the focus shifts from creation in general to human beings: the Word came forth from God as Life and Light, indicating ways in which God and the Word are present to sustain humanity. The Word became flesh in order to dwell among *us* (1:14). The Word's coming as Jesus is important for humanity; it is not an isolated marvel touching Jesus only. The purpose was to come to his own home and his own people (1:11), those prepared for such an event by centuries of God's self-disclosure, that they might believe in him and thereby be empowered to become offspring of God (1:12). This divine begetting supersedes the covenantal bond given through Moses (1:17). While John's Gospel assumes at all points the truth of the Israelite revelation—it is a piece of writing that makes no sense apart from the election of Israel by God—yet something went wrong with the plan, for God's own people "did not accept him" (1:11). Yet those who received the Word that became flesh were born anew, "not of blood or of the will of the flesh or of the will of man, but *of God*" (1:13). The story that follows is certainly not of John, nor of "Jesus Christ" only (1:17), but of a new race of humanity. Just as Genesis tells the origins of the cosmos and the human race, the Gospel of John tells a story "about fresh beginnings, a new human race."[11]

Essay 1: The Cultural, Religious, and Intellectual Background of John's Gospel

Having examined some of the essential background for the Gospel of John, we are left with the question of intellectual influence on the thought of the document as a whole. With what ideas had the Evangelist come in contact? What writings shaped his thought? Are there ideas and expressions in the Gospel on loan from elsewhere?

---

11. Sloyan, *John*, 15.

Without question, the Evangelist was significantly influenced by Jewish thought. This means that the Jewish scriptures and extrabiblical writings were part of the author's intellectual palate. There is evidence that the Judaism the Evangelist knew and may have embraced was not simply the rabbinic form of Judaism that became the mainstream tradition after the first century. John's dualistic imagery, for example, and other parallels between Johannine thought and the literature in the Dead Sea Scrolls, convinces us that the Evangelist was acquainted with a broad type of Judaism embracing a wide variety of forms and expressions. Such Judaism tolerated strict Pharisaism together with fervent apocalypticism; for a time it even tolerated the Christian movement within its midst.

This Judaism was receptive to influences from the Hellenistic world, including Greek philosophies, imported mystery religions, and even the Roman imperial cult. The writings of Philo of Alexandria, a first-century Jew, provide a sample of such "Hellenized Jewish" thought. An example is the concept employed at the start of John's prologue, the conceptually rich term *logos*. This term had deep roots in Greek philosophy, as we have demonstrated, yet it was also based on the concept in the Hebrew Bible of the Word of God, fleshed out with Jewish speculation concerning Wisdom. We can imagine that the author of the Fourth Gospel was conscious of the richness of such symbols and ideas, some of which may have been so commonplace that their richness was embraced by both author and readers. With this depth of background, the result was an Evangelist "peculiarly equipped to write a Gospel of exciting concepts and puzzling breadth."[12]

It is important to remember that during the first century the boundaries between Hellenism and Judaism were fluid. In its day, John's Gospel presented a new theological conception designed primarily for a Jewish audience—that the Word was God and became flesh—and repeats the singular morality found in Paul's writings and across the New Testament— that God's love, the hallmark of the new community, fulfills Torah.

That new community, which over the course of several centuries evolved out of Judaism into Christianity, was, for John (as for Paul) the New Israel, a community shaped by the words and deeds but particularly by the death and resurrection of Jesus Christ. This gospel was to be the community's New Torah. While John's Gospel may have included in its audience Jewish proselytes and Gentile converts, the categories by which

---

12. Kysar, *Maverick Gospel*, 32.

Jesus is described in John—Creator, Messiah, Life, Light, Prophet, Logos, King, Son of God, Son of Man, Lamb of God, Revealer of God, Shepherd, Bread, Vine, Giver of Spirit—are entirely comprehensible to Jews. This comprehension is further corroborated by the combination of biblical quotations and especially by allusions to the Old Testament such as the snake in the desert (3:14) and the manna from heaven (6:31–34). One thinks also of the way Jesus' person and work are tied in John 5—7 to elements in the Jewish feasts, where the major symbols in these chapters—bread, water, and light—are closely connected with their use in Jewish rituals connected to the Sabbath, Passover, Booths, and Hanukkah, or how no explanation is offered of "the Son of Man" (1:51), "the Prophet" (1:21, 25: 6:14), the devil (13:2) or of Satan (13:27). The story of Jacob's ladder is presupposed (1:51), even as the opening words of the prologue remind readers of the opening of Genesis.

John declares this agenda, this new understanding (see 6:32) of the Israelite paradigm, in his prologue (1:17), in a passage characterized by Hebrew poetic parallelism, contrasting Hebrew Torah (Mosaic Law) with the Grace and Truth of the Gospel and contrasting Moses with Jesus Christ:

> The law (Torah) indeed was given though Moses;
> Grace and truth came through Jesus Christ.[13]

John's message to his community is clear: the mission of Jesus, the long-awaited New Moses (see the discussion on "the Prophet" in John 1:25), is to reveal God by bringing New Torah to God's New People (1:9–13, 18). The twin tables of Torah are being fulfilled and superseded by the New Theology (Love of God) and the New Morality (Love of One Another; see Matt. 22:36–40; cf. John 13:34–35; 15:17).

The theme of John's Gospel is clear: if you want to know God, take a close look at Jesus. He is the Word bringing into being the new creation, through which God says once again: "Let there be light!" However, when God sends the Word into the world, specifically to Israel, the chosen people don't recognize him. This is the central problem that dominates John's Gospel. Jesus comes to God's people, and they do what the rest of the world does: they prefer darkness to light. That is why fresh grace is needed, on top of the grace already received (1:16). The Law, given by

---

13. As noted above, Hebrew poetry distinguishes between *synonymous* parallelism, *antithetical* parallelism, and *ascending* parallelism. How one interprets the pair in John 1:17 is critical. Does John have in mind synonymous, antithetical, or ascending parallelism? I argue the latter.

Moses, points in the right direction, but like Moses, it cannot take us to the Promised Land. For that we need the grace and truth that come through Jesus the Word, Messiah, and Son of God.[14]

Questions to Ponder

1. What does John's prologue tell you about God?
2. Describe your understanding of the Word's relationship to God? How can the Word both be with God and be God (John 1:1)?
3. What does it mean in John 1:14 that "the Word became flesh"?
4. What does John's prologue say about Jesus Christ's role as Revealer of God to Jews?
5. What does John's prologue say about Jesus Christ's role as Revealer of God to Gentiles?
6. Why is "light" an appropriate metaphor for the work of Jesus?
7. Describe the result (or the consequence) of disbelief in Jesus Christ.
8. What does it mean in John 1:17 that "grace and truth came through Jesus Christ"?
9. Do you find John 1:18 to be an adequate summary of the prologue? Why or why not?
10. How does John's message in the prologue compare with ideas about Christ in Philippians 2:5–11 and Colossians 1:15–20? In these passages, what are the most powerful images for you? Explain your answer.

---

14. Wright, *John*, 1:5.

PART II

The Public Ministry of Jesus

Phase One

(JOHN 1:19—4:54)

CHAPTER 2

The Initial Revelation of Jesus:
The First Witnesses
(John 1:19–51)

Summary: The Gospel now enters the realm of narrative. John the Baptist's witness to Jesus causes some of his disciples to begin following Jesus. Those disciples enlist others to "come and see."

Assignment: Read John 1:19–51

Key Passage: John 1:51

Central Theme: The Lamb of God Takes Charge

Key Symbols/Concepts: John (the Baptist), the Jews, the Messiah, Elijah, the Prophet, water, the Lamb of God, the Holy Spirit, Rabbi, Son of God, King of Israel, Son of Man

Learning Objectives
Participants will examine:
1. John's depiction of John the Baptist and his role as witness to Jesus
2. The nature and meaning of the Christological titles introduced in this section
3. What it means to be called to follow Jesus
4. The metaphorical meaning of John 1:51

Outline to John 1:19–51
  I. The First Witness of John the Baptist to Jesus 1:19–34
  II. The Calling of the First Disciples 1:35–51

Journeys into Discipleship

The narrative of Jesus' work as the Word incarnate in John 1:19–51 confirms the information given to the reader in the prologue, focusing on two interrelated themes basic to the Gospel as a whole: the identity of Jesus and the meaning of discipleship. The first chapter contains three recognition scenes: John the Baptist, Andrew, and Nathanael. The purpose of John the Baptist's witness is to reveal Jesus, who is the source of redemption for the world (1:29). John identifies Jesus with a traditional image from Judaism, Lamb of God, but his witness culminates with the central claim of the Fourth Gospel, that Jesus is the Son of God (1:34). Andrew, a disciple of the Baptist before following Jesus, recruits his brother Simon to join him, identifying Jesus as the long-awaited Jewish Messiah. Nathanael, the subject of the final discipleship story in chapter 1, demonstrates his move from skeptic to believer, though even this journey is incomplete.

In this segment we find an abundance of Christological titles; each disciple sees something different in Jesus and bears witness in his own way. Each comes to Jesus with different needs and expectations: one needs a teacher, another the Messiah, another the fulfillment of scripture—and each need is met. Yet Jesus suggests in 1:50 that none of these titles ultimately answers the question of his identity, for the testimonies of these witnesses are only the beginning: "You will see greater things than these." Verse 51 suggests that the reality of God in Jesus outruns traditional categories and titles. The rich variety of testimonies in 1:29–51 is "both cautionary and celebratory. It cautions the reader not to limit Jesus to preconceived categories and expectations but to keep one's eyes open for a surprising revelation of God."[1] The "I am" sayings of Jesus scattered through the Johannine discourses point to a similar "fullness" of grace in Jesus (1:16).

The Christological focus of this passage reveals much about the Evangelist's understanding of discipleship. The decision to be a disciple

---

1. O'Day, *John*, 533.

is inseparable from the decision one makes about Jesus' identity. As each new disciple comes to Jesus, the decision to follow Jesus is made in response to a statement about Jesus' identity (1:41, 45). These stories remind the church that discipleship is an active engagement with Jesus. John 1:19–51 consists almost entirely of dialogue, so that the readers themselves are drawn into the drama of discipleship, pondering Jesus' initial question to the first disciples, "What are you looking for?" (1:38) and his words of invitation: "Come and see" (1:39). The stories are dominated by verbs: follow, see, seek, stay, find. These verbs emphasize that discipleship is active and involves interacting with Jesus. For John, the ideal disciple is yet to be revealed, though his presence may be hinted at in 1:35–42, where an unknown disciple of John the Baptist joins Andrew as a follower of Jesus. Could this be the Evangelist's first reference to the Beloved Disciple?

Analysis of John 1:19–51

John 1:19–51 constitutes a narrative introduction to the Gospel. As the Gospel seems to have two conclusions (John 20:30–31 and John 21), so it has two beginnings (the prologue and 1:19–51). The narrative introduction presents the testimony of John the Baptist and the calling of the first disciples. A temporal framework, based upon a progressive typology, ties together the various stories in this segment. John appeared as the first witness to Jesus in the prologue, and his witness begins the Gospel proper. On the first day (1:19–28), John testifies that he is not the light; on the second day (1:29–34), John testifies to the light; on the third day, John testifies to his disciples, who in turn follow Jesus (1:35–42); on the fourth day, Nathanael (called a true "Israelite") encounters Jesus, the one "about whom Moses in the law and also the prophets wrote" (1:45), and testifies that Jesus is the Son of God, the King of Israel (note that Jesus is not here called King of the Jews, as in 19:19). Chapter 2 begins with yet another temporal reference: "On the third day." Scholars question whether John's seven-day sequence is an allusion to the week of creation in Genesis (the third day follows three days after the fourth-day sequence of chapter 1) or whether the phrase "[o]n the third day" in 2:1 might be a veiled reference to the day of resurrection (see 2:19–22).

In 1:19–28 "the Jews" from Jerusalem send a delegation to John the Baptist to ascertain his identity. It will become clear to readers of the prologue that these emissaries represent "the world" (see 1:10; 15:18), those in the earthly sphere that represent disbelief in Jesus and in his forerunner. This passage calls attention to the importance of confession (1:20). When confronted by the priestly and pharisaic delegation, John speaks in negatives (1:20–28). Not only is he not the Messiah, but he must not even say "I am." That title rightly belongs only to Jesus. It is not for John to say that he is Elijah or the Prophet (the expected "prophet like Moses"; see Deut. 18:15, 18–19). He is but a voice crying in the wilderness, making room for the coming of Jesus. Confronted by Jesus (1:29–34), John no longer speaks in negatives, for he has seen the one he calls "the Lamb of God" (1:29, 36).[2] By introducing this title early in the narrative, the Evangelist is agreeing with the other gospel writers that the movement of the plot is toward the cross and the resurrection.

Unlike the Synoptics, the Fourth Evangelist does not report the baptism of Jesus. Instead, he uses John the Baptist to introduce the coming of the Spirit upon Jesus, an important theme for the Evangelist (3:3; 14:17; 26; 15:26; 16:12–14; 20:22). John's faithful witness continues, culminating with John's second confession: Jesus is the Son of God (1:34).

The next section (1:35–42) begins with the same expression as verses 29 and 43: "The next day." The witness of John is not accepted by the crowd but by two of his own disciples. They do not understand who Jesus is, for they call him Rabbi, a title that in John's Gospel usually introduces an inadequate understanding, question, or action (1:49; 3:2; 4:31; 6:25; 9:2; 11:8; 20:16). The Evangelist assumes his readers are familiar with the earlier Synoptic tradition, where Jesus calls two pairs of brothers: Simon and Andrew, James and John (Mark 1:16–20 and Matt. 4:18–22). While two disciples of John the Baptist are mentioned, only one is named (Andrew). Verse 41 notes that Andrew first brought his brother Simon, suggesting that the other disciple also brought his brother. Because the Evangelist retains this disciple's anonymity, his identity belongs to the problem of the Beloved Disciple or to the "other disciple" who remains unnamed and who is said to be a close associate of Peter (13:23–25; 18:15, 16; 20:2–10; 21:7, 20–23; cf. 19:26, 27, and 35). While the Fourth Gospel never mentions John nor his brother James by name (only in the epilogue do we find reference to "the sons of Zebedee"; 21:2) the brothers are mentioned by name frequently in Luke, who also depicts John as close associate of Peter (8:51; 9:28; Acts 1:13).

2. For an explanation of this title and other Christological titles in 1:19–51, see essay 2: "John's Jesus—Then and Now."

If the identity of the second disciple in 1:35, 37 is the Beloved Disciple, the question arises as to why he is not named. This scene fits a pattern we will observe in later chapters, where the Beloved Disciple embodies the essential life of the entire Johannine community, transcending individual identity to typify faithful discipleship. In his association with Peter, reputed to be a pillar disciple in the church, the Beloved Disciple is sometimes elevated at Peter's expense.

The brief conversation between Jesus and the two disciples moves on two levels, educating readers in what to expect from this Gospel. The first words that Jesus speaks in John are "What are you looking for?" This is a natural question if two people are following you. At a deeper level, of course, it is one of the great existential questions of life: "What are you searching for?" The two disciples respond, apparently naively, "Rabbi, where are you staying?" In the Greek, the word for "to stay" is also translated "to abide," which brings out an important theme in John. In 14:2 Jesus will tell the disciples that he is going to prepare dwelling places (lit. "abiding places") for them, and in 14:23 he indicates that he and the Father will come to them and abide with them ("make our home with them"), a theme introduced in 1:14.

On one level, Jesus' answer to the two disciples is a word of invitation: "Come and see." But the response can be understood on a deeper level. The reader suspects that this is an invitation to discipleship. Seeing and believing is another important theme in the Gospel, and by the end of the Gospel, Jesus will call the disciples from believing in response to what they have seen (the signs) to believing without having seen (20:29).

John 1:42 alerts readers to the biblical pattern that one learns one's true identity when he or she discovers Jesus. Here Jesus gives Simon a new name: Cephas (an Aramaic nickname translated "Peter," from the Greek word for rock, *petra*). In the Synoptics, Peter receives primacy among the disciples for his confession that Jesus is the Messiah (Mark 8:29; Matt. 16:16-19; Luke 9:20), but in the Gospel of John, Peter's brother steals the scene early on, for it is Andrew who finds Simon and tells him, "We have found the Messiah" (1:41).

The disciples come to Jesus by different paths: two come in obedience to the words of John the Baptist, two because of a family tie, Philip as the result of a direct call given by Jesus, and Nathanael as the result of true Jewish skepticism. Nathanael's faith is real, though partial and inadequately grounded. While he rightly calls Jesus the Son of God, his understanding is limited to a Jewish messianic hope, much like the crowds at Jesus' triumphal entry into Jerusalem (12:13). Unlike Nathanael, who is not named in the Synoptics, Philip's role, minimal in the Synoptics, is expanded in the Fourth Gospel (6:5, 7; 12:21, 22; 14:8, 9). When Philip calls Jesus "son of Joseph from Nazareth" (1:45), commentators question whether the Fourth Evangelist was acquainted with the stories about the virginal conception of Jesus. In light of the ironic statement in 6:42, it may be that the Evangelist deliberately included Philip's remark early in the narrative to introduce a topic central to his thinking: misunderstanding Jesus' origins. The gap between the reader's knowledge and the information available to Philip allows the Evangelist to exploit the ironic potential of the narrative situation, drawing the reader to the narrator's omniscient perspective while watching characters fumble in ignorance. The choice between identifying with the narrator or with the inexpert disciples is easy: readers side with the narrator in knowing that Jesus comes from above (3:31).

Nathanael qualifies as a witness because he seems an honest Jewish person who requires evidence before believing in Jesus. His reply, the now-famous remark "Can anything good come out of Nazareth?" means that God would not bring the Messiah from such an obscure village. Nathanael represents skepticism, as if the author were suggesting that it is better to doubt openly than to be easily deceived, or better to question than to be a Judas who betrays Jesus while acclaiming him Master. The reference to Nathanael's being under a fig tree (1:50) may be an allusion to the traditional place where a teacher would study the Torah, in which case the Evangelist may be portraying Nathanael as an expert in the scriptures, a type of the true Israelite who recognizes Jesus to be the Messiah, the true King of Israel.[3]

Though we are told that the disciples believed (1:50; 2:11), we are not told precisely what the content of their faith was. Their belief was partial, for they were only on the way to becoming full-fledged disciples. The entire Gospel is in many ways about discipleship, about the pilgrimage that leads to a fully adequate faith in Jesus. The Evangelist intimates that fully adequate understanding and faith come only after Easter. This

---

3. Building on a possibility first introduced by E. F. Scott early in the twentieth century, John Shelby Spong makes an interesting case that Nathanael is not an actual person, but a veiled reference to the apostle Paul. John "could have chosen in this manner to signify his appreciation of Paul and at the same time reveal to his readers that this Johannine character and John's entire gospel needed to be read non-literally," *Fourth Gospel*, 72.

means that the characters in this drama, including Jesus' mother, Nicodemus, the Samaritan woman, the blind man, and others, are not yet full-fledged Christians but rather examples of ways to come to adequate faith in Jesus. Full-fledged faith is only disclosed in chapter 20, when Thomas declares Jesus "Lord" and "God" (20:28).

John 1:51, the key passage of this unit, introduces the phrase "Son of Man," which appears thirteen times in John, often in contexts discussing revelation (6:27, 53), Jesus' death (3:14; 8:28), and the authority of Jesus (5:27; 9:39). Historically speaking, the title Son of Man was the designation Jesus felt most comfortable using of himself. The background of that title lies in the Hebrew scriptures, most likely Daniel 7:13–14, a passage that seems to stress the theme of Jesus' heavenly origin and destiny. Paradoxically, what the title does not convey in John is Jesus' humanity.

John 1:51 alludes to Jacob's dream at Bethel (Gen. 28:12), in which he saw a ladder with angels ascending to heaven and descending to earth. Here, however, the angels are said to be ascending and descending upon Jesus. The words about the opening of heaven refer to having a vision, in this case a vision that unveils the truth about Jesus—something that can be known only by revelation. The language of vision here is quite similar to what is said about the Baptist's seeing the Spirit descending upon Jesus in 1:32. The meaning is that Jesus is the new Bethel, the place where heaven and earth, God and humanity, meet. The angels ascend from and descend to the Son of Man because he has become the place on earth where the heavenly and earthly realms come together. By alluding to Bethel, the Evangelist prepares for the discussion in 2:19–22 about Jesus being the temple of God. It is in Jesus, not in the temple, that one finds the presence of God perfectly joined with a human being. In such a context, worship need no longer be place-centered but rather person-centered (4:20–26).

In Genesis, the Bethel narrative concludes with Jacob's exclamation: "How awesome is this place! This is none other than the house of God, and this is the gate of heaven" (Gen. 28:17). The Johannine response seems to be: "How awesome is this person, who is the locus not only of God's revelation but also of God's presence on earth." Chapter 1 of John is connected by powerful Christological affirmations: the prologue speaks of the Word become flesh (1:14), John the Baptist's testimony informs us that "this is the Son of God" (1:34), and the final segment ends with the pronouncement that Jesus is the Son of Man (1:51).

Essay 2: John's Jesus—Then and Now

Who is Jesus Christ, and why is he so important for the Christian faith? The Christian doctrine of the person of Christ, known as Christology, sets out to explore why the church believes that Jesus of Nazareth, a first-century Galilean peasant, holds the key to the nature of God and of human destiny.

One of the perennial tasks of Christian theology has been the clarification of the relationship between human and divine elements in the person of Jesus Christ. The Council of Chalcedon (451) laid down the controlling principle for classical Christology, accepted as definitive by most Christian theologians: "provided that it is recognized that Jesus Christ is both truly divine and truly human, the precise manner in which this is articulated or explored is not of fundamental importance."[4]

It can be argued that there are three fundamental concepts of Christ in the New Testament: adoptionist, agency, and incarnational. (1) *Adoptionist Christology* suggests that Jesus was a man who, because of his obedience to God, was adopted as God's Messiah. This adoption may have taken place sometime during the ministry of Jesus, such as at his baptism or his transfiguration, but more often it is associated with the resurrection. The presence of early adoptionist Christology has been found in Acts 2:36; 3:13; and Romans 1:2–4. (2) *Agency Christology* is more common in the New Testament. This view understands Jesus to be God's agent, sent as God's personal representative to perform a revelatory and saving function. This kind of thinking is present in passages which stress that God "sent" Jesus. It is one of John's favorite expressions (3:34), but it is found elsewhere in the New Testament as well.[5] (3) The boldest of the claims for Christ is embodied in *incarnational Christology,* which stresses Christ's preexistence with God as well as his incarnation in human flesh. The prologue to John is the clearest statement of incarnational Christology in the New Testament, though Colossians 1:15–20 and Philippians 2:6–11 express similar views.

While the topic of Christology is central to the Gospel of John, the topic is not approached abstractly or metaphysically but relationally, in association with discipleship, with what it means to be a believer. While religious traditions rooted in a historical figure develop claims for the uniqueness of the founder as well as his or her revelation,

---

4. McGrath, *Christian Theology*, 284.
5. A fuller discussion of agency language in John is found at the start of chapter 4.

for John it is not Jesus' experience that is central but rather it is the believers' experience of Jesus.

The explanation of the nature of the founder is an early and vitally important stage in the emergence of every religious tradition, and that is certainly the case with Johannine Christians. The New Testament provides us with ample evidence of the efforts of the early Christians to formulate an understanding of Jesus' person and work. The results are complex and diverse, for the New Testament writings do not present a single or even a consistent view of Christ. The Fourth Gospel represents an important contribution to the emerging view of Christ among first-century Christians. It takes a unique and sometimes radical approach to Jesus, one that that is not altogether consistent, for the Gospel presents diverse assertions about Christ. The following topics provide an overall understanding of John's Christology: (1) the Logos or Word Christology of John's prologue; (2) the variety of Christological titles employed in 1:19–51; (3) the Son of Man and the Father-Son relationship in the Gospel; (4) the importance of the "I am" sayings for Christology; and (5) the work of Christ accomplished in his death.[6] We will discuss the first three here and the remaining points in other essays.

1. The presence of Logos Christology, inserted in the prologue but obviously central to the Evangelist, takes a concept current in Hellenistic philosophies but also central to Jewish thought and plies its imaginative richness to suggest that in one person Jesus fulfills simultaneously the variety of religious and philosophical views of the universe. Christ is Stoic Logos, Hebraic Word of God, and Jewish Wisdom all in one. The thrust of the prologue, however, seems to be that for the Christian, Logos is a person and not an abstract philosophical concept.

Of the many affirmations about the Logos, the first constitutes the highest: the Logos existed from the beginning, before things began. For John, as for the Synoptic Evangelists, Christ is so vital that he could not have come into being like any other person or object. The authors of Matthew and Luke implied this when they incorporated the stories of Jesus' Virgin Birth and his conception by the Holy Spirit. The Fourth Evangelist goes one step further to say the same thing: Christ existed before creation, meaning he is not a created being. Another affirmation about the Logos is that he was the agent of creation: "All things came into being

---

6. This segment is adapted from Robert Kysar's essay "The Father's Son—Johannine Christology" in *Maverick Gospel*, 37–56.

through him" (1:3). As agent of creation, he is the source of a new kind of life, a life attuned to the divine purpose for human existence.

A central concern in John is the relationship of this preexistent, creative Logos to God. If we ask whether the Evangelist is suggesting full divinity, along the lines of the later Nicene or Chalcedonian Christology, such formulation presses the imagery too far. In 1:1, a key text for John's Christology, the author may simply be teasing the reader: "The Logos was with God, and the Logos was God." Insofar as the preposition "with" suggests relationship, this sentence makes two different claims: the Logos is a distinct being, yet identical with God. This means there is both *individuality* and *identification* in the relationship between God and Logos. That's as far as John goes. We should not make the prologue read like a treatise on the Trinity, since it was written long before the church wrestled with this concept.

Yet we find here the paradox at the heart of Christianity, that somehow individuality (distinctiveness, twoness) and identity (equivalence, oneness) coexist in the person of Jesus. Robert Kysar addresses the paradox by appealing to the analogy of personality, which views persons as having two sides or dimensions, an inward side, known only to themselves and rarely expressed, and an outward side, revealed to others. Understood in this way, the Logos is the expressive outward side of God. This does not mean that God is exhausted in the Logos, but that the Logos is that dimension of God that has come to expression for the comprehension of humans.

This leads to 1:14, the most complete statement of incarnational Christology in the New Testament: "And the Word became flesh and lived among us." Here the divine nature of the preexistent Logos is most clearly affirmed, and here the humanization or enfleshment of that Logos is openly declared. Such claims and understanding are poetic and imaginative in the most profound sense. John's Logos imagery, expressed in the language of liturgy, articulates a model of meaning and a cosmic perspective that encompasses the experience of a worshipping community. The prologue cannot be confined to historical or factual descriptions but rather bursts out of the mundane to tell us something about early Christians and their perception of reality.

Apart from the prologue, John never expressly states that Jesus is the divine Logos. However, he affirms that Jesus utters the *logos* of God (the revelation or Word of God), which, in accordance with Jewish and Christian tradition, is conceived as embodied in scripture. In a profound sense the Word of God is found in the words of Jesus. So in 17:14 Jesus says, "I have given them your word (*logos*), to which he adds, "your word is truth" (17:17). Thus the *logos* of Jesus is the *logos* of God. In view of the equation of the divine *logos* with "truth," it is significant that Jesus says, "I am the truth" (14:6). Hence Jesus not only gives the word of God, which is truth, he *is* truth; he not only gives life, but *is* life; he not only gives the bread of life, he *is* the bread. As we discover in 6:63, Jesus' words are "spirit and life." It is only a step from that to say: "Jesus is the Logos."

2. John 1:19-51 is packed with Christological affirmations. A survey of these titles is a summary of the varied ways by which the Fourth Gospel explains its understanding of Christ:

(a) The first title in this passage is spoken by John the Baptist: *Lamb of God* (1:29, 36). This title evokes numerous meanings, including Passover imagery of liberation from bondage; the sacrificial lamb, symbolic of the remorse of the sinner and the removal of human sin; the Suffering Servant of Isaiah (Isa. 53:7) whose suffering atones for the sin of others; and the conquering lamb of God, which according to Jewish apocalyptic literature, is expected to appear at the end of time to destroy evil in the world.[7] The Passover reference is appealing, since according to John, Jesus is crucified precisely at the time the Passover lambs are being slain in preparation for the meal (19:14). The text from Isaiah 53:7 is applied to Jesus in Acts 8:32, so comparing Jesus to a vicarious suffering lamb was known to early Christians. However, for John, the death of Jesus is not so much a sacrifice as an ironic means of exaltation of Jesus. So we are left with the idea of the horned lamb as leader of the flock of God, a symbol of the Messiah as "King of Israel" (1:49), who comes to abolish or do away with sin. To make an end of sin is a function of the Jewish Messiah, quite apart from any thought of a redemptive death. Primitive Christianity retained and emphasized this function of the Messiah (Matt. 1:21; Acts 5:31). Thus the expression "Lamb of God who takes away the sin of the world" (1:29) is entirely intelligible on the basis of primitive Christian messianic belief, apart from any theology of atonement.[8] Therefore, it is likely that the Evangelist wants readers to ponder the liberating qualities of Christ, understood in broader terms than that of an expiatory death. The Lamb of God is the liberating revealer of God: "You will know the truth, and the truth will make you free" (8:32). To know Christ is to know

---

7. Brown, *John*, 1:58-63.
8. Dodd, *Interpretation*, 237-38.

the truth, according to the Fourth Gospel (14:6); to know him is to be freed from the sin of disbelief.

(b) The next title, *Messiah* (1:41), is related to the expression "King of Israel" in 1:49 and to messianic ideas in 1:45. These are all ways of referring to the special agent of God who is to come, including images of an ideal Jewish king who will rule justly. By the first century AD, messianic titles included more than political rule; they suggested economic as well as political rescue, religious justice, correction of falsehood, and destruction of the forces of evil in the world. Such a redeemer was variously thought of as a human, a super hero, and even an angelic type of divine creature. Messianic titles in John 1 emphasize the conviction that Jesus was the fulfillment of a host of expectations relative to a future savior figure.

(c) Related to these expectations is the title *Son of God* (1:49), a term whose historical and biblical precedents appear in close connection with the messianic title. In 1:49 Nathanael uses the title as a synonym for King of Israel. In this case the title has a traditional messianic sense, but in 1:49 Jesus is more than that. This is made clear in the persistent theme of the relationship between Jesus and John the Baptist in chapter 1, where Jesus is said to be greater than the Baptist (1:27, 30) because (1) he was before him (a possible reference to the preexistence of Christ); (2) because he baptizes with the Holy Spirit (1:33), unlike John who baptizes with water; and (3) because he is the light, whereas John is only a witness to the light (1:8). While the Baptist had acquired a large following, not only in Palestine but as far across the Roman world as Ephesus (Acts 19:1–7), the Evangelist's claim is that Jesus is in an entirely different category from the Baptist.

(d) The climax of the identity of Jesus comes in the last title, *Son of Man* (1:51). While for John Jesus is the Messiah in the sense that all previous titles suggest, his real identity is surely found in the meaning of Son of Man. Jewish speculation had conceived of a heavenly human who resided with God from creation, designated a divine agent of God. A complex figure, combining messianic and eschatological roles, he would come among humans at a time of God's choosing to overcome evil and establish the reign of God on earth (Dan. 7:13–14). While the title is prominent in the Synoptic Gospels, it seems to be John's preferred title for Jesus, a title he regularly simplifies to *Son* (used eighteen times of Jesus in John).

Despite the different literary and cultural trajectories underlying the Johannine titles Son of God and Son of Man, there is some overlap in their usage by John. Nevertheless, it is not inaccurate to say that John associates the Son of Man title more with Jesus' historic revelatory work and Son of God with his relationship to the Father. On the other hand, it would certainly be misleading to suggest that in the Gospel of John Son of Man refers to Jesus' human nature and Son of God to his divine nature.[9]

3. The Son of Man and Son titles constitute the heart of Johannine Christology as well as of the Father-Son relationship. The following assertions summarize the relevant passages:

(a) Jesus is the Son of Man (9:35-38), indicating what for John is an obvious point, namely that the man Jesus of Nazareth was indeed this mysterious Son of Man.

(b) Jesus' home is in the heavenly realm with God (3:13-15). The Son of Man originates in that heavenly home, descends into the human world, and will once again ascend to his home (3:13; 6:62; 16:28). The Messiah's origin was a validating credential for Jews in the first century, and the Evangelist uses that concern to make the point repeatedly that the Son of Man has no earthly origin. The descent and ascent themes confuse the opponents of Jesus (6:42-43; 7:41; 8:22), demonstrating the crowd's complete misunderstanding of Jesus' words.

(c) The Son has been sent by the Father. This idea confirms Jesus' heavenly origin and destination (3:34; 4:34; 8:26; 9:4; 17:3). Jesus, the agent of God, is no mere prophet; he is none other than the Son of Man.

(d) The Son of Man will be "lifted up" and ascend into heaven. Three times Jesus speaks of his being "lifted up" (3:13-15; 8:28; 12:32). For John this term refers to the act of crucifying (lifting the victim onto the cross), but it also means exaltation (as in exalting a king to his throne). Throughout the Gospel Jesus' death is the revelation of his identity, for John's passion account is not of a victim suffering disgrace and humiliation but of the Son being glorified.

(e) The functions of the Son are the functions of God. The Father gives to the Son those tasks that are thought to be God's. In the matter of judgment, the Son judges on behalf of the Father (3:18; 5:22, 27). Likewise, the Son of Man (or Son) is the giver of eternal life (3:15; 6:27, 53). The Son also reveals the glory of God (in the Hebrew Bible, glory denotes the very presence of God). In saying that the Son reveals the glory of God (13:31), the Evangelist is asserting that the presence of God is in the presence of the Son.

---

9. Smith, *Theology*, 132.

(f) The Son carries the full authority of the Father, bearing the Father's divine "seal" (6:27). The authority of the Son is asserted as well in Jesus' insistence that his glorification is that of the Father (13:31). This matter of divine authority residing in the Son may well represent the enigmatic statement at 1:51, an image suggesting that the lines of communication are always open and active in the relationship between the Son and the Father.

(g) While the Father and Son are represented as one (10:30, 38; 17:22), the Son is said to be obedient to the Father (4:34), which implies distinct individuality. Similarly, the Father loves the Son (3:35). Can there be love without individuality? Finally, the Father is greater than the Son (14:28), which contradicts any conclusion that the Father and Son in the Fourth Gospel are fully one and equal.

(h) The Evangelist calls Jesus the "only Son" (3:16, 18, and possibly 1:18). The word "only," meaning "one of its kind," makes clear that the sonship of Christ is absolutely unique. Possibly the qualification means to suggest the absolute distinction between Jesus' sonship and any ideas of humans as sons of God (since they may be "children of God." 1:12). In addition, whatever other divine beings there may be, Jesus is superior to them in his unique sonship.

(i) Finally, the Evangelist wants readers to know that to respond to Jesus is to respond to God (5:23). The point of John's discussions of the identity of Jesus is not metaphysical or purely theological but practical. How one responds to the Son constitutes one's response to God. Accept him and you accept God; reject him and you reject God.

Readers of John must be aware that the Evangelist loved paradox. While we may not be altogether clear what the author had in mind Christologically, we must assume that he must have known. He was not groping for clarity on that topic, but speaking rather to a unique relationship that is unlike any human association. The result is paradoxical: the Son is one with the Father but not identical; he is divine, yet he is subordinate to God. The author is struggling to communicate his understanding of the relationship to God of the founder of his faith, but has no pat solutions to offer. "What is clear is that the Son is the divine agent who participates in the being of the Father, yet has a distinct individuality of his own. The relationship is in the final analysis a mystery."[10] Whatever Christological meaning present-day Christians attribute to Jesus,

---

10. Kysar, *Maverick Gospel*, 55.

whether as pastors, theologians, or lay people, they should heed John's approach, valuing relational categories over metaphysical ones. As Fred Craddock notes, "any single title by which one confesses faith in Jesus is insufficient and reductionistic."[11]

Having emphasized the understanding of Jesus based upon Christological titles, we must not ignore the assumption of the gospel writers that Jesus had a normal, progressive human consciousness, and that awareness of what God wanted him to do did not come all at once, whether at his birth, his baptism, or his temptation, but over the course of time and as a result of certain things that happened during his ministry. God gradually guided and instructed Jesus, and there were clearly times of deep insight into what would transpire. This is the portrayal of Jesus, not only in the Synoptics, but also in John. This portrayal is of great importance, for it means that Jesus was a human who learned as time went on (see Luke 2:52), who suffered hunger, thirst, and exhaustion (John 4:6), who questioned (Mark 5:30) and admitted there were things God had withheld (Mark 13:32). In other words, each gospel, including John, makes clear that in becoming human Jesus also took on limitations of time, space, knowledge, and endurance. This paradox is not resolved in John, or in the rest of scripture.[12]

Questions to Ponder

1. When you examine the Synoptic account of John the Baptist, what general impression do you get? How would you describe his lifestyle and his message, and why might others think he was the Messiah?
2. Is the Baptist's role in the Fourth Gospel different from his role in the Synoptic Gospels?
3. What was the Baptist saying about Jesus when he described him as the "Lamb of God"?
4. What is the meaning of the Baptist's reference to the Holy Spirit in 1:32–34?
5. In John, what new titles did Nathanael use for Jesus? What do they signify?

---

11. Craddock, *John*, 37.
12. Witherington, *John's Wisdom*, 112–13.

6. Which Christological title best summarizes the meaning of Jesus for you? Why?

7. What is the Johannine meaning of John 1:51 in the overall context of John's Gospel? What meaning(s) might this verse impart to Christians today?

CHAPTER 3

Belief and Disbelief: The Early Signs and Discourses
(John 2:1—4:54)

Summary: Jesus performs his first sign at a wedding in Cana. The scene shifts from Galilee in the north to Jerusalem in Judea, where Jesus drives the animal sellers and money changers from the temple. By way of explanation, Jesus indicates that he is both fulfilling scripture and anticipating his death and resurrection. Jesus then embarks on two long discussions, one with the Pharisee Nicodemus and the other with the Samaritan woman at the well. The discussion with Nicodemus focuses on spiritual birth, belief, and the consequences of disbelief, while the discussion with the woman focuses on Christology. The passage concludes with Jesus' return to Cana, where he performs his second Galilean sign, the healing of an official's son.

Assignment: Read John 2–4

Key Passages: John 3:16; 4:42

Central Theme: Jesus is the Giver of Life

Key Symbols/Concepts: wedding feast, wine, sign, glory, Passover, temple; Kingdom of God, spiritual birth, the Spirit, lifted up, eternal life, light, darkness, judgment, Samaritan, living water, truth, Messiah, harvest, Savior

Learning Objectives

Participants will examine:

1. The relationship between Jesus and Judaism
2. The role of symbolism and of "signs" in John's Gospel
3. The concept of spiritual birth
4. The meaning of judgment and condemnation in 3:16–21
5. The nature of Jesus and the gifts he brings to humanity from God
6. The nature of mission in 4:34–38 and its relationship to Christian discipleship

Outline to John 2:1—4:54

I. The First Sign: The Wedding at Cana 2:1–12

II. Cleansing the Temple 2:13–25

III. Jesus and Nicodemus 3:1–21

    A. The New Birth 3:1–11

    B. Belief and Disbelief: Salvation and Judgment 3:12–21

IV. The Final Witness of John 3:22—4:3

V. Jesus and Samaritans 4:4–42

    A. Jesus and the Samaritan Woman 4:4–30

    B. Jesus, Disciples, and Mission 4:31–38

    C. Jesus, Samaritans, and Mission 4:39–42

VI. The Second Sign: Healing the Officer's Son 4:43–54

Jesus as the Source of Life

Chapter 2 begins the public phase of Jesus' ministry (2:1—12:50). It also provides the first demonstration of the "greater things" promised to Nathanael in 1:50–51. Chapters 2—4 stand out as a distinct unit that is marked off geographically and thematically. John 2 begins in Cana of Galilee (the home town of Nathanael, according to 21:2) and John 4 brings the unit to a close, again in Cana. The events of the opening account, a wedding feast, are referred to by John as the first of Jesus' "signs"

(2:11), whereas the closing account, the official's son, is called the second of Jesus' signs (4:54), and these are the only two signs that are numbered. In the Fourth Gospel, the actions of Jesus are consistently named signs (2:23; 4:54; 6:2, 14, 26; 7:31; 9:16; 10:41; 11:47; 12:18, 37; 20:30). Signs in the Gospel are not narrated as prodigies or wonders to evoke curiosity or even awe, but are more properly parables of the nature of Jesus' work: they manifest his glory (1:14; see 7:4; 21:1).

Chapters 2—4 are also marked off thematically in that they develop the theme of Jesus as the giver of life. The prologue introduces the Word as Life (1:4; cf. 1 John 1:1, where Jesus is called "the word of life"), and the purpose statement in John's first conclusion urges readers to believe, in order that they may "have life" (20:31).

The theme of Jesus as the source of life is central in this section. For example, at the wedding feast (2:1–12), both wine and weddings celebrate the goodness of life. In the next episode (2:13–25), Jesus explains that he will raise the temple in three days, referring to his death and resurrection to life. In the story of Nicodemus (3:1–21), Jesus challenges the Jewish leader to be born anew, this time from above, and 3:16 explains that Jesus comes to give life. In the account of John the Baptist (3:22–36), the Evangelist's pronouncement statement indicates that those who believe have "eternal life" (3:36). In his encounter with the woman at the well (4:1–45), Jesus offers living water (4:10–15), and in the closing episode (4:46–54), Jesus gives life to the nobleman's son.[1]

Analysis of John 2:1—4:54

The Wedding at Cana (Chapter 2:1–12)

While the wedding at Cana is absent from the Synoptics, it is inserted by John from his sources to underscore uniquely Johannine themes. The story of Jesus changing the water to wine is the first of a series of acts and pronouncements in which Jesus offers himself as the fulfillment of traditional Jewish ceremonies and festivals. He replaces the water used for ritual cleansing with wine at the marriage ceremony. Then, in the temple he offers his body as the new temple, the new place where one meets God, a point of emphasis already anticipated in 1:51. In these episodes, the focus is not on the actual events so much as on their meaning and significance.

---

1. These points are taken from Culpepper, *Gospel and Letters*, 129.

The wedding episode begins with a temporal reference: "On the third day" (2:1). Noting the temporal references present in the preceding verses (1:29, 35, and 43), some scholars read John's seven-day sequence literally, as a chronological timetable of Jesus' first week, counterbalancing the seven-day post-resurrection sequence of appearances by Jesus in chapter 20. Others find allusion to the week of creation in Genesis (the third day completing the four-day sequence of chapter 1). Since John has already drawn attention to creation in the prologue, the good news he proclaims in this Gospel reflects a new creation. Yet a third possibility interprets the setting "[o]n the third day" from a post-Easter perspective (see 2:19–22).

This last interpretation is promising, for the text abounds with resurrection motifs. In Hebrew thought, the phrase "three days" did not constitute a reference to calendar time, but carried symbolic significance (see Gen 42:17–18; Exod. 3:18; 10:22; 19:11; 2 Kgs. 20:5, 8; Hos. 6:2; Jonah 1:17). Reference to "three days" was in many instances either the critical Day of Judgment or the day when a new reality dawned. The third day also had eschatological overtones, evoking images that Jews associated with the climax of history (Isa. 25:6–8), the Day of the Lord. As in Jewish history, so Jewish Christians began to assert that on the third day God had raised Christ and exalted him to God's right hand. For Christians, the third day became the day of resurrection. To literalize its meaning in the New Testament would be to miss its meaning. The third day came to symbolize the presence of the living Christ (Mark 2:18–20) and of the eschatological banquet (Rev. 19:7–9) that the church shares with Christ. Christians living at the time of John's writing, near the end of the first century, would have associated the wedding feast of Cana not only with God's decisive act in Christ but would also find Eucharistic significance in the miraculous changing of water into wine. For them, the Kingdom of God had come: the bridegroom was present, and the church was celebrating marriage with Christ as its Bride (Rev. 21:2, 9).

Jesus' snub of his mother in this passage puzzles many readers (2:4). Though it seems insensitive, it fits a pattern in John in which Jesus refuses to do what others ask him to do, but later does of his own accord and in his own time (cf. 7:3, 8–10; 11:3–7). In these cases the author is indicating that Jesus cannot be coerced but rather does everything of his own free will. Jesus' relationship with his mother here, while perplexing, needs to be read in the context of discipleship. Like the disciples, Mary too is depicted as a person on the road to full comprehension and full discipleship. As "woman," Mary must resolve the tensions between her physical family, from which Jesus is disengaging (see 7:1–5), and the family of faith. Mary later joins the family of faith at the cross, as an archetypal female disciple (as "woman"), rather than as Jesus' mother.[2]

The reference to six water pots, used by the Jews for ritual cleansing and said to be empty, symbolizes the incompleteness of the traditional Jewish ritual, which Jesus literally fills (that is, fulfills). Stone jars, in contrast to earthen jars, are said to be free from the possibility of Levitical impurity (Lev. 11:33). The purification rites mentioned in 2:6 probably refer to the ritual cleansing of hands at meals (see 3:25). The large size of the pots accentuates the great quantity of wine that is produced. Wine was a powerful symbol associated with spiritual joy (Eccl. 9:7; Gen. 27:28), eschatological hope (Zech. 10:6–7; Joel 2:19), and abundance (Joel 2:24; 3:18; Amos 9:13). The wine's redness also made common the association with blood, making wine secondarily associated with suffering and death.

The surprise of the passage comes near the end, with the chief steward's declaration that the host has kept the best wine for last. The wine, of course, had not come from the host but from Jesus. Just as the best had been served last at this banquet, so God's most powerful and life-giving force has been released at the end of the age. As the wedding, including a meal with wine, was the normal image of eschatological fellowship in early Judaism, John 2 clearly alludes to the eschatological age, which is said to have arrived in Christ. God has saved the best for last, whether it be the best revelation, the most life-giving one, or the joy and fellowship of Christian communion, an expression of this new wine. For John, as for early Christianity, the very presence of God has now appeared on the human stage, signaling the coming of the messianic age of miracles and blessing for God's people, the climax of the human drama of redemption. By changing water into wine, Jesus accomplished what only the Word could do, "bring all things into being" (1:3). Here, in the only scene in which Jesus' mother appears until his death on the cross, Jesus states, "My hour has not yet come" (2:4), an obvious Johannine reference to the time of Jesus' death. The narrator notes that Jesus "revealed his glory" and then reports that "his disciples believed in him" (2:11).

This section revisits the theme of Jesus as the giver of life, introduced in 1:4 and developed more fully in chapters 3 and 4. Here Jesus' disciples believe in him, yet they do not speak their confession, for there is still much they do not understand about who Jesus is. Much of the

---

2. Witherington, *John's Wisdom*, 79.

Gospel account is devoted to the disciples' struggle to understand more about the one in whom they believed as a result of Jesus' signs. The signs, in and of themselves, are not the complete revelation, nor do they lead to full discipleship.

This account poses hard questions for modern readers, as it surely did for ancient readers, because the force of the miracle derives precisely from its extraordinariness. If the contemporary reader does not experience a sense of dissonance when faced with this miracle, then the wonder of the miracle may not be experienced either. This story cannot be approached in terms of whether one believes in miracles; to be forced to choose between the claims of religious faith and those of modern science begs the question. In this story, the reader is asked to push beyond the literal to its application. The miracle is one of grace and abundance, of transformation and new possibilities, offering a glimpse of Jesus' glory (2:11). "The interpretive task is not to put the miracle in a framework in which it 'makes sense' (like the attempts of the steward in 2:9–10), but to free the faith community to receive the extraordinary gifts this miracle offers. . . . The story invites the reader to see what the disciples see, that in the abundance and graciousness of Jesus' gift, one catches a glimpse of the identity and character of God."[3]

Cleansing the Temple (Chapter 2:13–25)

While John regularly follows the Synoptic chronology of events in the life of Jesus, at least in its general contours, this chapter demonstrates John's radical departure from the Synoptic pattern when it suits his purpose. The cleansing of the temple is recorded in all four Gospels, but the Synoptics place it at the end Jesus' ministry, whereas in John it is Jesus' first public act. While the Synoptics may recall a more accurate chronology, John's placement of the event is essential to his purpose. Commentators suggest three distinct explanations for this dislocation, each quite plausible. The Fourth Evangelist may have moved the scene (a) to introduce the allusion to Jesus' death and resurrection in the context of his "third day" reference, (b) to allow the raising of Lazarus to be climactic sign of his public ministry, or (c) to demonstrate Jesus' relationship to Judaism. For it is in the temple, at the very heart of Judaism, that Jesus reveals himself, demonstrating that Judaism's institutions needed a major reformation.

---

3. O'Day, *John*, 540.

BELIEF AND DISBELIEF: THE EARLY SIGNS AND DISCOURSES   69

This account furthers the theme, already noted in this Gospel, of Jesus fulfilling and thus superseding the ritual institutions of early Judaism.

John reports the first journey of Jesus to Jerusalem in 2:13, at the time of the first Passover mentioned in the Gospel. This verse marks the first of three journeys from Galilee to Jerusalem (cf. 5:1; 7:10). Jerusalem at the time of the Passover was the appropriate place and occasion for Jesus to inaugurate his mission and explain its significance (see 5:1; 6:4; 11:55; 18:38, 39; 19:14). Passover was one of the annual pilgrimage festivals, when thousands of faithful Jews traveled to Jerusalem. Two other Passovers (6:4; 11:55; with 5:1 a possible reference to a fourth) in John provide the basis for thinking that Jesus' ministry lasted about three years. A further chronological note appears in 2:20; if one begins with the chronology of the eighteenth year of Herod the Great's reign, the reference in 2:20 to the Herodian temple taking forty-six years to build means that the temple construction began about 20-19 BC, and forty-six years brings us to AD 27-28, the likely start of Jesus' ministry. That would place Jesus' death around AD 30.

When Jesus drove out the moneychangers, such action does not mean that he brought to a halt the lucrative temple industry, as some scholars suggest. This was most likely a limited action, meaning that it was primarily symbolic in nature, demonstrating the need for the cleansing of the temple. Only John mentions that Jesus made a whip out of cords, and we are not told that Jesus used it on the merchants. This passage is frequently interpreted as an example of Jesus' anger, but such attempts to focus on isolated attributes or emotions as proof of Jesus' humanity is to remain on the surface without perceiving the deeper reality. The scandal of John 2:13-22 is not Jesus' anger as proof of his humanity, but the authority this human being claims for himself through his words and actions. Jesus, an outsider to the power structure of the temple, issues a challenge to the authority of the temple that disrupts the temple system during one of the most significant feasts of the year, causing a commotion that began that day and culminated in his crucifixion.

As unusual as this action seems, particularly for Jesus, he must not be seen as exceeding the parameters of the Jewish religion or as advocating the superiority of one religion over another. Jesus was neither anti-Jewish nor non-Jewish on this occasion but radically Jewish, acting in line with the institutional challenges of prophets like Amos and Jeremiah, challenging a religious system so embedded in self-perpetuation that it is no longer open to fresh revelation from God, a temptation that exists for contemporary Christians as well.

Two pronouncements, each followed by a parenthetical reference to what the disciples remembered later, guide the reader's understanding of this event. Verse 16 is seen as an allusion to Zechariah 14:21 and verse 17 to Psalm 69:9. The religious authorities speak in Johannine terms at this point, asking what "sign" he could show them (this is the same term used in 2:11 to describe the Cana miracle). Their demand for a sign is in reality a question about Jesus' authority. Jesus responds by pointing to the ultimate sign, his death and resurrection. The reference to three days causes misunderstanding because the interrogators focus on the literal, missing what Jesus is really talking about. Irony and misunderstanding are prominent features in John (3:3–10; 6:41–59; 11:4–53).[4] Explanations that clear away such misunderstandings are common in John (6:64, 71; 7:5, 39; 11:13, 51–52; 12:6, 33; 20:9).

In 2:22 the narrator adds a comment ("after he was raised from the dead") that clarifies the point of view from which the entire Gospel is written, namely a post-Easter perspective. The reference to what the disciples remembered points ahead to the primary role of the Beloved Disciple (21:24), whose process of recalling and reinterpreting the tradition will be understood as the work of the Paraclete (14:26). The Gospel, by its own admission, is not a historical record of what eyewitnesses saw and heard (12:16) but a later, post-Easter reflection on both the significance of Jesus' ministry in the light of his resurrection and on the church's study of the scriptures.

The end of chapter 2 presents a further challenge for the reader. The narrator reports that when Jesus confronts the money changers in the temple, the authorities fail to recognize his identity, though "many believed in his name because they saw the signs that he was doing" (2:23). Their lack of understanding is underscored by the statement that despite their belief, Jesus "would not entrust himself to them . . . for he himself knew what was in everyone" (2:24). The issue at hand is to understand what constitutes an acceptable response to Jesus. The prologue states that "all who received him, who believed in his name," he empowered as "children of God" (1:12). Yet here we learn that despite the faith of many who believed in his signs, Jesus would not entrust himself to them because he knew what was in them. In chapter 3 we will encounter Nicodemus,

---

4. See essay 9, "John's Use of Misunderstanding and Irony as Literary Techniques."

another uncommitted Judean Jew. For the Evangelist, inadequate faith is not completely rejected, however (cf. 10:32–38); it is simply insufficient and can lead to misunderstanding Jesus' purposes and character. The Gospel warns against shallow responses and calls for readers to move to deeper levels of understanding and commitment. Only the disciples are depicted as models at this point, and even in their case it is clear that they understand only after Jesus' resurrection.

The Evangelist apparently wants his audience to read the Gospel in light of this event. By setting this account at the beginning of Jesus' ministry, the author can present that ministry, especially from chapter 5 on, as the story of a legal investigation, leading to a trial and an execution. Seen in this light, various other actions of Jesus will be taken as precipitating confrontations between him and the Jewish authorities. Because Jesus died by crucifixion, the apologetic purposes of this Gospel cannot be overlooked; one of the driving passions of John is to present the course of events that led to Jesus' death in such a way as to convict his adversaries and exonerate him and his followers of any wrongdoing.

The two accounts in chapter 2 are similarly shaped. Both the wedding story and the temple cleansing are revelatory (they manifest the glory of the Son); both are third-day stories (they display resurrection symbolism); both focus upon a sign; both carry a polemic about Jewish rituals (water of purification and temple rites); and both conclude with references to disciples believing. There is, however, a major difference between them: the Galilean passage is about life, the Judean passage is about death. For the Evangelist, they are inseparable, pointing forward to the conclusion of the drama in the death and resurrection of Jesus. The intrusiveness of the Evangelist near the end of the chapter (2:21–22) suggests that the audience needs a theological explanation to understand the larger significance of the story. The narrator's summations at the end of the wedding (2:11) and at the end of the confrontation with the money changers (2:23) raise questions about the nature of belief, the basis for belief, and the relation of belief to the recognition of Jesus as the Word made flesh.[5] Both events in chapter 2 point to Jesus' glorification, for John the climax of his account.

---

5. Culpepper, *Gospel and Letters*, 79.

Jesus and Nicodemus (Chapter 3:1–21)

At this point, the focus shifts from the public arena to Jesus' interaction with individuals of highly diverse backgrounds and needs: Nicodemus (3:1–10); a Samaritan woman (4:1–26); a royal official (4:43–53); a man at the pool of Bethesda (5:1–15); and more. In this passage, the Evangelist is contrasting Jesus' teaching with that of the Pharisees, personified in the teacher Nicodemus. This section thus brings Jesus in direct contact with the Jewish establishment, disclosing the perspectives and assumptions that will lead to ever deepening conflict. The passage consists of two parts: the dialogue itself (3:1–10) and a discourse by Jesus (3:11–21). This material provides the first instance of a common Johannine pattern, in which a significant event is followed by a discourse that draws general theological themes from the preceding event.

It is noteworthy that in this first Johannine discourse, Jesus is speaking to a Jewish rabbi (in 3:10 he is called "*the* teacher of Israel," suggesting he is Israel's leading sage) who is likely a member of the Sanhedrin, the ruling body in Palestinian Judaism. The presence of "we" in 3:2 makes it clear that John's characters have a representative and therefore a legitimate point of view. Nicodemus is a type of the sympathetic Jewish seeker; he represents learned Jews, who are said to recognize Jesus as a teacher sent from God, yet still remains "in the dark." Unlike the common people, who believe in Jesus because of signs of healing (2:23), Jesus desires real disciples. As a theologian, Nicodemus is bound by tradition and religious perspective. So the Evangelist uses him as a foil, not so much speaking with him but through him to the readers of the Gospel, for Nicodemus soon disappears as he came, into the darkness of the night.[6]

The discussion about birth and new birth begins at 3:3, and much has been made of the fact that *anōthen* can mean "above" as well as "anew." This double meaning is not only possible in Greek, it seems intentional. Jesus' expression is a deliberate challenge for Nicodemus to move beyond surface meanings to a deeper meaning. The intentional double meaning of *anōthen* must be kept in mind when reading this verse in order to discern Jesus' full meaning and the nature of Nicodemus's misunderstanding. Readers may well connect spiritual birth with the phrase "to become children of God" in 1:12–13.

---

6. Nicodemus does not disappear altogether, however; see 7:50–52 and 19:38–42, where he reappears in a more positive light.

The notion of spiritual birth should not be dissociated from that of the Kingdom of God, with which it is joined. Reference to the Kingdom of God is rare in John (3:3, 5; see also 18:36), unlike the Synoptics, where it is a frequent metaphor of eschatological newness. To connect "to be born *anōthen*" with Kingdom of God references suggest that the new birth of which Jesus speaks is also an eschatological category. Nicodemus assumes Jesus is referring to another physical birth by the phrase "born anew," whereas Jesus is referring to a birth of a different sort, caused by the work of the Holy Spirit, God's eschatological gift to his followers. Nicodemus's incredulous response in 3:4 is part of the recurring pattern of misunderstanding followed by explanation in John's Gospel. As an educated Jew, Nicodemus thinks of the Kingdom of God as participation in the new order God would bring about at the end of history. He cannot believe that the transformation of an individual's character is a requirement for entrance into the Kingdom and therefore is amazed by Jesus' explanation (3:7, 12).

Being born from above is further explained in 3:5, where it means being born "of water and Spirit." Christian readers detect a baptismal reference here, but the emphasis throughout is on birth through the Spirit. If water/baptism is so important for entering the Kingdom, it is surprising that the rest of the discussion never mentions it again; the entire focus is on the work of the Spirit (3:8), the work of God (3:16–17), and the place of faith (3:15–16). The analogy between the mysterious wind and the sovereign work of the Spirit (3:8) becomes very strange if Spirit-birth is tied to baptism.[7] While the expression "born of water and Spirit" is not found in the Old Testament, water and spirit appear in Ezekiel 36:25–27, where hope for the future is tied to spiritual rebirth, imagery that anticipates the vision of dry bones in Ezekiel 37:1–14.

Assuming that John 3:6 describes two births, one from flesh to flesh and the other from Spirit to spirit, some interpreters propose that "born of water and Spirit" in 3:5 similarly refers to two births, natural procreation and the other supernatural, birth by the Spirit. To support this view, "water" is taken as a reference to the amniotic fluid that breaks from the womb before childbirth. Such a view, attractive on many levels, cannot be substantiated from ancient records, for there are no ancient sources that picture natural birth as "from water." Furthermore, the

---

7. For an extended discussion of this topic see essay 8, "John's Sacramental Language." A good case can be made that the phrase "water and" in John 3:5 is a later editorial addition by a sacramentalist; see Randel Helms's explanation in the Introduction.

Greek construction does not favor two births here but one, since we have but one preposition (*ek*) before "water and Spirit," meaning they refer to one and the same birth. Verses 7–8 make clear that John is speaking only of spiritual regeneration, not about a physical and a spiritual birth. The analogy here between "wind" and the work of the Spirit is apt not only because one can detect the presence of the wind or Spirit by their respective effects, but also because in this Gospel *hearing*, not seeing, the Word is the prerequisite to new birth and entering the Kingdom of God.

It becomes apparent at 3:11 that what began as a story about a private dialogue becomes a public discussion. Original Greek copies of the New Testament had no punctuation marks, so translations often cannot indicate where (or if) the speech of Jesus ends and John's commentary begins. The "we" references in this verse ask readers to think not only of what Jesus once might have said but also of what the Johannine community continued to say to people of their age. It is of course difficult to know exactly where Jesus stops and the comments of the Evangelist and his community begin, but these verses mark the transition. In 3:16–22 we are hearing the voice of the narrator commenting on the significance of Jesus' words.

Chapter 3:11–21, the first of many discourses in John, is not so much *a* discourse as *the* discourse, the subject-matter of which is repeated in all subsequent discourses. Here Jesus discloses the fundamental themes of his mission: repentance, the death of the Son of Man, the love of God, judgment and salvation, and works and faith.

Verses 11–12 are significant in that they address a topic that is of concern to every Christian, the content of revelation. The Evangelist's favorite way of communicating revealed truth is through bearing witness. There are numerous witnesses in the Fourth Gospel, beginning with John the Baptist (1:7, 24) and including the Evangelist, the last of a long line of witnesses of which his Gospel speaks (21:24), but the truth to which they testify is always the same: the person of Jesus. This, after all, is the only truth with which the Gospel is concerned. The revelatory role of Jesus in John's Gospel is to reveal the Father (1:18), but the content of that revelation is never divulged. There is one apparent exception to this, one tantalizing hint: "Very truly, I tell you, we speak of what we know and testify to what we have seen; yet you do not receive our testimony. If I have told you about earthly things and you do not believe, how can you believe if I tell you about heavenly things?" The moment, however, passes, without any satisfactory account of what these "heavenly things" may be.

BELIEF AND DISBELIEF: THE EARLY SIGNS AND DISCOURSES   75

The real irony, as John's readers discover, is that the heavenly truths are to be found in the earthly reality of Jesus' presence. In this case the "heavenly things" and the "earthly things" are the same. What looks like an exception turns out to conform to the general Johannine pattern of witness. Ultimately all truth is self-authenticating, for there is nothing outside of his revelation to which Jesus can call for support. The witness and his testimony belong indissolubly together, as we learn in 3:31–36, a passage that represents the Evangelist's final thought on the subject of revelation.[8]

We are left, then, with a Gospel, whose frequent references to revelation resemble a promise that is regularly reiterated but never fulfilled. But the promise is unfulfilled only because it is unfulfillable, since there are no heavenly mysteries revealed to Jesus by God except those disclosed in his own life and death. No wonder, then, that any attempt to separate the message from the life results in an empty revelation form. "No understanding of [John] is possible if one loses sight of the simple fact that it is not a theological tract but a Gospel. What the divine agent 'heard' from God is disclosed not in words but in his life; the 'what' is displayed in the 'how.' The matter of the Gospel, its true content, is indistinguishable from its form: the medium is the message."[9]

Three big questions raised in John's Gospel: Who is Jesus? Where did he come from? Where is he going? run rampant throughout this discourse. In 3:13 these questions are clearly answered. Verse 13 indicates that Jesus, the Son of Man, came from heaven and will return there. His ascension is addressed obliquely in 3:14, via the cross. Verse 14 refers to the Old Testament book of Numbers 21:4–9, which John connects to the crucifixion. To be "lifted up" in John always refers to the cross (see 8:28 and 12:32).

The "why" of Jesus' coming is spelled out distinctly in 3:15–17. His coming saves from spiritual death—from alienation from God—by opening the way to eternal life. The reference to "eternal life," appearing for the first time in John, properly means "life in the age to come." For John that life may be experienced before the end, just as in the Synoptics the Kingdom dawns before the end. The eternal life begun by the new birth is for John nothing less than the life granted by the eternal Word (see 1:4). Entrance to that life is predicated upon one's belief in Jesus (3:15). The term "believe" is central to the message of the Fourth Gospel. It is used ninety-eight times in John, where it means "to trust in such a

8. Ashton, *Understanding*, 491–502.
9. Ibid., 529.

way that one's actions stem from that trust." In John, love, trust, and belief always result in action.[10]

John 3:16–18 has been called "the Gospel in miniature." John 3:16, the most quoted verse in the New Testament, sums up the preceding verses by reiterating the salvific dimensions of Jesus' death, but moves the argument forward with its reference to God's love. This is the only place in the Fourth Gospel that says that God "gave" his Son to the world. The more common expression is that God "sent" Jesus, as in 3:17. To send Jesus is more clearly associated with God's will for the world, whereas to give Jesus underscores God's love for the world. This passage is the only one in John where God's love is directed toward the world, a term generally associated with that part of humanity that is at odds with Jesus and God (1:10; 7:7; 15:18–19). Elsewhere God's love is directed to the disciples.

God's love is expressed in what God does, which is to give (that is, to give over to death) the "only Son," a possible allusion to Abraham's willingness to sacrifice his only son Isaac (Gen. 22:1–18). The purpose of Jesus' coming is to turn the world—all humanity—toward God and toward God's gift of life in Christ. Jesus' purpose in coming is not for the purpose of passing judgment, but rather for the purpose of turning people to God. The context makes clear that God gives Jesus in love to everyone, though only believers accept the gift. Verse 16 restates the theme of eternal life in 1:15, but advances the argument by naming the alternative to eternal life: to "perish." This verse makes clear that there is no middle ground in John's perspective. God's gift in Jesus, which culminates in the death, resurrection, and ascension of Jesus, decisively alters the options available to the world. If one believes, "one's present is altered by the gift of eternal life; if one does not believe, one perishes."[11]

John's Gospel is propelled by conflict between belief and unbelief as responses to Jesus. The centrality of this conflict is confirmed by the fact that almost half of the occurrences of the verb "believe" in the New Testament are found in John (98 out of 239). Lest there be confusion, however, John states clearly that the divine purpose of the mission of Jesus is salvation and not judgment, eternal life and not destruction. Jesus does not come to pass judgment, and indeed it is not necessary that he do so. People judge themselves by their response to Jesus, who is the light (3:19–21). Those who hide from this light experience the judgment of

---

10. Miller, *That You May Believe*, 29.
11. O'Day, *John*, 553.

the world, which has already begun. Because the mission of Jesus brings out the radical distinction between those who believe and those who do not, the theme of judgment persists throughout John's Gospel (5:22–30; 8:15–16; 12:31, 47, 48; 16:11) and is used in 9:39 to define the purpose of his coming: "I came into this world for judgment so that those who do not see may see, and those who do see may become blind." John 3:18 explains this judgment, exemplifying what is known as "realized eschatology," meaning that God's long-awaited eschatological transformation of reality, including judgment of evil, is underway in the present, initiated by Jesus' coming into the world (see 3:36). The very presence of Jesus in the world confronts the world with a decision, to believe or not to believe, and making that decision is the moment of judgment. If one's life is characterized by transformative belief, so that one's deeds are "done in God" (3:21), then one is saved; if one does not believe, one is *already* condemned. In John's Gospel, believing is always tied to the actions that comprise a person's life. Belief is never simply a matter of agreeing with a set of ideas. To believe is to do what is true (see 1 John 1:6).

The distinction between two kinds of action is absolute in John. Doing the truth, which means living by the truth, makes room for the righteousness of God. Such deeds require faith, for they are incomplete. Deeds of darkness exclude faith, for they are self-sufficient. This way of life defines humans who cling to their sin, unwilling to repent and yield to the work of God's transformative Spirit. The mission of Jesus compels a final distinction between these two ways of living (see 9:39–41).

Verses 19–21 portray the intricate balance between judgment and decision in the metaphorical language of light and darkness. This language recalls the imagery of the prologue (1:5, 9–10). To love darkness more than light is the same as not believing; such love results in judgment. The way people act—whether good or evil—is directly related to the decision they make regarding Jesus. Christology and anthropology are thus inseparably linked in the Fourth Gospel. One's identity is determined by one's response to Jesus; Nicodemus did not believe (3:12), so he remains in darkness.

The Final Witness of John (Chapter 3:22—4:3)

In this section, John the Baptist makes his final appearance in the Fourth Gospel. At 3:22 Jesus withdraws into the Judean countryside and will move next to the boundaries of the Jewish world (Samaria). But before Jesus' ministry expands, the Baptist gives his final witness. Jesus' first ministry among "his own" (1:11) is framed by the witness of John (1:19–34; 3:22–30). While the placement of 3:31–36 suggests that these words are those of John the Baptist (as punctuated by the NIV Bible), the unit resonates with Johannine subjects and characteristic expressions, leading us to interpret this material as either a displaced discourse of Jesus or as the Evangelist's commentary (as in the NRSV Bible). This material may have been of special importance if there was an ongoing witness to the Baptist's followers in Ephesus, where this Gospel was published. The Evangelist's technique here, as elsewhere in the Gospel, is to address his audience by means of progressive repetition.

In this passage the Evangelist claims that the ministries of Jesus and John overlapped. The narrator's remark in 3:24 about John's arrest makes that clear. If this passage is misplaced (Raymond Brown suggest it may have been originally between 1:34 and 35), this might explain the awkwardness of 4:2, which disrupts the grammar of verses 1 and 3 (these verses are one sentence in the Greek) and directly contradicts 3:22, 26 and 4:1. Brown sees 4:2 as indisputable proof that several hands were responsible for the final form of the Fourth Gospel. The presence of this interruption in the text can be explained only as the correction of a later editor who feared that the evidence that Jesus himself baptized disciples would support claims that Jesus was an imitator of John the Baptist (see 1:29–34 and 3:30, which may have been inserted to contradict such an impression).

The introduction of the disagreement between an unknown "Jew" and John's disciples about purification (3:25) seems awkward as well, since its meaning and its relationship to the rest of the story are unclear. The substance of the disagreement about impurity is never specified, nor is it even alluded to in the disciples' complaint to John in verse 26. The suggestion that "Jew" is a textual corruption of "Jesus," which makes the best sense of the verse, lacks manuscript support.

In the Baptist's response to his disciples (3:27–30), he tells a parable of the bridegroom and his friend to highlight the difference between their roles—in a wedding, the friend of the bridegroom was responsible for all the nuptial arrangements but still had a secondary role—and yet highlights their shared joy. John views himself as the friend, who is delighted with the greater response to Jesus. The statement in 1:30 made clear that John's ministry of baptism was for the purpose of revealing Jesus to Israel (1:31). At that time, John had testified that Jesus was the "Lamb of God who takes away the sin of the world" (1:29). Now, he declares that Jesus is Israel's bridegroom.[12] In both cases, John's role is anticipatory and explanatory: John is not the light; Jesus is the light (1:8–9).

John 3:31–36 appears to be a doublet of 3:11–21, elucidating earlier themes. The following examples make that clear: (a) verse 31 returns to the contrast between the earthly and the heavenly (cf. 3:12); (b) the themes of bearing witness to what one has seen and heard in verse 11 are echoed in verse 32; (c) the reference to the one whom God has sent in verse 34 parallels verse 16, (d) as do the affirmations in 3:16 that "the Father loves the Son" (3:33) and that the one who "believes in the Son has eternal life" (3:36); as in 3:19–21, the discussion of eternal life in verse 36 leads to its corollary: the judgment ("wrath of God") rests on those who refuse to believe.[13] Despite the ambiguity of the identity of the speaker, recapitulating earlier themes brings the chapter to a forceful conclusion.

Jesus and Samaritans (Chapter 4:4–42)

In chapter 4 Jesus' ministry enters a new phase. He leaves the confines of traditional Judaism and turns to those whom his Jewish contemporaries considered outsiders and enemies: the Samaritans. While the breach between Jews and Samaritans went back to the Assyrian occupation of Israel in 721 BC, the most intense rivalry began around 200 BC. The source of enmity was a dispute about the proper place of worship, whether at the temple in Jerusalem or at the Samaritan shrine on Mt. Gerizim (4:20). The Samaritans recognized only the Pentateuch as sacred scripture, denying the role of the Hebrew prophets, and when they thought of a redeemer figure, they conceived of him as being like Moses (see Deut. 18:18–22) or even as Moses come back from the dead. They called this redeemer prophet the Taheb (the Restorer). Jews avoided Samaritan territory, detouring along the east side of the Jordan River rather than taking the direct Samaritan route whenever they traveled from Jerusalem to Galilee. Jesus doesn't take the detour; rather he walks deliberately through Samaria.

John 4:4–42 is an important example of the complex interweaving of dialogue and narrative that characterizes much of the Fourth Gospel. This lengthy narrative consists of two main blocks of conversation, Jesus

---

12. In the Old Testament, Israel is presented as the bride of God (Isa. 61:10; Jer. 2:2; Hos. 1–2); the use of bridal imagery in John has Christological implications.

13. Culpepper, *Gospel and Letters*, 138.

and the Samaritan woman (4:7–26) and Jesus and his disciples (4:31–38), surrounded by narrative frames. The episode concludes with an encounter between Jesus and Samaritan townspeople (4:39–42).

The story of Jesus' encounter with the Samaritan woman at a well is a beautifully constructed literary pattern known as a "type scene," particularly a type of "well story" familiar from patriarchal narratives, where a hero meets his bride at a well in a "far country." The scene, whether of Isaac, Jacob, or even of Moses, always serves to highlight something significant about the hero's character. Jesus is depicted in this narrative as the giver of living water and thus of life, and the Samaritan woman as a marginalized Samaritan. The tension between Jesus and this woman crosses four boundaries: gender, nationality, race, and religion. Yet none of these stop Jesus from approaching her. In the course of the conversation, all four barriers are crossed and community is created. The Samaritan woman is in many ways the opposite of Nicodemus, a respectable Jewish leader.

This story is the Johannine equivalent of the story in Acts 8 about how the gospel reached the Samaritans. Raymond Brown, in *Community of the Beloved Disciple*, discerned in John a concern with the early Christian mission, reading John 4 as a story about the relation between Johannine Christians and Samaritans rather than as an isolated incident in the life of Jesus. The Gospel of John clearly devotes unusual attention to the Samaritans. Interestingly, the last reference to the apostle John in the book of Acts leaves him in Samaria (8:25). Were Johannine Christians engaged in mission work among the Samaritans? Did Samaritan converts join in sufficient numbers that they influenced the Johannine community's self-understanding? While Brown's approach contributes significantly to our understanding of the history of the Johannine community and to the compositional history of John's Gospel, John 4 is best read biographically and literarily.

One of John's distinguishing features is its depiction of Jesus as the Revealer of the Father and of the various human responses to that role. The narrative draws readers to affirm the narrator's perception of Jesus' identity through a series of episodes that describe attempted, failed, and occasionally successful "recognition scenes."[14] The encounter with Nicodemus represents such a scene, as does the encounter with the Samaritan woman. The notion of a recognition scene is made clear by Jesus' challenge in 4:10: "If you knew . . . who it is that is saying to you, 'Give me a drink,'

---

14. Ibid., 71.

you would have asked him, and he would have given you living water." In the course of the conversation that follows, the woman comes step by step to recognize who Jesus is and to share her recognition with others in the town. The conversation progresses from "you, a Jew" (4:9) to "Sir, I see that you are a prophet" (4:19), to the woman's invitation to her townspeople, "Come and see a man who told me everything I have ever done! He cannot be the Messiah, can he?" (4:29). The story concludes with the recognition by the Samaritans that Jesus "is truly the Savior of the world" (4:42). The key to the narrative is the recognition that the Samaritan woman and her fellow villagers are depicted as examples of those moving from no faith to some faith in Jesus, making progress toward an adequate faith.

Jesus initiates the conversation on the level of common physical need: "Give me a drink" (4:7). The request carries radical implications because Jesus, a Jewish man, was offering to drink from the vessel of a Samaritan woman. In doing so, Jesus was setting aside powerful social conventions and ignoring centuries of hostility between Jews and Samaritans. The conversation progressively addresses and transcends each of the barriers that separate Jesus and the woman, while Jesus develops the symbolism of "living water" and the woman grows in her perception of Jesus' identity.

Jesus' reference to "living water" is ambiguous, as was *anōthen* in 3:3, because literally it would have meant running or flowing water. As in the scene with Nicodemus, Jesus words are misunderstood because the woman is thinking of earthly things while Jesus is speaking of heavenly things. The woman raises several questions in response. Where would Jesus get the "living water"? Jacob had dug the well to provide people of this region with water. Was Jesus greater than the patriarch? This second question is ironic because it presumes a negative response, but the reader knows from the prologue that Jesus is certainly greater than the patriarchs.

After the woman asks for living water (4:15), the conversation enters its second phase (4:16–26), and the topic of living water is not mentioned again. Instead, the conversation focuses on the woman's marital background, Jesus' identity, and the differences between Jewish and Samaritan worship. The second part of the conversation, like the first, is initiated by Jesus, who tells the woman to get her husband. When she responds that she has no husband, Jesus demonstrates that he knows what is in each person's heart (cf. 1:48; 2:24–25) by confirming that she has spoken the truth. She has had five husbands, and the man with whom she is living is not her husband. Readers have presumed the woman's immorality, but it is important to note that Jesus does not judge her. There are many possible reasons for her marital history other than moral laxity.

The woman uses Jesus' perception to test his response on the differences between Jewish and Samaritan worship practices. If Jesus had said that Jerusalem was the proper place for true worship, she would have rejected him as a false prophet, for her allegiance centered around the cultic center on Mt. Gerizim. But Jesus elevates the conversation to a new level, rejecting her either/or approach by indicating that what really matters is the manner of worship ("in spirit and truth"), not the place. While Samaritans may worship the true God, they lack in understanding, for salvation is "from the Jews" (4:21). By this statement Jesus may well be indicating the origins of monotheistic worship. He is clearly not making an exclusivist statement, but rather is affirming a form of worship that transcends gender and ritual restrictions, since salvation is for everyone, not just the Jews.

When the woman alludes to the coming of the Messiah, Jesus says, "I am he" (4:26). Scholars debate whether John's use of *egō eimi* in this context should be interpreted in an absolute sense, as a Christological title, or whether one should take the most natural meaning here, as indicating an implied predicate. Perhaps the Evangelist means this reply as at least a partial revelation of Jesus' identity, since it prompts the women to return to town with the news.[15]

The scene shifts with the return of the disciples in 4:27. They marvel not that Jesus was talking with a Samaritan, but that he was talking with a woman. The woman returns to the city, forsaking her water jug, and the conversation turns to food. Just as water has symbolic significance, so too does food (Jesus has bread to eat that the disciples do not know of, meaning not literal bread but doing the will of the one who sent him; 4:34). Two agricultural proverbs follow, implying that the harvest has come, that disciples often share in a harvest for which they are not primarily responsible, and that Samaritans—outsiders—are to be included in the community of those who receive the gospel. The Samaritan mission thus serves as a concrete example of Johannine realized eschatology (see 12:20–24, where the beginning of the Gentile mission is also imbued with eschatological significance and illustrated with agricultural imagery).

Verses 39–42 are the climax of this intricate story. The woman functions as an effective witness to her people, bringing them to Jesus. The

---

15. For a discussion on John's use of "I am" sayings, see essay 5.

disciples had brought Jesus food, but the woman brought an entire city! While the Samaritans believed her witness, this served as a catalyst for them to go and find out things for themselves and to believe on the basis of hearing Jesus' own word, a testimony he continued during the days he stayed with them. The use of the Greek verb *meno* for "stay" recalls 1:38 and Jesus' meeting with his first disciples. To stay with Jesus is to enter into relationship with him (see 15:4, 7). The story is brought to a dramatic climax by the confession that Jesus is truly the savior of the world, not just of Jews but also of Samaritans. Again, the recognition of Jesus is the focal point on which the story ends. Belief has been confirmed by their own hearing (4:42), a faith based not on signs but on Jesus' word (4:41). The Samaritans' acclamation of Jesus as the savior of the world has been described as "the most sweeping Christological confession yet encountered in the Gospel."[16] Salvation may be from the Jews (4:22), but it is not limited to the Jews.

There is a continuity of themes in John 2—4, all of them having to do with water and its various metaphorical meanings. In John 2 it is purification water; in John 3 entrance into God's Kingdom by being born "of water and Spirit"; in John 4 it is drinking water. In this latter narrative Jesus persuades a woman that she needs to exchange drinking water for living water. It should be noticed that unlike the stories in John 2 and 3, the Samaritan woman is responding to Jesus' word, not to any signs he has performed. While this story deals with the process of coming to faith, the Samaritan woman's faith is clearly an advance over earlier accounts. This account also continues the theme of temple worship and true worship first introduced in 2:13-22 and now more fully explored in 4:20-24.

The Second Sign: Healing the Officer's Son (Chapter 4:43–54)

Contrary to the proverb that John quotes in 4:44, that "a prophet has no honor in the prophet's own country" (a saying found in all three Synoptic Gospels as well), Jesus has now gained at least some credibility among the Galileans. The statement in 4:45 about the Galileans welcoming Jesus because "they had seen all that he had done in Jerusalem" is ultimately ironic, for a faith based on signs or works will not only prove insufficient but in due course will also turn into rejection.

---

16. O'Day, *John*, 570.

Jesus returns to Cana, where he had turned the water into wine, and this time he heals the son of a royal official. The royal official may well be serving in the court of Herod Antipas, a Jewish puppet king of the Roman government. He is unlikely a Gentile, as is often assumed, but rather Jewish. We find here a pattern common to John (seen previously in the changing of water to wine): Jesus does not do what others request, in this case leave Cana for Capernaum, as the father requests, but he does assure the father that the child will recover. The healing scene is reminiscent of a healing at Capernaum recorded in Matthew 8:5–13 and Luke 7:1–10. In this instance Jesus also heals the stricken person from a distance. The father "believed the word that Jesus spoke to him" (4:50) and returned to his home. That his faith is real is obvious from the fact that the man left without having seen any sign. His faith, confirmed by the son's healing, results in the conversion of his household.

This brief account marks the end of this section of the Gospel. The first Cana sign revealed Jesus' glory (2:11); this sign advances the theme important throughout this section, that Jesus is the giver of life.

Essay 3: John's Dualistic Imagery

Readers do not get far into the Fourth Gospel before they encounter dualistic symbols. The first dualism in John's prologue is that of light and darkness (1:5). Of course, pairs of opposites are commonly found in the New Testament, as in the Hebrew Bible. What is unusual in John is their prominence. It would appear that the whole system of religious thought presented here requires a dualistic framework. In addition to light and darkness, dualistic pairs in John include: above and below (8:23), spirit and flesh (3:6), life (eternal) and death (3:36), belief and disbelief (3:18), truth and falsehood (8:44–47), heaven and earth (3:31), God and Satan (13:27), and Israel and "the Jews" (1:19 and 47). Why does the Evangelist resort to dualistic thinking? The obvious answer is that he is following common intellectual and theological practice. In addition, he is dealing with a problem so massive, pervasive, and ambiguous that in order to find clarity he resorts to a reductionistic conceptualization that he finds meaningful, one that enables him to bring certainty and security to his audience. Nevertheless, his use of this literary approach is sophisticated.

A major concern for humans, no matter their race, background, or creed, is the problem of evil. The reality of evil, whether natural (in the realm of nature) or anthropological (in the human realm), has been particularly problematic for monotheists, who must reconcile the presence of evil (including suffering and death) with belief in the goodness of the God who created the world. Why does evil exist, and why is its impact seemingly disproportionate to human character and behavior? Or, to put the dilemma in modern terms, why do bad things happen to good people and good things to bad people? Questions regarding the fairness of life and the justice of God surface wherever tragedy strikes, in every age and place across the globe.

In antiquity, the simplest religious explanation was to attribute evil to the actions of the gods. They seemed capricious, and if humans were to survive, they needed to appease the deities. Eventually, more complex answers arose. Some treated evil as illusory; others envisioned it as cosmic, attributing equal status to evil and good. Some acknowledged its presence within the rhythm of nature and simply learned to cope, while others limited it to human decision-making and behavior. Whatever its nature, evil affects humans where they live and must be understood on that level.

Early Christianity inherited a "modified dualism" from Judaism. During the period of the Babylonian Exile (586–539 BC) and its aftermath, Jews grappled with theodicy, developing an understanding that posited a force that thwarted the divine will. That opposition, however, was believed to be short-lived, for in a climactic event in which the long-awaited Messiah would appear, opposition to the will of the sovereign Creator would be overcome. While evil was viewed as real, it would soon be defeated decisively. Early Christians inherited this perspective through their Jewish tradition, coming to see in the life and person of Jesus of Nazareth the answer to the rule of evil, personified by the rule of Satan. Christians felt they were living in an interim period, between the first coming of Jesus, whose mission inaugurated God's rule on earth, and the second coming of Jesus, whose second appearance would eliminate all traces of evil. Theirs was both a cosmic dualism (seeing evil and good as dimensions of reality, symbolized by earthly and heavenly realms) and a temporal dualism (consisting of a past age of evil and a future age of bliss). The former influenced the vertical dimension (the realm of space), and the latter the horizontal dimension (the realm of time or history).

The Fourth Gospel presents a revision of the dualistic thought of the New Testament. While it is among the most dualistic of New Testament books, it is not a simple continuation of this early Christian view. Scholars generally examine Johannine dualism under two headings: cosmic and eschatological. Our discussion will address its cosmic or existential nature.[17]

Rather than examining John's dualistic pairs individually, we will explore his dualism by investigating one of his most important symbols, "world" (*kosmos*). It is important to note that John does not use the term consistently. Where the term is employed in a neutral or even an affirming sense, it refers to the creation, the physical reality of the earth (1:9; 3:16; 16:21; and 17:24). However, when John uses *kosmos* in a negative, dualistic sense, it does not refer to the physical world in which we live. This approach often mistakenly led Christians in the past to devalue the physical world, as though it were somehow evil. But John views the created earth as the object of God's love (3:16), as the realm in which the light operates (1:9).

So what does the writer mean when he uses *kosmos* negatively? In those cases, the symbol represents the realm of unbelief, the realm that rejects the truth of God as revealed in Christ. It symbolizes ways of life that deem relationship with God unnecessary, ways opposed to God and God's divine plan of salvation for humans. When John uses the term *kosmos* dualistically, he means to distinguish between two ways of being human, two forms of self-understanding: (a) *self-consciousness*, an autonomous, self-serving, self-sufficient sphere of living shrouded in darkness (8:12) and ruled by Satan (12:31), and (b) *God-consciousness*, characterized by dependence upon God and others. The first way of living is declared distorted, whereas the second is declared authentic.

In John 8:23 and 13:1, the domain of the divine is set against the sphere of "this world." Jesus' home is elsewhere, and he comes into the worldly sphere only temporarily, to offer redemption and restoration. The distinction between these spheres is synonymous with several others in the Fourth Gospel, such as "earth and heaven" and "below and above."

At this point readers might question the relationship between the cosmic and human dualisms implicit in the use of the word "world." How literally did the Fourth Evangelist and the Johannine church embrace this cosmic dualism? Did they really believe in two different worlds? Were they able to conceptualize the cosmic dualism as representing the human dualism, or is this a modern distinction?[18] We can be fairly certain that the

---

17. This segment represents an adaptation of the discussion in Kysar's essay "Two Different Worlds—Johannine Dualism," in *Maverick Gospel*, 73–80. Readers interested in Johannine eschatology may consult essay 7.

18. The modern existential approach is often associated with biblical theologian

distinction modern people make between literal and poetic description, objective and subjective reality, reason and faith, fact and meaning, is a modern one. It is one that Christians and Jews of the first century did not make. They lived in a prescientific age and did not use modern distinctions. But even if the first readers of the Gospel did not consistently apply cosmic dualistic language to human self-understanding, the vital issue was not whether they thought in terms of a two-story cosmos but whether they viewed themselves as God's creatures, with all that implies, and whether they viewed life independent from God as defective and inauthentic. For them as for us, the human and the cosmic dualisms mesh.

Surprisingly, the Gospel of John says very little about Satan's role. There is only one use of the title "Satan," and that occurs as a way of explaining the motivation for Judas's betrayal (13:27). More common in the Gospel is the title "ruler of this world" (12:31; 14:30; 16:11), an evil figure associated exclusively with the crucifixion of Jesus, with the realm of error and unbelief that underlie evil. "The Gospel has little interest in the image of a cosmic figure responsible for evil, and in that lack of interest departs significantly from much other New Testament literature. Our Gospel is more concerned with the way in which human existence is deformed by misunderstanding and seems almost intent on avoiding the temptation to abdicate responsibility for that deformity by thrusting culpability on to some cosmic embodiment of evil."[19]

With this key in hand, modern readers are able to unlock the meaning of other Johannine dualistic symbols. On the negative side, there is a polarity that describes the state of misdirected and confused human life, a state John describes variously as darkness, falsehood, flesh, death, Satan's realm, and the realm below. Even the term "night" suggests the darkness that characterizes erroneous human self-understanding (3:2; 13:30). The positive polarity is symbolized as light, truth, spirit, life, eternal life, God's rule, and the realm above. The various symbols mean the same. The positive images represent God's revelation in Christ—truth—while the evil of the world is rooted in misconstrued self-understanding.

If people act in evil and hurtful ways because they belong to the world and its values, how then can human evil be overcome? John's answer sounds simple: by walking in the light, a form of discipleship

---

Rudolph Bultmann, whose ground-breaking commentary on John promoted his demythologizing/remythologizing hermeneutical agenda, interpreting the biblical message as distinguishing between authentic and inauthentic ways of living.

19. Kysar, *Maverick Gospel*, 79.

described as living life abundantly (10:10). As simple as it sounds, John's two realms represent different identities. The journey from one to the other requires continuous transformation of the self, a process John entrusts to the Holy Spirit.

Questions to Ponder

1. For whose benefit does Jesus change the water to wine? Why?
2. In John's Gospel, what function does the cleansing of the temple have?
3. Does the concept of spiritual birth have relevance in the modern world?
4. For John, what is the meaning of the word "believe" (belief)? How is this concept related to "faith"? Are they the same? If not, how are they different?
5. What, for John, is the opposite of "life" or "eternal life"?
6. In John 4:10, what does Jesus mean by "living water"?
7. What implications can you draw from the healing of the official's son? Do you believe this sort of healing can take place today? Support your answer.
8. Do you conceive of evil as essentially cosmic or anthropological in nature? Explain your answer.
9. Why might John's early readers have found it helpful to think dualistically about realities in their lives?

PART III

The Public Ministry of Jesus

Phase Two

(JOHN 5–12)

CHAPTER 4

Jesus, the Sabbath, and Exodus Imagery
(John 5:1—6:71)

Summary: John 5 reveals a common Johannine pattern: an event (in this case the healing of the man at the pool of Bethesda) followed by an extended discourse (on the authority of the Son and on the witnesses to Jesus). With chapter 5, the tone of the Gospel changes substantially. Whereas previously those who encounter Jesus may question his authority or simply be confused by him, the story of the healing on the Sabbath results in concerted opposition. Jesus' enemies are threatened by him and their response is to initiate a judicial process that culminates in a trial. Jesus is seen to violate Jewish law, and his opponents see it as their religious duty to prosecute him. Jesus' defense is a soliloquy about his relationship to the Father and about judgment. Chapter 6, which recounts the incident of the feeding of the five thousand, followed by the account of Jesus walking on the water, focuses on the metaphor of bread. There are connections to the manna stories in the Old Testament and references to the Eucharist, which taken literally cause many of Jesus' disciples to turn away from him.

Assignment: Read John 5–6

Key Passages: John 6:35; 6:38

Central Theme: Jesus is the Bread of Life

Key Symbols/Concepts: the Jews, the Sabbath, (eternal) life, testimony, glory, Passover, Son of Man, manna, bread of life, belief in Jesus, flesh and blood of the Son, words of life

Learning Objectives

Participants will examine:
1. Christological agency language in John
2. The nature of Jewish opposition to Jesus
3. Jesus and the Jewish Sabbath
4. The metaphorical meaning of Jesus as the bread of life
5. The Eucharistic overtones of John 6:52–58
6. The nature of discipleship in John 6:60–71
7. The meaning of the term "the Jews" in John's Gospel

Outline to John 5:1—6:71

I. Jesus Heals on the Sabbath 5:1–18
   A. The Healing of the Man at the Pool 5:1–9a
   B. Aftermath of the Healing 5:9b–18

II. Jesus' Discourse 5:19–47
   A. The Authority of the Son 5:19–30
   B. Witnesses to Jesus 5:30–47

III. Feeding the Five Thousand 6:1–15

IV. Jesus Walks on the Water 6:16–21

V. Discourse on Jesus as the Bread of Life 6:22–59
   A. Introduction to the Discourse 6:22–24
   B. The Bread of Life 6:25–51
   C. The Food of the Faithful 6:52–59

VI. The Faith of the Faithful 6:60–71

Christological Agency Language

In John's prologue we learn that Jesus is God's Word come in the flesh. This declaration is followed by copious witnesses to Jesus, a series of people approaching adequate faith in Jesus. The first two signs recorded in the Fourth Gospel, primarily private affairs, took place in Cana, but in chapters 5–6 Jesus goes much more public with his works and words, and we find increasing claims made by and about Jesus matched by a rise of opposition to him from a distinct segment of Jewish society. The reason for this opposition is made clear in the first miracle story of this unit, in which Jesus is said to make himself "equal with God" (5:18), confirming that the attributions to the Word in John 1 are true. Later in the Gospel we learn that the appropriate confession of Jesus involves the recognition that "before Abraham was, I am" (8:58) and that "the Father and I are one" (10:30). It is ultimately these sorts of claims, by word and by deed, that scandalize "the Jews" and lead to the trial, conviction, and execution of Jesus. The Evangelist flashes back and forth between Jerusalem and Galilee to show the mounting tide of opposition to Jesus in both places. The judicial process has been set in motion, and Jesus is now a marked man.

One of the most important advances in understanding Johannine language about Jesus comes by exploring how "agency language" is used to describe the relationship between the Son and the Father.[1] The Jewish concept of agency can be summed up in the phrase: "A person's agent is as himself." An agent is a person legally authorized to perform a set of tasks and thus empowered to speak and act for the sender. This agent was to be treated as the sender would have been treated had that one come in person. In many ways this was also how ambassadors or envoys were viewed in the ancient world.

This notion is crucial to John's intent, as the following points indicate: (1) John's Gospel repeatedly stresses that Jesus is the Father's unique and special Son. In family affairs, the agent of first choice for any family business would be the eldest son, who was the primary heir, and if he were the only son, he would be the sole heir of the father's estate. (2) This son could be authorized to undertake a mission for the head of the family, and would be empowered to say or do whatever necessary to accomplish the task. In this case the son would not only act and speak for the father, but also as the father would act. The son could do nothing beyond the

---

1. This discussion on agency language is adapted from Witherington, *John's Wisdom*, 140-41.

scope of the power and authority given to him. If the Fourth Evangelist is using this Jewish concept of agency to describe Jesus' relationship with the Father, this would explain why it is said that the Son can do only what the Father authorizes (5:30). Jesus, the only Son, is his Father's sole agent on earth, commissioned and sent so that anyone who hears his word and believes has eternal life (5:24). (3) Whoever honors the Son honors the Father, but whoever dishonors the Son dishonors the Father who sent him (5:23). If and when the Son is rejected, then the Sender has been rejected as well, and some type of judgment must follow: "The Father judges no one but has given all judgment to the Son" (5:22).

The agency model explains how Jesus can be both equal in power and authority to the Father and yet clearly subordinate to the Father. It also partially explains why it is necessary for Jesus to return to the Father. All agents report directly to the sender about the outcome of their (joint) venture. While agency language appears regularly in John, it is only at Jesus' crucial last meal with his disciples where Jesus reveals this truth: "Very truly, I tell you, a slave (*doulos*) is not greater than his master, nor is the apostle (*apostolos*) greater than the one who sent him" (13:16; my translation). Here Jesus authorizes the disciples as his agents, his apostles (*apostoloi*): "I have set you an example, that you also should do as I have done" (3:15). The discourse culminates at 13:20, where Jesus pronounces the fundamental truth about a person and his agent: "whoever receives one whom I send receives me; and whoever receives me receives him who sent me."

The concept of agency may not adequately summarize all that the Fourth Evangelist wants to say about Jesus' equality with the Father, but it does unlock many puzzling doors in the world of Johannine Christology. The Synoptics as well, in the famous parable of the vineyard (Matt. 21:33–46; Mark 12:1–12; Luke 20:9–19), tell an agency story of an only son sent by a father to deal with wicked tenants in the owner's vineyard, a son recognized as the heir and thus the ultimate agent of the father, who gets himself killed in the bargain. Both John and the Synoptics agree that Jesus presented himself as God's unique agent, the only Son of the Father.

Analysis of John 5:1—6:71

Jesus Heals on the Sabbath (Chapter 5:1–18)

As previously noted, John 5 follows a common pattern, consisting of a healing story and a discourse by Jesus that sets forth the theological implications of that event. By constructing the Gospel in this way, the fourth Evangelist provides readers with requisite theological categories through which to interpret the story of Jesus. In the case of John 5, those theological categories involve the introduction of the controversy between Jesus and the Jewish authorities.

The context for the story in chapter 5 is Jerusalem during an unnamed Jewish festival. The festival could be any of the three pilgrimage festivals (Passover, Pentecost, or Tabernacles), but the identity of the festival is not important, for the account has to do with the Jewish Sabbath (5:9). The rising hostility is introduced by the explanation in 5:16: "Therefore the Jews started persecuting Jesus, because he was doing such things on the Sabbath; see also 5:18). These statements foreshadow the role of "the Jews" in the rest of the Gospel. The discourse that follows cites witnesses to Jesus (5:30–47) as though he were already on trial. In the next episode the people murmur against Jesus (6:41) and then argue with one another (6:52). The level of hostility escalates in the ensuing debate, where we learn that "the Jews" are seeking to kill Jesus (7:1). John 8 contains the most hostile exchange between Jesus and "the Jews," who accuse Jesus of being demon-possessed and attempt to stone him (8:59; see 10:31, 33). Jesus eventually withdraws from Jerusalem (10:40), but returns because Lazarus is at the point of death. Jesus delays and then returns to raise Lazarus from the dead. The response of the authorities is to plot Jesus' death, a plotting that leads to the events of Jesus' passion and bring to a close his public ministry.

Biblical scholars have long pointed out the presence of editorial seams at the start of chapters 5 and 6. The abrupt beginning of chapter 5, followed by verses rife with textual variants (5:2–3), points to the independent nature of the scene. Likewise, the lack of smooth transition between chapters 5 and 6 further suggests that something is amiss chronologically. The problem is compounded by geographical inconsistencies. In 5:1 Jesus goes to Jerusalem, where he spends the entire chapter healing and teaching. In this context, the editorial comment in 6:1 is puzzling: "After this, Jesus went to the other side of the Sea of Galilee." How could

Jesus go to the other side of the sea if he is not already on one of its sides? Chapter 5 tells us that Jesus is nowhere near the Sea of Galilee, since he is in Jerusalem. Following Bultmann, some scholars transpose these chapters, placing chapter 6 after chapter 4.[2] This solution provides geographical continuity and minimizes some of the problems. For example, the remark in 7:1 about Jesus not traveling in Judea for fear of being killed follows logically on 5:18, without the interference provided by a lengthy chapter 6 spent in Galilee. Similarly, the "one work" of 7:21 is best explained by the more recent healing of the paralytic at the sheep pool in 5:2–15. Since these peculiarities don't much affect the meaning of these passages or their interpretation, we will follow the traditional order. This approach is confirmed by the manuscript tradition, which provides no evidence for transposition, meaning that any transposition must belong to a stage prior to the publication of the Gospel.

The account of the healing of the cripple at the pool of Bethesda (5:1–18) includes details that can be easily allegorized. For example, did John's Jewish audience think to connect the length of the cripple's thirty-eight years with the thirty-eight years that the Hebrews had wandered in the desert (Deut. 2:14)? The healing story is also one of the most enigmatic in John. Unlike most healings in John, where people in need come to Jesus, here Jesus takes the initiative, asking the cripple, "Do you want to be made well?" (5:6). Surprisingly, there is no response of faith (cf. 2:11; 4:55). The man simply goes away (5:15). Parenthetically, Jesus' command to the man by the pool to rise, take up his pallet, and walk, is the longest verbatim parallel between John and the Synoptics (see Mark 2:9). Only when the man has been healed are we told that it was the Sabbath (5:9). This timing, then, is crucial about this miracle, for it precipitates conflict with "the Jews" (5:10, 15–18).

As noted above, it was not Jesus' custom to seek out people to heal; rather they come to him. The one exception to this rule, however, is when the healing occurs on the Sabbath. Both the Synoptics and the Fourth Gospel stress that Jesus deliberately sought out opportunities to heal on the Sabbath, which raises the question of whether he did so as a provocation. For Jews, observing the Sabbath was one of the distinctive marks of being Jewish. And yet Jesus felt free to act in ways he knew would be seen as deliberate violations of the Sabbath. The cripple did not have to be healed that day; he did not even request the healing. Clearly Jesus could

---

2. As Gerard Sloyan does in his commentary on John in the Interpretation series.

have waited one more day, and yet Jesus chose to act. By violating regulations concerning the Sabbath, Jesus would have been seen as encouraging others to break with tradition. The consequences of Sabbath violation could be as severe as death by stoning, and John's Gospel makes it clear that it was these sorts of actions on the Sabbath that caused some Jews to begin taking action against Jesus.

Ben Witherington gives various plausible explanations for Jesus' behavior: (1) Jesus believed he was bringing in the eschatological age, when Sabbath regulations were no longer in force; (2) Jesus believed he was divine and therefore not subject to such regulations; and (3) Jesus believed he was fulfilling the true intent of sabbatical rest by healing on the Sabbath.[3] This third explanation illustrates further the Johannine theme of Jesus' replacing the institutions of Judaism with something he considered superior and more lasting, perhaps best describing the Evangelist's perspective.

N. T. Wright's offers a delightfully different explanation.[4] He speaks of attending a conference and of sharing a room with a distinguished Indian scholar. He awoke one morning at four o'clock to hear his roommate speaking with his wife on the phone. When the conversation ended, Wright chided the scholar with the words: "Come on! It's four in the morning! It's time for rest!" His friend replied that it was seven o'clock where his wife lived and that he needed to speak with her before she went to work. Applying this awareness to the account of the healing of the man on the Sabbath, Wright notes that it was as if Jesus and his Judean (Jewish) opponents were working in two different time zones, not geographical but theological. While Jesus' Jewish opponents were thinking it time for rest, Jesus was awake and busy with the theological business of his "day." Jesus was simply living in a different time zone. His Father was at work, and so should he be. For John, the battle of time zones continued until it reached its climax on the cross (note Jesus' uniquely Johannine words: "It is finished" in 19:30).

Once the man had been healed, the story continues by saying that sometime later Jesus found the man in the temple, at which time he reminded him to stop sinning, lest something worse happen to him (5:14). The reference to sickness and sin, as though they were directly connected, is problematic. In light of what is said in John 9:1–4 about the

---

3. Witherington, *John's Wisdom*, 135.
4. Wright, *John*, 1:58–59.

man born blind (cf. 9:39–41), it seems wrong to read Jesus words in 5:14 as affirming the traditional linkage of sin and illness (see Job 5:17–18; Mark 2:5–10; 1 Cor. 11:29–30).

Another perceived misconception appears in 5:15, commonly read as an indication of the healed man's ingratitude, as though his response to Jesus was to "turn him in" to the authorities. Such a reading is not suggested by the words themselves. The verb used to describe the man's speech is "to announce," used elsewhere in John as a positive announcement of the activity of the Messiah (4:25) and of the Paraclete (16:13–15). The man is not turning Jesus in for violating the Sabbath law but rather is announcing him as the one who made him well. The response of the Jews, translated as "persecute" in 5:16, is better translated as "prosecute," meaning to bring to trial. What we have here is akin to pretrial hearings. Verse 18 needs to be interpreted carefully as well, for it records a statement by the narrator, not by Jesus; the text does not say that the Jews were charging him with claiming to be equal to God—that comes later, after further confrontations (10:33; 19:7). The fact that Jesus calls God his Father is sufficient cause for indictment. In Jewish eyes, the charges against Jesus are twofold: Sabbath violation (5:16) and blasphemy (5:18). The latter charge forces readers to ask: "In what sense is Jesus equal to the Father, especially in light of his evident subordination to the Father?" (5:19).

Jesus' Discourse (Chapter 5:19–47)

In light of the discussion earlier about agency Christology, much of what follows in John should be easier to understand. For instance, the strong assertion (note the double "amen" in 5:19, translated as "very truly") about the Son's subordination to the Father is part of an intimate relationship between the two. Sonship means obedience, not independence. That Jesus is the Son means that his works *are* the works of God. The Father authorizes the Son to give life, including being able to raise the dead, a power Jews believed was solely in the hands of God. In addition, 5:22 states that the Son is given the power to pass ultimate judgment, again a role that is exclusively God's. As is true with an agent, anyone who doesn't honor the agent doesn't honor the sender (5:23). The Son's words are in fact the words of "him who sent me" (5:24), so that to hear and believe the Son's words is to hear and believe the Father's words.

Fulfilling expectations about the apocalyptic Son of Man, Jesus is able to raise the dead and give life. John 5:25 extends the theme of Jesus as the giver of life in 1:4 and foreshadows the raising of Lazarus in chapter 11. For John, eternal life begins here and now, and those who hear Jesus and believe already have eternal life. Nevertheless, Jesus also looks ahead to the time when the dead will hear his voice and rise, to resurrection or to condemnation.

John 5:27 speaks of the Son's authority to execute judgment. Judgment is a key Johannine term capable of subtle distinctions of meaning. Verse 29 implies that judgment is rendered on the basis of deeds, but this is not viewed as contradictory to grace, in part because the chief work or deed said to be necessary in this Gospel is "belief" in the Son, viewed as a gift rather than as a requisite work or deed. John 5:30 concludes the discussion of agency, reiterating the principle with which it began, that the Son does not seek to act independently but rather to do the Father's will. In this passage "judgment" is synonymous with witness or knowledge, though elsewhere it can mean condemnation (see 8:15–16).

Having defended his authority to heal on the Sabbath and to call God his Father (5:19–29), Jesus now calls forth witnesses to his defense, including John the Baptist (5:33–35), the works he performs (5:36), the Father (5:37–38), and the scriptures (5:39). In 5:33–40 Jesus speaks as his own defense attorney; the verb "witness" occurs seven times in 5:31–40 and the noun form of the verb occurs four times. In a limited sense, the reference to Jesus' "works" in 5:36 indicates his miracles, but the expression is used more generally to refer to Jesus' ministry in its entirety (see 4:34). The whole discourse takes on the atmosphere of a trial scene in which charges are brought, the accused responds, and witnesses are summoned. According to Jewish law, testimony had to be confirmed by two witnesses (Deut. 19:15), but Jesus adds several others, appealing eventually to the testimony of Moses (5:45–47).

The audience is said to be caught in the cycle of relying on human testimonies and accepting glory from one another, rather than accepting the testimony God sent in Christ and the glory that comes from God alone. We find here yet another two-level discussion: Jesus is speaking and acting on a spiritual level while the audience is operating and thinking on a mundane level. In a surprising turn, Jesus indicates that Moses, far from testifying against him for what he does on the Sabbath, will testify against his accusers. Now it is "the Jews," not Jesus, who are on trial. If his accusers had believed Moses, they would believe Jesus, "for he wrote about me" (5:46). The discourse then comes to an abrupt end, but the reader knows this is only the first round in an ongoing controversy. The Evangelist leaves no doubt that the issue under debate is not simply over Jesus' sayings or deeds but about his identity. It is evident as well that John's perception of the Hebrew scriptures in general and Moses' law in particular is that they testify about Jesus. For John, the Old Testament seems to have a rather exclusively Christological function.

Feeding the Five Thousand (Chapter 6:1–15)

Chapter 6 presents Jesus as the bread of life. This passage may once have been an independent homily, since it is closely related to Exodus 16, Numbers 11, and other Old Testament passages. The story of the miraculous feeding was popular in the early church because of the Eucharistic interpretation to which it lent itself, an interpretation I find to be minimal if at all present in this context.

Whether chapters 5 and 6 were originally transposed (since the geographical indicators flow more smoothly when the chapters are reversed), the present order allows chapter 6 to develop the theme of the witnesses to Jesus (God, scripture, Jesus' works, and Moses) introduced in chapter 5, for each plays an important role in John 6. In addition, the request by Jesus' brothers that he go to Jerusalem and show himself (7:3) loses much of its force if that passage follows the story of Jesus in Jerusalem in chapter 5.

The Old Testament background to which this account alludes is the wilderness feeding of the Hebrew multitudes with manna, the bread that came down from heaven. That story, as this one, includes a large group of Jews who benefit from the manna and a smaller group that murmurs and complains, as "the Jews" do in John 6:41 and 52. Here Jesus fulfills the role of Moses by feeding the multitude in the wilderness (6:1–15) and crossing the sea (6:16–24). The discourse that follows the accounts of the feeding of the five thousand and Jesus walking on the water (6:22–59) treats only the bread, not Jesus on the water. Its inclusion in the chapter shows that these events were firmly linked in the tradition, as their presence in the Synoptics attest.

The chief symbolic association of this story with the various Jewish manna traditions is where Torah (or Wisdom) is alluded to as manna/bread from God that feeds people. The Jewish Wisdom traditions are especially important in this case. For example Proverbs 9:5 reads, "Come, eat of my bread and drink of the wine I have mixed." In the rabbinical tradition, this verse in Proverbs is linked to Exodus 16:4: "Because I will cause to rain bread from heaven," the former text being seen as the explanation of the latter.[5] Philo, the first-century Jewish philosopher, is more explicit. In commenting on Exodus 16:4 he remarks: "Of what food can he rightly say that it rained from heaven, save of heavenly Wisdom?"[6] As John Painter notes, there is a close parallel between John 4 and 6. In one there is the offering of life-giving water and in the other the offer of life-giving bread.[7] Both water and bread are well-known symbols for Wisdom, which is often identified with Torah. The Fourth Evangelist is taking these traditions and depicting Jesus as greater than Torah (see the discussion on 1:17), which enshrines God's wisdom, for Jesus is Wisdom/Torah/Logos in the flesh. This interpretation further supports the contention that John 6 is about Christology, not about the Eucharist.

John 6 is the only chapter where the Evangelist treats in any depth the Galilean phase of Jesus' public ministry, and it is not an accident that he chose the one incident (feeding the five thousand) that brought that phase to a crisis, causing the withdrawal of Jesus, the falling away of peripheral disciples, and finally the confession of the faithful few. The audience narrows progressively as the narrative unfolds. At first the discussion is with the crowd (6:25–40), then with "the Jews," a smaller group of objectors within the crowd (6:41–59), and finally with the disciples again (6:60–66), narrowed to the inner circle of the Twelve (6:67–71).

The first four verses set the scene: on the other side of the Sea of Galilee, the crowd follows Jesus up a mountain at the time of Passover.[8] While crowds of pilgrims are making their way to Jerusalem to celebrate, another crowd throngs around Jesus in Galilee. John explains that the crowds came because of the signs that Jesus had performed in healing the sick. By the end of the chapter, those with shallow ("signs") faith will have left Jesus. The reference to going up on a mountain (6:3) evokes memories of Moses on Mt. Sinai and the giving of the Law. The men-

---

5. *Exodus Rabbah* 25:7.
6. Cited by Witherington, *John's Wisdom*, 149.
7. Painter, *Quest*, 242.
8. As Koester notes, there are good reasons to think that the expression "the other side" or "across the sea" (6:1, 17, 22, 25), often taken to mean that people were traveling east to west across the sea, means traveling the stretch of water between Tiberius and Capernaum, both on the western side of the lake, *Symbolism*, 55 n. 35.

tion of the Passover in 6:4 introduces the exodus theme, for that festival celebrates God's deliverance of the Jews from slavery in Egypt, including the giving of manna from heaven (Exod. 16:9–35; exodus imagery figures prominently in John 6:5–59, particularly in 6:12, 31–32, 49, and 58).

The feeding of the five thousand is the only miracle related in all four gospels. In the Johannine telling of the story, Jesus is the focus of attention: it is he rather than the disciples who distributes the bread and fish (6:11), whereas the Synoptics include the disciples in that role. In John, Jesus uses the occasion to test one of the disciples, Philip. As elsewhere in John, a disciple fails the test by thinking only on a mundane level. Only the Fourth Gospel mentions that the loaves ae barley loaves, an allusion to the story of Elisha feeding a hundred people with twenty barley loaves, with some left over (2 Kgs. 4:42–44). In John's version, Jesus' actions do not reflect the more liturgically stylized actions of the Synoptic accounts (Mark 6:41; Luke 9:16), but rather reflect the actions of a host at a Jewish meal. John 6:11 tells us that the people ate as much as they wanted, and that the fragments that resulted left more bread than when they started. The gathering of twelve (or seven) baskets full of fragments (6:13) is standard in the Synoptic tradition, but Jesus' words in 6:12 ("Gather up the fragments left over, so that nothing may be lost") are unique to John's version and make an important connection between this story and the manna story of Exodus 16:19–20, where leftover manna "bred worms and became foul." The connection between the feeding miracle and the manna story, pivotal to John 6:25–59, is thus introduced early on. The feeding of the multitude—in the wilderness, at the time of Passover, with barley loaves—is a clear affirmation in narrative form that Jesus is the fulfillment of Moses and the prophets. He is the expected Prophet like Moses who will again deliver his people.

The crowd's response to make Jesus king because he is "the prophet who is to come into the world" (6:14) is ambiguous from John's perspective, since the confession rests on the evidence of signs. The people's confession continues the exodus imagery because it recalls the promise of a prophet like Moses (Deut. 8:15). The kingship of Jesus is an important theme in the Fourth Gospel, but for John Jesus will be king only according to his definition of kingship (18:36–38), not according to the world's definition. The kingship theme reaches its resolution in the crucifixion narrative in John 18—19.

Jesus Walks on the Water (Chapter 6:16–21)

Having fed the people as Moses did in the wilderness, Jesus now performs a sea miracle, akin to the parting of the sea at the exodus. Walking on the water, like the multiplication of loaves, again demonstrates Jesus' sovereignty over the created order as the creative Logos incarnate. Both creation and exodus motifs are prominent in passages such as Psalm 77:16, 19, which speak of how God came to his people in the exodus, making his way "through the sea" and his path "through the mighty waters." The admonition to the disciples not to fear (6:20) is typical of scriptural theophanies and angelophanies (see Gen. 15:1; Jud. 6:23; Matt. 28:5; Luke 1:13, 30; 2:10). The expression "It is I" (*egō eimi*) can be taken as reassurance, but it can also be translated to mean "I am," the formula of divine self-disclosure (Exod. 3:14; Isa. 43:3, 11, 13). If so, the account of the walking on the water is once again a revelatory event, disclosing that Jesus is the incarnate Logos and therefore one greater than Moses.

Discourse on Jesus as the Bread of Life (Chapter 6:22–59)

A brief transitional passage (6:22–24) brings us to 6:25–59, a profound and beautifully developed discourse on the identity of Jesus as the bread of life. The meaning of the discourse is found in its contrast between belief (faith) and unbelief. For John, this is where all disciples find themselves: midway between the ministry of Jesus and the eve of his crucifixion, midway between the satisfaction of food and drink and the final meaning of Jesus' life and death.

In the ensuing dialogue with the crowd, Jesus does not answer their question but moves the conversation to another level. The two-level discussion once more comes into play. It is important to recognize that Jesus provides both physical and spiritual food, not simply the latter. It would not be correct, then, to limit the Johannine Christ to purely spiritual things, nor helpful to simply call John the "spiritual" Gospel, particularly since it is this Gospel that most clearly focuses on the incarnation.

In John 6:27–30 the crowd picks up on Jesus' admonition that they should perform the works of God. Their focus is on doing good works, but Jesus subordinates the doing of good works to the priority of the one good work, believing in him (6:29), that is, recognizing that he is God's revealer, on whom God has "set his seal" (6:27). The crowd asks for a validating sign to be given (6:31), alluding to Psalm 78 and its reference to the manna story of Exodus 16.[9] The ensuing dialogue revolves around the proper meaning of Psalm 78:24, with Jesus correcting their misunderstanding of that text, which provides the three-part structure for the rest of the discourse: (1) First, Jesus explains that Moses did not give their ancestors the bread from heaven—God did (6:32–34); (2) then, Jesus explains that he is the true bread from heaven that gives life (6:35–51); (3) lastly, he explains that eating the bread of life means eating his body and drinking his blood (6:52–58).

John's aim in 6:32–34 is to portray Jesus as one greater than Moses. This leads to the famous "bread of life" saying in John 6:35, the first of the "I am" sayings with an explicit predicate (a noun as an object). Here Jesus claims that those who come to him will not hunger or thirst, but will have eternal life (coming to Jesus and believing in him are synonymous here; see also 7:37–38). Verses 36–40 follow a chiastic structure (ABCB'A'). The frame of the chiasm is "seeing and believing" (6:36 and 40), a linkage central to the Johannine understanding of faith (see 4:48; 6:30; 20:25, 29; for the Fourth Evangelist, to see rightly is to believe). The statement in verse 38: "I have come down from heaven," represents the central element of the chiasm, clarifying that Jesus is the true bread from heaven that gives life.

The statement in 6:37 "Everything that the Father gives me will come to me, and anyone who comes to me, I will never drive away" (6:37), suggests the issue of election, a divisive doctrine throughout Christian history. If humanity is divided into two groups, either "from above" or "from below" (8:23), can all come to Jesus? While it is true to say that none come to Jesus unless the Father draws them, John does not disclose on what basis God draws some and not others. By contrast, when the author speaks about the human response he speaks of individuals, not of a group: "anyone who comes to me I will never drive away" (6:37b). God's will is that Jesus lose none of those the Father has given him, but rather raise them up on the last day (6:39). That is God's will, but we are not told that someone God draws may not commit apostasy or rebellion. Indeed, 6:70 tells us that while Judas Iscariot was one of the Twelve, he turned out to be "a devil." Thus, even though the Fourth Gospel has a strong view of divine sovereignty (6:44; 15:16), it also recognizes things that happen contrary to God's desires and will. While God's role in the relationship with humans is decisive, the fact remains that God does not and will not force people to be faithful. Even though human response

---

9. The reference to "manna" in John 6 is the only mention of the term in the gospels.

is enabled by God's grace, God will not save a person apart from faith. While all humans may be drawn by the Father, all may resist. The key to maintaining the balance between God's initiative (6:37, 39) and human faith (6:36, 40) is expressed in verse 38: Jesus has come down from heaven to make God's will visible and accessible to humanity. Faith in Jesus is impossible without God's initiating will for the world, but human beings are responsible for the decisions they make in response to God's initiative. In 6:36–40, that decision is expressed in terms of either seeing and not believing (6:36) or seeing and believing (6:40).[10] Despite emphasizing realized eschatology, the Gospel still asserts that Jesus' work will culminate in the future: "and I will raise them up on the last day" (6:38, 40, 44, 54).

At 6:41 the issue of Jesus' true identity predominates, and as we saw previously, the key to Jesus' identity is his origin and his destiny. This chapter has the heaviest concentration in the Gospel of language of Jesus' heavenly descent. Introduced in 3:13, the language is used in chapter 6 to solidify the connection between the manna miracle and Jesus' revelation of himself as the bread of life. Descent language does not recur after this chapter.

Having been impressed by Jesus' signs, the crowd's response to Jesus' words is unbelief. In John, individual sins are subordinated to unbelief, the foundation of all sin. For the first time in chapter 6, the crowd is identified as "the Jews." The change in reference is not so much due to a change of audience as to the crowd's resistance to Jesus. The word "complain" in 6:41, another example of exodus imagery at work in John 6, is carefully chosen for its use in the Septuagint (the Greek version of the Old Testament), where it describes the Israelites' grumbling and complaining in the wilderness (Exod. 16:2).

The Jews' claim to know Jesus' parentage (6:42) seems out of place in a Gospel that contains no infancy narrative and makes no direct reference to Jesus' birth. It seems likely that this reference is an ironic allusion to those traditions (see also 7:41–42). The Jews' misplaced certitude about Jesus' origins blinds them to his true origin.

At 6:46 Jesus makes the claim that he has seen God, implying his origin in heaven. The ensuing verses make clear that certain interpretations of the doctrine of election are incorrect. While God's chosen people were led out of Egypt and into the wilderness en masse, many died on

---

10. For an extended discussion of divine determinism and individual free will, see essay 6, "The Paradoxical Nature of Faith."

account of their rebellion. It was only the faithful that either saw or entered the Promised Land. The manna offered in the wilderness did not provide eternal life; Jesus alone is the bread of heaven, which provides eternal life. While he is the living bread, paradoxically, the dying Jesus is bread as well, for eternal life cannot be provided unless Jesus dies (6:51). The phrase "flesh and blood" (6:53), a common way of referring to one's humanity or mortality (cf. Matt. 16:17; 1 Cor. 15:50), can represent Jesus as living or as dying. It is not surprising, in light of the extreme aversion Jews had to meat eaten with its blood that the Jews are portrayed as completely offended by Jesus' graphic remarks at 6:52–58.

The insistence in 6:53 on eating "the flesh of the Son of Man" and "drinking his blood," which some interpret Eucharistically, may reflect an editorial attempt to counter docetic or gnostic tendencies within the Johannine community to deny bodily aspects of Christ and of Christian experience. However, it is noteworthy that nowhere in 6:53–59 are the Eucharistic elements of bread and wine mentioned. The Evangelist's focus remains on the flesh and blood of Jesus, not their sacramental representations, in order to underscore Jesus' gift of his whole self on the cross. A comparison of 6:40 and 54 shows that eating Jesus' flesh and drinking his blood parallels "seeing" the Son and "believing" in him.

People partake of the crucified Jesus by faith; "to eat" is "to believe." The centrality of faith is introduced at the beginning of the discourse, when Jesus reminds the crowd that their priority is to believe in him (6:29). When Jesus identifies himself as the bread of life, he states that those who believe in him would not hunger or thirst (6:35). Finally, he promises eternal life and resurrection to those who believe in him (6:40, 47), repeating the same idea in 6:54: "Those who eat my flesh and drink my blood have eternal life, and I will raise them up on the last day." Jesus warns that those who do not eat and drink of him do not have life (6:53), as elsewhere he cautioned that those who do not believe face the prospect of death (3:18, 36; 8:24). To partake of Jesus as the bread of life is to believe that the crucified Messiah is the source of eternal life with God.[11] At the heart of 6:56 ("those who eat my flesh and drink my blood abide in me, and I in them") is the verb "abide," a key Johannine term that expresses the interrelationship of Jesus and believers (15:4), understood as an extension of the interrelationship of the Father and Jesus (6:57).

---

11. Koester, *Symbolism*, 103.

The statement in 6:59, "He said these things while he was teaching in the synagogue at Capernaum," indicates that a shift in locale had taken place earlier (perhaps beginning at 6:47 or more likely 6:53; in both cases we find a reprise of familiar Johannine themes, marked by the expression "Very truly I tell you," which signals the beginning of a new section in the discourse; cf. 5:19, 24–25; 6:32). This segment of the discourse seems to reflect actual or hypothetical synagogue debates, since Johannine Christians themselves likely participated in such debates at key times in their experience.

The Faith of the Faithful (Chapter 6:60–71)

This section can be subdivided into two units: 6:60–65, which focuses on doubt and rejection among Jesus' disciples, and 6:66–71, which focuses more narrowly on the faith response of the Twelve. In the face of Jesus' most explicit and far-reaching offer of himself and the gift of life to believers, these verses form a fitting conclusion to chapter 6.

The similarity between certain of Jesus' disciples and the crowd is established by the repetition of the verb "to complain" (6:61; cf. 6:41). When the disciples find the teaching about consuming (eating and drinking) Jesus offensive (6:60–61), he replies that if they were to see the Son of Man ascend, they might be even more scandalized. One of the keys to rightly understanding the entire discourse is the statement in 6:63 that Jesus' words, not sacramental action, give life. The emphasis here is that salvation comes through revelation and the resultant transformation. John 6:64–65 returns to a theme that recurs through the discourse, namely, the tension between divine initiative and human choice (6:65; see 6:37, 39, and 44). The stress again is on the primacy of God's initiating act: "no one can come to me unless it is granted by the Father."

In 6:67 Jesus presents the Twelve with a choice: "Do you wish to go away?" The Twelve remain loyal, at least for the moment, and after the other disciples have left, Simon Peter, speaking for the Twelve, confesses that Jesus alone has the "words of eternal life" (6:68). The prominent role of Peter in 6:66–71 suggests that the Evangelist draws on traditions similar to those drawn on by the Synoptics (Matt. 16:13–20; Mark 8: 27–33; and Luke 9:18–20). Peter's response indicates that he has heard and learned from the bread of life discourse: "Lord, to whom can we go? You have the words of eternal life" (6:68; see 6:40, 47, 51, 54, and 58). Peter's confession continues in 6:69: "We have come to believe and know that you are the Holy One of God." "Believe" and "know" here function as synonyms, as they do elsewhere (10:38; 14:7; 16:30). The Christological title "the Holy One of God" appears only here in John. The meaning is similar to the expression "the one whom the Father has sanctified," that is, "made holy," in 10:36. Curiously, when the title appears in the Synoptics, it appears on the lips of demons (Mark 1:24; Luke 4:34).

Instead of embracing Peter's confession, Jesus raises again the question of election and choice. This time it is Jesus' act of election, not God's, on which Jesus focuses (6:70). Even Judas's selection into the Twelve is no guarantee of a faith response, as 6:71 makes clear. In that verse Judas is described as a devil (cf. 13:2, 27) meaning that he is drawn more to evil than to God (cf. 3:19–21). "Election is no substitute for the decision of faith."[12]

John 6:67 and 70 are the first mention of "the Twelve" in John, a term found only in this passage and in 20:24. Because the Beloved Disciple was *the* apostle of the Johannine community, the Twelve are not as important in John as they are in the Synoptic Gospels.

Essay 4: Jesus and "the Jews" in John's Gospel

In John's Gospel, we find numerous occasions when a group of individuals designated "the Jews" seem to come under harsh scrutiny, coming across as villains. They persecute Jesus (5:16), they misunderstand him (8:22), they attempt to stone him (8:59) and they are responsible for his arrest and crucifixion (18:12; 19:12). Most characteristically, they are the ones who refuse to believe in him (10:31–39).

To understand the polemical treatment of "the Jews" in John, it is important to review the situation in which the Gospel was written. The era of successful and concerted Christian missionary inroads into Judaism has passed. Jesus had been preached to the Jews both in Palestine and the Diaspora, and the decision for or against Jesus had been made. For the most part, the Jews who had accepted Jesus have simply become Christians and part of the Church. When the Gospel was written, many of the religious distinctions and groupings of Jesus' time no longer applied; the destruction of the temple and of Jerusalem in AD 70 had simplified Judaism. Thus, only the chief priests and the Pharisees are portrayed in John—the chief priests because their role in the Sanhedrin and in the

---

12. O'Day, *John*, 611.

trial of Jesus was too essential a part of the story to be ignored, and the Pharisees because they are precisely the Jewish leaders who survived the calamity of 70. Pharisaic Judaism was the form of Judaism dominant in the period when the Gospel was written. It is this dominance that explains the use of the term "the Jews" in John (see also Matt. 28:15). The Fourth Evangelist is using the term with the meaning that it had in his own time.

If John desires to disuade Diaspora Jews from committing the same errors and sins that many Palestinian Jews committed, it is not surprising that he should use strong language to denounce "the Jews." This expression, found seventy times in the Fourth Gospel, commonly designates those who oppose Jesus (7:1). Some see in this usage evidence of Christian anti-Semitism; most think it refers primarily to Jewish leaders and not to Jewish people at large; some think it reflects geography (Judean Jews as opposed to Galilean Jews); and still others think the diversity of usage in John reflects the way Johannine Christians were treated at certain stages of communal experience by Jewish leaders at nearby synagogues.[13]

In light of John's usage of the term we must note that the Evangelist is deliberately inconsistent. Passages such as 4:22, which state that "salvation is from the Jews," make clear that one cannot declare the Evangelist or his Gospel as anti-Semitic or even as anti-Jewish. Whatever hostilities are present in John turn on theological issues related to the acceptance or rejection of Christian belief, and not on race. How could race be a factor, when all of the first Christians were Jews, and when the Fourth Evangelist and his readers were Jews? Those who respond to Jesus, whether Jews, Samaritans, or "other sheep" (10:16) yet to be added to Jesus' fold, are blessed; those who ignore him or reject him do so out of unbelief, disobedience (3:36) and culpable blindness (9:39-41), not genes.

While in many passages "the Jews" seem to be a way of referring to Jewish authorities (1:19; 5:10, 15, 16, 18; 7:1, 13; 8:48, 52, 57; 9:18, 22; 10:31, 33; 11:8), on occasion an individual or individuals who are Jews are distinguished from "the Jews" (5:15; 7:13; 9:18, 22; 11:8). In some cases the expression seems to denote the common Jewish people, "the crowd" (6:41, 52; 7:11-12, 15, 31, 35; 8:22, 31; 10:19, 24; 11:19, 31, 33, 36, 42, 45, 56; 12:9, 11). Some members of this crowd question Jesus while others believe (12:17-19, 34). Elsewhere in John "the Jews" bears

---

13. The expression "put out of the synagogue" occurs at three places in the Gospel (9:22; 12:42, and 16:2). Whether this expression refers to actual practices or to hypothetical situations is highly debated by scholars.

decidedly positive overtones: Jesus himself is a Jew (4:9) and certain Jews believe (11:45; 12:11), though others, unfortunately, come to faith but then turn away (8:30–59). Most commonly the expression refers to the Jewish leaders, especially in Jerusalem and Judea, who are depicted as actively opposing Jesus, to the point of seeking his death (11:57). Not all Jewish leaders, however, are presented negatively: Nicodemus and Joseph of Arimathea fare much better (3:1–21; 7:50; 19:38–42).

John's opposition to Judaism is neither moral nor legal, as it was earlier for Paul. John does not treat the Law as either a problem or as an enemy; it has simply been superseded by God's covenantal act in Jesus Christ (1:17). The Law affects Jews, not Christians, and so Jesus speaks of it to the Jews as "your Law" (8:17; 10:34; see 15:25). The contrast between the disciples of Moses and the disciples of Jesus continues that line of thought. It should be noted that John does not react to Jewish claims about Moses by denigrating Moses; in John's thought, if the Jews truly believed in Moses, they would also believe in Jesus (5:46).[14]

In reading John, we cannot simply dismiss or ignore the Gospel's use of the expression "the Jews." The symbol is part of the broader Johannine dualism. With this reference, John may be using a distinction already found in the prologue, referring to those who belong to "the world" (1:10), that is, to those human beings who cling to selfish pride, who cannot accept the self-understanding presented in Christ, and therefore to that segment of humanity opposed to Jesus and his gospel. Surely this is the broader meaning intended, for when the Fourth Evangelist speaks of "the Jews" pejoratively, he has in mind a broad class of opponents, those who reject Christ as well as his followers. In this sense one thinks of the apostle Paul, whose conversion brought about the realization that those who persecute disciples of Jesus persecute Jesus (Acts 9:1–5). When we read the Fourth Gospel today, we should understand the term "the Jews" to designate a type of individual and not a particular religious body of persons. An examination of Nathanael's story in John 1 indicates that the positive pole of the dualistic pair in this case may be "Israelite," John's reference to one who accepts the revelation (1:47; see 1:31).

---

14. Brown, *John*, 1:lxxii–lxxiii.

Questions to Ponder

1. In your estimation, did Jesus deliberately contravene Jewish Sabbath regulations by healing people on that day?
2. In your view, are sin and suffering connected in any direct way?
3. Why were "the Jews" so determined to kill Jesus? Why do some people take religious offense so personally and to such extremes?
4. What does John 5:16–30 indicate about the relationship between Jesus and the Father? How does this relationship compare to 1:18?
5. Which of the witnesses to Jesus in John 5:31–47 do you find most compelling?
6. What relationship exists between the Jewish celebration of Passover and the feeding of the five thousand related in John 6? Can you find correlations between the Passover and the account of Jesus walking on the water?
7. What meaning do you find in the reference to Jesus as "bread of life"?
8. What for you is the meaning of the discussion in John 6:53–58? Do you believe the Evangelist is utilizing Eucharistic imagery or exodus imagery at this point? Explain your answer.
9. What do you learn about belief and unbelief in John 6:60–71?

CHAPTER 5

Jesus and Jewish Festivals: Part One
(John 7:1—8:59)

Summary: By the time readers reach John 7, Jesus has left Galilee for good and will be in or near Judea for the remainder of his ministry. There is little action in this middle section of the Gospel; the story mainly proceeds through dialogues and discourses. The festival of Booths (Tabernacles) provides the backdrop as Jesus promises "rivers of living water." Throughout chapters 7 and 8 there is great controversy about the true identity and nature of Jesus, beginning with his own brothers and carrying through to his opponents. The questions "Who is Jesus?" and "Where did he come from?" are constantly asked and answered. The story of the woman taken in adultery (7:53—8:11), a late addition that should be treated as an extracanonical text, demonstrates the growing hostility between Jesus and the Pharisees. An acrimonious debate between them forms most of chapter 8, ending with an attempt on Jesus' life.

Assignment: Read John 7–8

Key Passages: John 7:37–38; 8:31–32

Central Theme: Jesus is the Light of the World

Key Symbols/Concepts: festival of Booths, the world, the Messiah, rivers of living water, the Spirit, light of the world, darkness, truth, freedom, to glorify

Learning Objectives

Participants will examine:

1. The growing opposition between Jesus and "the Jews"
2. The Jewish festival of Booths (Tabernacles) and its relation to the themes of water and light in John 7 and 8
3. The story of the woman caught in adultery (7:53—8:11) as extracanonical gloss
4. The metaphorical meaning of Jesus as the light of the world
5. The role of freedom as a mark of true discipleship
6. The meaning of the enigmatic "I am" sayings in John

Outline to John 7:1—8:59

I. Jesus Travels to Jerusalem for the Feast of Booths 7:1-13

II. First Teaching Episode and Response 7:14-36

III. Second Teaching Episode and Response 7:37-52

IV. The Woman Caught in Adultery 7:53—8:11

V. Third Teaching Episode and Response 8:12-30

VI. A Debate between Jesus and his Opponents 8:31-59

Jesus on Trial

John 5—12 is marked by cycles of increasing hostility against Jesus set in the context of Jewish festivals. The progression of festivals in John is significant, for at each festival Jesus does or says things that show that he is the fulfillment of the festival's celebration. The healing of the man at the pool occurred on the Sabbath (5:9, 10, 18), so in chapter 5 we were alerted to ways in which Jesus is said to fulfill the meaning of the Sabbath. The same applies to the Passover (6:4), the festival of Booths (7:2), the festival of the Dedication/Hanukkah (10:22), and Jesus' entry into Jerusalem for his final celebration of the Passover in 12:1.

Chapters 7:1—10:21 take place in Jerusalem at the festival of Booths. When Jesus goes to Jerusalem for this festival, the hostility toward him escalates dramatically. The controversy with the religious authorities in John 5 continues in chapter 7, leading some scholars to argue for the reversal of chapters 5 and 6, but as we have noted, such transposition creates more problems than it solves.

Chapters 7—10 lack the literary cohesiveness of other extended Johannine texts because they seem to be composed of fragments from the Jesus tradition brought together by the Evangelist to create a picture of the increasing conflict between Jesus and his opponents. In chapter 7 the conflict is played out in a sequence of short scenes in which Jesus presses his case with Jewish crowds at the temple, while the religious authorities plot against him behind his back. In chapter 8 these mini-dramas converge into a larger drama as Jesus and his enemies engage in direct accusations and recriminations.

This material demonstrates considerable understanding of Jewish judicial procedures and the legal ramifications of Jesus' remarks.[1] The judicial process has developed further from the deliberations we saw in John 5, so that now not only do we hear charges against Jesus, but his opponents are also prepared to carry out the sentence of stoning (8:59). The charges of blasphemy, based on statements such as "Before Abraham was, I am" (8:58) and "the Father and I are one" (10:30), must be defended using, among other tactics, polemics. The legal process is clearly defined in these chapters: "No other New Testament writer . . . offers such a compelling account of why Jesus was brought to trial by his fellow-Jews."[2] The sticky point, however, was that it was impossible for Jesus to prove his claims to be God's agent in the flesh. Exodus 22:8–9 was clear that if someone swore an oath falsely, God would judge that person. And that's exactly how traditional Jews would have understood Jesus' death on the cross: such a person was cursed by God (Deut. 21:23; but cf. Gal. 3:13). This judicial setting hovers over these discourses, set in a temple and festival framework.

Analysis of John 7:1—8:59

Jesus Travels to Jerusalem for the Feast of Booths (Chapter 7:1–13)

John 7:1-13 can be subdivided into two sections: Jesus and his unbelieving brothers (7:1–10) and the initial response to Jesus in Jerusalem

---

1. A. E. Harvey, *Jesus on Trial*.
2. Ibid., 58.

(7:11–13). Earlier we noted how the Evangelist stresses that Jesus replaces or fulfills the institutions of Judaism. Chapter 7 demonstrates how this holds true with the festival of Booths. Originally a fall harvest festival, Booths received theological significance by its identification with the wilderness journey after the exodus. In New Testament times the festival had grown to an eight-day celebration centered at the temple. The temple court and the streets of Jerusalem would be filled with temporary shelters in which the celebrants lived. At the end of the first day, four large lampstands, which lit the entire city, were set up in the Court of Women, symbolizing the light of God. The joyous festivities involved dances in the evening. Another ceremony, occurring on each of the seven mornings, involved a procession down the hill from the temple to the Gihon spring, which supplies the pool of Siloam (see 9:7). There a priest filled a laver with water and carried it up the hill to the altar as a libation. The seventh day included a procession during which people waved branches, marched around the altar seven times, and prayed for rain and a good harvest in the coming year. This day also commemorated the water from the rock (Num. 20:2–13), another exodus theme. The festival concluded with solemn worship on the eighth day. This is the setting of John 7—8; what was offered and depicted in the feast, Jesus claims to give—water and light to God's people.

The festival of Booths was one of three pilgrimage feasts observed during New Testament times; the others were Passover and Pentecost. Their popularity explains the demand of Jesus' brothers that he go to Judea and show himself "to the world" (7:4). The attitude displayed by his brothers recalls the crowd's demand for a sign in 6:30. In 7:5 the narrator makes explicit their lack of faith. Jesus' response is framed by references to "his time" (7:8), a synonym for the more common "hour" of Jesus' glorification, a reference to his death, resurrection, and ascension. The "hour" is part of God's timing and is not subject to human demands. The brothers misunderstand his relationship to "the world" (7:4, 7), thinking that Jesus is someone who will impress with his works and thus cause the world to embrace him; but they are wrong, for the world represents all that is opposed to him. Jesus brings the world to the moment of judgment by testifying to the nature of the world's works (see 3:19–21). The difference in the world's response to Jesus' brothers reinforces their distance from Jesus: "the world cannot hate you, but it hates me" (7:7).

Jesus stays in Galilee, but then goes up to Jerusalem in secret. Repeatedly in John's Gospel Jesus acts in accord with his own time and not with the demands of others (see 2:4; 11:3–7). Verses 11–13 are framed by references to "the Jews," reminding the reader of the ever-present threat to Jesus. The term "Jews" cannot be an ethnic designation, since the crowd is itself Jewish, but rather is a symbol for Jesus' opponents. The crowd is divided in its response to Jesus, and similar division will characterize its response throughout John 7.

First Teaching Episode and Response (Chapter 7:14–36)

This passage is said to occur "about the middle of the festival" (7:14), whereas the remainder of the chapter takes place "on the last day of the festival" (7:37). The action takes place in the temple, Judaism's most sacred place. As Jesus teaches, the crowd responds in astonishment at the depth of his teaching, but he responds using agency language (7:16–18). Jesus incites the crowd by accusing them of not keeping the revealed will of God in the Mosaic law (7:19). The dialogue becomes exceedingly contentious as Jesus is accused of having a demon, though the crowd indicates surprise at the charge that someone is attempting to kill Jesus.

Scholars may be correct in suggesting that 7:22–24 belong with the Sabbath discussion in John 5, but in this context, the passage provides a good defense of Jesus' action on the Sabbath. John 7:25 opens a new subsection of the ongoing dialogue, for the crowd begins to wonder if perhaps the authorities are convinced Jesus is the Messiah, since Jesus has not been arrested. Verse 27 repeats the Johannine refrain that to understand who Jesus is one must understand where he comes from. The dialogue is deeply ironic at this point, because the real origins of the Son appear to be unknown to the crowd and the authorities. Yet Jesus says they really do know where he is from, they just don't want to accept it. The real problem, says Jesus, is that they do not know the One who sent him; otherwise they would recognize the Son as God's agent. There follows an unsuccessful attempt to arrest Jesus, but the Evangelist makes clear that Jesus' hour has not yet come, meaning God is in control of these events.

In 7:33 Jesus announces his departure, and the misunderstanding of the crowd results in a double meaning; the remark is intended on one level, but is heard on another. The Jews ask if Jesus intends to instruct the Greeks in the Diaspora (7:35), a question that has fueled significant disagreement among interpreters. Scholars debate whether the expression "among the Greeks" refers to Jews outside of Israel, as the term "Dispersion" suggests, or to Gentiles, in which case the crowd's misunderstanding becomes doubly ironic, an unconscious prophecy of the future of the Christian movement (cf. 12:20). Whatever its meaning, the reference holds particular promise for the Johannine community, undoubtedly located "among the Greeks."

Second Teaching Episode and Response (Chapter 7:37–52)

The next two subsections of the ongoing temple dialogue (7:37–52 and 8:12–59) demonstrate how Jesus fulfills what the festival of Booths celebrated, the giving of water (rain) and the celebration of lights. The quotation in 7:38 is problematic, both regarding its source and its meaning: "out of the believer's heart shall flow rivers of living water." It probably originated as a sapiential saying, like Ben Sira's declaration, "As for me, I was like a canal from a river, like a water channel into a garden . . . And lo, my canal became a river, and my river a sea" (Sir. 24:30–32). The point in John is that those who believe in Jesus can become a reservoir of water they no longer need to seek. Indeed one can become a dispenser of water when one believes in Jesus (see 4:14). As the parenthetical remark in verse 39 indicates, water here refers not to baptism but to the Holy Spirit that is yet to be given. As God gave water from the rock in the desert to those perishing from thirst, so the Spirit would be given freely to those who thirst for God and for true life. By postponing the gift of the Spirit to Jesus' glorification ("for as yet there was no Spirit, because Jesus was not yet glorified"; 7:39b), the Evangelist is not denying the earlier presence of the Spirit. Indeed, the Spirit of God had descended on Jesus at his baptism (1:34). The author is simply saying that the Spirit as it is known in the life of the church did not yet exist, because the Spirit is redefined in the light of Jesus' death, resurrection, and ascension.

The response to Jesus' words on the last day of the feast is mixed. Some believe that he is the Messiah while others once again question Jesus' Galilean origins, meaning he is not from Bethlehem, the place traditionally associated with David and hence with the Messiah (Mic. 5:2; Matt. 1:18–2:12). According to 7:45 the temple police return to the authorities and indicate they are impressed by Jesus. Nicodemus, one of these authorities, objects to arresting Jesus without giving him due process, in the form of a hearing. Since Nicodemus "had gone to Jesus before" (7:50), he alone among the Pharisees has given Jesus the hearing the law requires. The Pharisees' response to Nicodemus in 7:52 is problematic ("Search and you will see that no prophet is to arise from Galilee"), for as 2 Kings 14:25 indicates, the prophet Jonah had Galilean origins. Far from being superior to the crowd, the Pharisees are subject to the same faulty judgment, based on appearances (7:24).

The Woman Caught in Adultery (Chapter 7:53—8:11)

This passage was not originally part of the Gospel of John, but found its way into some manuscripts of the Gospel at a later date. The testimony of the church fathers is striking: none comment on these verses, even when they are writing commentaries on the Gospel. They simply skip from 7:52 to 8:12 without acknowledging the passage. None of the Eastern (including Greek) church fathers mention the passage before the tenth century AD. Where the passage does appear in the manuscript tradition, some insert these verses elsewhere in John and even after Luke 21:38. Furthermore, the text of John reads quite smoothly if one skips the passage in question altogether. While the account of the woman taken in adultery is clearly an interpolation, this does not deny that it may preserve an authentic story about an episode in the life of Jesus. One must remember, as the Evangelist tells us in 20:30, that there were many other things Jesus did and said that were not recorded in the canonical gospels.

John 7:53—8:2 provide the setting: early in the morning Jesus comes to the temple to teach. A trap is set for Jesus (8:6), which pits him against the Mosaic law. There are irregularities in the accusers' story, for the authorities provide no witnesses to sustain their case that the woman was caught in the "very act" of adultery (see Deut. 17:6; 19:15). Furthermore, the authorities ignore the fate of the male sexual partner, who is also subject to the death penalty (Deut. 20:20; 22:22). Twice Jesus writes on the ground, and twice he speaks. While the story has held great fascination for preachers and scholars alike, the words that Jesus speaks form the climax of the story. The noun translated "the one without sin"(8:7) occurs only here in the New Testament, and the notion that sin is linked to actions rather than to a person's refusal to recognize Jesus as the Son (8:24; 15:22–24) is unusual for the Fourth Gospel.

While vividly depicting Jesus' grace toward the woman, the account stresses that all humans are sinners, even the most revered members of the Jewish community. Jesus supersedes legal stipulation, challenging both the woman and her accusers to lay aside the question of guilt or innocence and to enter into a new life based on mercy and forgiveness. It is easy to see why the church chose to include this story, even though it was not originally part of the Fourth Gospel. First, it provides an illustration of the conflict that animates the dialogues of John 7 and 8. Second, the central conflict in this story concerns the proper interpretation of the law, a topic addressed in John 7 (see verses 19-24 and 48-49). Third, one can read this story as an illustration of 7:24, the difference between judging by appearance or by right judgment. The theme of judgment continues in John 8:15-17.

Third Teaching Episode and Response (Chapter 8:12-30)

The debate with the crowd at the end of John 7 continues in this section. Many of the themes in this debate had arisen in John 5, particularly the issue of Jesus' relation to the Father and the Father's witness to him. As Jesus claimed to be the source of living water (7:37-39), now, by announcing that he is the "light of the world" (8:12), he introduces a second image associated with the festival of Booths. Once again, Jesus claims to be the fulfillment of a Jewish festival. This saying is the second in a series of "I am" sayings that occurs in the Gospel of John.

Light is an important theme, not only for John, but for the Jewish people, making its prominence in this section serve a double purpose, as reminder of the centrality of light in John's prologue (1:4-9) and as preparation for the story of giving sight (and therefore light) to the blind man in John 9. It also anticipates the festival of Dedication (Hanukkah) in John 10:22, a festival of lights celebrating the Maccabean victories and the cleansing of Jerusalem.

Light is a frequent image also in the Old Testament, where it is associated with the first act of creation (Gen. 1:3-4). In the exodus and wilderness traditions, light functions as a symbol for God's presence with his people (Exod. 13:21). Light also refers to the knowledge of God that illumines one's path (Ps. 119:105). In the Wisdom tradition, light is associated with truth and is a symbol for Torah (Prov. 6:23; Wis. 7:26; 18:4) and for Wisdom itself, said to be the first act of God's creation (Prov. 8:22). In Hellenistic Judaism as well as in the Dead Sea Scrolls and in Gnosticism, light also figures as a symbol of God or God's Word, though the Fourth Evangelist gives that symbol new meaning by identifying it with the revelation of God in Jesus. John 8:12 makes explicit the soteriological dimensions of Jesus as the light; the presence of Jesus as the light of the world presents the world with two choices, to follow Jesus in the light or to walk in darkness. The verb "follow" in John represents discipleship (1:37–38, 40, 43; 10:4–5).

John 8:13–20 continues the legal discussion of whether Jesus should testify on his own behalf, and whether his testimony is valid. The Pharisees declare Jesus' self-witness invalid, for Jewish law held that a person's self-witness is inadmissible (see 5:31); there must be at least two additional witnesses. In 5:31–40 Jesus presented other witnesses on his behalf. This time he utilizes a different strategy, seemingly contradicting his earlier tactic. In the present text, Jesus distances himself from his opponents' categories ("your law" in verse 17) and counters with his own juridical categories: "you judge by human standards; I judge no one. Yet even if I do judge, my judgment is valid" (8:15–16). The heavy concentration on the adjective "valid" or true (*alēthēs* in 8:13–14, 17 and *alēthinos* in 8:16) points to the heart of the debate; only one perspective can be valid or true. This debate undoubtedly reflects Johannine church-synagogue disputes about the validity of Jesus' claims (see 5:31–40; 7:12; 15:26–27; 16:1–2, 8–11). Jesus' knowledge of his origin and his destination (8:14) validates his self-witness because it derives from his relationship to God as God's Son. Jesus' words, therefore, are not self-interested witness. Rather, Jesus can bear witness "on his behalf" because he has seen God and can make God known (1:18). His opponents cannot recognize the validity of his witness because they do not share his knowledge (8:14). In 8:17–18 Jesus ends his argument with an ironic twist: he meets the Pharisees' demand for two witnesses by offering himself and God. The irony arises because Jesus gives the Pharisees what they ask for, but in terms they can neither recognize nor receive, because they judge "by human standards" (8:15). The unit concludes with an echo of 7:30: it is God's timing, not human intentions, that governs Jesus' life (8:20).

Like the discussion in John 6, Jesus' remarks become more and more offensive. The reference to "sin" in 8:21 and 24 ("you will die in your sin") is not to individual deeds but instead to unbelief (not recognizing God in Jesus), for John the central and decisive sin (see 1:29; 8:24; 9:41; 15:22–24; 16:9). At 8:24 and 28 we find the absolute use of "I am" (*egō eimi*), a possible reference to God's self-designation (see Isa. 41:4; 43:25; 51:12; 52:6 and Exod. 3:14). Notice that *egō eimi* does not constitute a claim to *be* the heavenly Father or to exhaust the Godhead, as 8:28 makes evident. While it may be seen as a claim to eternal existence, it is not a claim to self-existence, for Jesus is dependent on the Father and, while on earth as his agent, is subordinate to him.[3]

For John, knowledge of Jesus's identity is not fully available until the Son of Man is "lifted up" (8:28), a term with a double meaning (it refers to being lifted up on a cross but also to being exalted by God). For this reason, prior to the crucifixion, none of the potential converts portrayed in John can be viewed as models of Christian faith and confession; they are simply those who are on the way to fully adequate faith in Jesus. This faith includes that expressed by some of the "Jews" in 8:30–31. For the Fourth Evangelist, knowledge of the full mystery of Jesus' identity is not possible before his crucifixion and resurrection, which occur prior to the bestowal of the Spirit.

A Debate between Jesus and his Opponents (Chapter 8:31–59)

John 8:31–59 has been called the *locus classicus* of Johannine theology.[4] In these verses we find the fundamental lines of debate and disagreement between Judaism and Christianity. The dialogue of this passage proceeds carefully, each verse building on the preceding to convey the intensification of the theological debate. At issue is the truth of Jesus' testimony (8:32, 40, 45–60, and 55) and the falsehood of those opposed (8:44–45). The repeated references to Abraham (8:33, 37, 39–40, 52–53, 56, and 58), the only such in John, provide a key to the development of the debate. The debate shows that one's relationship to Abraham is ultimately determined by one's relationship to God (8:39–47).

John 8:31–32 identifies Jesus' audience as "the Jews who believed in him." The harsh nature of the debate that follows raises questions about this identification. Jesus' words to those who believe in him ("If you continue in my word, you are truly my disciples, and you will know the truth, and the truth will make you free") speak of a process; continuing in Jesus' words leads not only to true discipleship but to knowing the truth, which in turn leads to being set free. While in early Judaism Torah was viewed as the truth (Ps. 119:160), and studying Torah made a person free, John 8:32 claims that believing in Jesus and his story does this. As 8:40

---

3. Witherington, *John's Wisdom*, 175.
4. Dodd, *Historical Tradition*, 330.

shows, "truth" does not denote the typically Greek view of divine reality but conveys the sense of revealed truth, the revelation Jesus imparts to humanity as the Word of God. And that revelation is Jesus himself and his career—he is both revealer and the revelation, for in him the divine plan of salvation is unveiled and comes to fruition.

The centrality of Jesus' word (*logos*) in 8:31–59 is highlighted in several ways: by frequent use of the term *logos* (8:31, 37, 43, 51–52, 55); by three occurrences of "very truly, I say to you" (8:34, 51, 58); and by Jesus' repeated references to his speaking (8:38, 43, 45–46, 55). All that Jesus promises in 8:32 depends on the listener's continuing relationship to Jesus' word. The truth and freedom that Jesus promises are not abstract principles, but like light and life, are bound to the Word. The truth is the presence of God in Jesus.

In 8:33 the Jews counter Jesus' claim that his truth brings freedom by arguing that as Abraham's descendants they had never been enslaved. The irony, of course, is that their response ignores the time when the Israelites were slaves in Egypt and that even in the present they are in servitude to Rome. Perhaps they are thinking of a different sort of slavery, but so is Jesus. His point is that everyone who sins is a slave to sin. The Jews' rebuttal of Jesus' words is another instance of the Johannine use of misunderstanding. Jesus speaks of the freedom that results from knowing the truth, but when the Jews repeat Jesus' words in 8:33, they misquote him by leaving out the reference to truth. In 8:36 Jesus repeats the promise of freedom, substituting "Son" for "truth," and thus makes explicit the link between truth and his identity.

For John, freedom is possible only if one recognizes that Jesus is the Son. Whereas the Jews argued that they were free through physical descent from Abraham and because Abraham's righteousness had been passed on to all descendants according to the flesh, the Fourth Gospel, with the entire New Testament, represents one long protest. For John, the disciples are set free forever, so long as they "abide" in Jesus' word (8:31). Those who believe temporarily but lapse into the crowd of unbelievers fall back into slavery.

When Jesus says in 8:39 that if they were Abraham's children they would do what Abraham did, he is likely alluding to the story of Abraham's reception of the divine messengers in Genesis 18. The overriding complaint is that if they truly knew the Father, they would recognize his Son. Failure to recognize the latter indicates they do not know the former. Their angry retort at 8:41, "At least we are not illegitimate," has been seen as an attack on rumors about Jesus' birth, but this seems unlikely given that the Jews here remain on the defensive and don't go on the offensive until 8:48.

The polemic becomes increasingly vitriolic, and one that has led to terrible atrocities in the name of Christianity, for in 8:44 Jesus accuses his opponents as being children of the devil. Speaking of the devil, John resorts to thorough-going dualistic thought here, contrasting the devil with Jesus; both are described as being from the beginning. The devil is a liar and the father of lies, while Jesus tells the truth. The devil speaks from himself, unlike Jesus, who speaks what the Father provides. The underlying assumption throughout the discussion is that one's origin determines one's character.

In response to Jesus' charges, his opponents resort to "name calling" (8:48): Jesus is said to be demon-possessed or an unclean Samaritan, probably a frequent charge concerning Jews who came from the north and were suspect. Their attack is similar to the one Jesus had used against them. Just as Jesus denied their claims to be children of Abraham (8:39), calling them children of the devil (8:44), so the Jews now deny Jesus' Jewish heritage by calling him a Samaritan and identifying him with the "demonic."

When Jesus claims that his followers will never taste death (8:51), this is taken as ludicrous by his opponents and as proof that Jesus has a demon. The dialogue comes to a dramatic halt with Jesus' claim in 8:58: "Before Abraham was, I am." This is clearly the culminating teaching of the entire debate, for Jesus' use of the absolute form "I am" points to his preexistence with God as well as to his unity with God (cf. 1:1). Jesus' words thus prove true the irony of the Jews' words in 8:53: Jesus *is* greater than Abraham because Jesus is one with God. Jesus' statement produces the expected response when devout Jews believe they have witnessed blasphemy: they seek to stone Jesus, but he mysteriously slips away, for his hour had not yet come.

Thus ends the first act of the three-act drama of the middle section of John that centers in the temple. The second act follows in the story of the blind man, followed in turn by the good shepherd discourse and its aftermath. Both events are connected ingeniously with the festival of Hanukkah, the celebration of the liberation of Jerusalem by the Maccabees in the second century BC, which serves as backdrop to Jesus' offer of a new sort of liberation by a new sort of shepherd for God's people.[5]

---

5. Witherington, *John's Wisdom*, 178.

Essay 5: The Johannine "I Am" Sayings

The paradoxical nature of the Fourth Gospel is displayed in the way John portrays Jesus, the eternal Word of God become incarnate. As the Jewish Messiah, Jesus is also the Son of the Father as well as the Son of Man. While participating fully in the being of God, Jesus has individuality from the Father. John's Christological presentation is compounded when we examine the enigmatic "I am" sayings. The Greek expression "I am" (*egō eimi*), placed regularly on the lips of Jesus, is used by John to help explain Jesus' identity. It is a statement attributed to Jesus in which an emphatic construction appears in the Greek. The normal way one would say "I am" in Greek is *eimi* (the first-person pronoun "I" is implicit in the form of the verb). For emphasis one might add the first-person pronoun *egō*. The result is repetitive, something like "I, I am."

This peculiar construction seems to have additional meaning in John, as it does for example in Matthew's antithetical sayings in the Sermon on the Mount (Matt. 5:22, 28, 32, 34, 39, and 44), where the emphatic use of the personal pronoun (*egō de legō*, "but I say to you") anticipates and reinforces the crowd's response at the end of the sermon: "the crowds were astonished at his teaching, for he taught them as one having authority, and not as their scribes" (Matt. 7:28–29). What might this usage suggest about the view of Christ in the Fourth Gospel?

Grammatically, the expression *egō eimi* is used in the following ways:

- In an absolute sense (without a predicate): "before Abraham was, *I am*" (8:58);
- With an implied predicate: "But he said to them, '*I am*; do not be afraid'" (6:20);
- With an explicit predicate (a predicate nominative): "*I am* the bread of life" (6:35).

Most interpreters agree that the "I am" sayings are more than simple emphatic statements. They find John's usage to be profoundly Christological, in part because these sayings have affinity with similar sayings in other religious traditions. Among certain religions of the Hellenistic world of the first century, revealer gods spoke with the emphatic *egō eimi*, particularly with predicates. For example, the god Isis is quoted in inscriptions using the "I am" saying. Parallels occur in the Hermetic literature, particularly where Poimandres reveals himself to Hermes: "The messenger of light I am," and in the Mandaean literature: "A shepherd I am, who loves his sheep." Some believe that the "I am" sayings in John are intentionally modeled after these uses, such as in John 10:14.

There are seven instances in John's Gospel where Jesus speaks of himself figuratively, using the emphatic "I am" expression with a predicate nominative:

- "I am the bread of life [living bread]" (6:35, 51);
- "I am the light of the world" (8:12; 9:5);
- "I am the gate" (10:7, 9);
- "I am the good shepherd" (10:11, 14);
- "I am the resurrection and the life" (11:25);
- "I am the way, and the truth, and the life" (14:6);
- "I am the [true] vine" (15:1, 5).

The use of the predicate is not an essential descriptor of Jesus; rather it tells something of his role in relation to humanity. In his mission, Jesus is the source of eternal life for humans (vine, life, resurrection); he is the means whereby humans find life (way, gate); he leads human beings to life (shepherd); he reveals truth to them (truth), which nourishes their life (bread). These predicates are not static titles but are means of divine self-disclosure, revelations of the divine commitment involved in the Father's sending of the Son. Jesus is these things for humanity because he and the Father are one (10:30) and because he possesses the life-giving power of the Father (5:21). Statements such as "I am the truth, the light, the vine" are similar to statements about the Father's relation to human beings: "God is Spirit" (4:24) "God is light" (1 John 1:5), and "God is love" (1 John 4:8, 16). Some scholars find parallelism between this class of "I am" sayings and the Synoptic parables that begin with "The Kingdom of God (heaven) is like." "I am" statements with a nominal predicate are also found in the book of Revelation, but while in John's Gospel the predicates are adaptations of Old Testament symbolism (bread, light, shepherd, and vine are used symbolically in describing the relations of God to Israel), in Revelation the predicates are frequently taken directly from Old Testament passages. See for example "I am the Alpha and the Omega" (Rev. 1:8) and "I am the first and the last" (Rev. 1:17), divine titles derived from Second Isaiah (41:4; 44:6; 48:12).

Scholars find precedents for John's "I am" sayings in the Hebrew Bible, where we find the absolute usage, without predicates. A classic example is Exodus 3:14, where the meaning of the sacred name is revealed to Moses. The NRSV reads: "I AM WHO I AM," meaning something like "I AM! That is who I am." In Isaiah 43:10, Yahweh says that he has chosen his servant Israel, "that you may know and believe me and understand that *I am he*." In John 8:28 Jesus promises that when the Son of Man is lifted up, "then you will realize that *I am he*." Jesus' use of the expression *egō eimi* often prompts extreme behavior on the part of his audience. In 8:58, the Jews try to stone him; in 18:5, the soldiers and police sent to apprehend Jesus fall to the ground. If the Fourth Evangelist is alluding to the sacred name for God in these instances, this may help to explain the many Johannine references to the divine name that Jesus bears. In his ministry Jesus reveals the Father's name to his disciples (17:6, 26); he comes in the Father's name (5:43) and does works in his Father's name (10:25); indeed, he says that the Father has given him his name (17:11, 12). This usage may explain why for John the great sin is to refuse to believe in the name of God's only Son (3:18), or why the Paraclete is said to be sent by the Father in Christ's name (14:26), or why the glorification of Jesus (12:23) means the glorification of the Father's name (12:28).

When we turn to the Septuagint, the Greek translation of the Hebrew Bible commonly used by Greek-speaking Jews and Christians in the first century, we find that the translators used the emphatic *egō eimi* to render the Hebrew expression "I, Yahweh" (Isa. 41:4; 45:18). In some passages in Isaiah in which the Hebrew reads "I, I am He," the Greek translation is "I am I am." Such passages emphasize the oneness of God's existence.[6]

On the basis of these precedents, we can begin to construct the meaning of John's "I am" sayings. Three claims can be made with some degree of certainty: when Jesus says "I am," he is (a) communicating God's revelation to humans; (b) disclosing that he is the true divine revealer (as Yahweh is the one true God, so Christ is the one true divine revealer); (c) he is uttering the very name of God. Taken together, these constitute the highest New Testament claims for Christ's divinity. If John held Christ to be God, at least on some level, that would help explain the unusual (and

---

6. This segment is adapted from Robert Kysar's essay "The Father's Son—Johannine Christology" in *Maverick Gospel*, 56–60. See also Brown's appendix on "I am" sayings, *John*, 1:533–38.

preferred) reading in 1:18: "It is *God the only Son*, who is close to the Father's heart, who has made him known."

All three views above seem consistent with John's view of Jesus presented in other parts of the Gospel. They are consistent with the prologue's insistence that Christ is more than the Jewish Messiah, and with the Son of Man and Father-Son relationship passages (see essay 2 above). What they specifically underscore is the functional equivalency of God and Christ, suggesting that "so far as human concerns go, Christ and God are one and the same. The words of Christ are God's words. The actions of Christ are God's actions. The human response to Christ is the response to God. For all human purposes, then, the Christ figure is God."[7]

Questions to Ponder

1. In John 7:14–24, what does Jesus' teaching reveal about God's will for humanity?
2. According to John 7:32–36 and 8:21–23, where is Jesus going that will prevent others from finding him? How does this relate to his claims to be the Messiah?
3. In your estimation, if the passage about the woman caught in adultery (John 8:1–11) was not part of the original Gospel, should it be included in the Bible? Explain your answer.
4. What do "light" and "darkness" signify in John 8:12?
5. In John 8:12–18, how does Jesus use the Jewish law (Torah) to show that his testimony is valid?
6. In John 8, how does Jesus' relationship with the Father set him in opposition to the Pharisees?
7. What do you think Jesus means by "truth" in John 8:32? How will this "truth" set them free?
8. In John's Gospel, why do people continually misunderstand Jesus?
9. In one sentence, summarize the Christological meaning of John's "I am" sayings. Which "I am" saying do you find most significant? Why?

---

7. Kysar, *Maverick Gospel*, 60.

CHAPTER 6

Jesus and Jewish Festivals: Part Two
(John 9:1—10:42)

Summary: Chapter 9 contains the story of the healing of a man born blind and of the reactions to that healing. The theme is blindness and sight, a reference to those who believe in Jesus and those who don't. The story illustrates how even a blind man can "see" who Jesus is. Chapter 10 uses the allegory of the good shepherd and the sheep to depict Jesus as the good shepherd who calls his sheep by name and lays down his life for the sheep. The opponents of Jesus are depicted as hirelings, robbers, and wolves. It is winter, the time of the festival of the Dedication (Hanukkah), and Jesus demonstrates that he is the fulfillment of that to which the festival points. His remark that "The Father and I are one" in 10:30 causes the people to attempt to stone Jesus. He defends himself with rabbinical arguments, again avoiding arrest.

Assignment: Read John 9–10

Key Passages: John 9:5; 10:11, 30

Central Theme: Jesus is the Good Shepherd

Key Symbols/Concepts: blindness and sight, sheep, the gate, the good shepherd, festival of Dedication

Learning Objectives
Participants will examine:
   1. The meaning of sin and its relation to physical suffering

2. The ongoing conflict between Jesus and the Pharisees in John's Gospel
3. The metaphorical meaning of light (sight) and blindness in John's Gospel
4. The metaphorical meaning of Jesus as the gate for the sheep
5. The metaphorical meaning of Jesus as the good shepherd
6. The metaphorical meaning of "abundant life" in John 10:10
7. The Jewish festival of Dedication (Hanukkah) and its relation to the festival of Booths
8. The paradoxical nature of faith in John's Gospel and its relation to seeing, hearing, and knowing

Outline to John 9:1—10:42

I. The Healing of the Blind Man 9:1–12

II. The Pharisees Interrogate the Blind Man and His Parents 9:13–34

III. Jesus Questions the Blind Man 9:35–41

IV. The Parable of the Good Shepherd 10:1–21

V. Jesus at the Festival of Dedication 10:22–42

Natural and Spiritual Blindness

In crucial ways, John 9—10 is an exposition of 3:16–21. In that earlier passage the Evangelist laid out the heart of his eschatology, describing how the incarnation altered eschatological expectations: (a) God's judgment is no longer reserved for a future age, because the presence of Jesus in the world brings human beings to crisis, requiring decision; (b) the offer of God's love, available to everyone through Jesus, is the eschatological moment; (c) good and evil are defined by people's response to Jesus; the good are those who come to the light, the evil those who remain in darkness.

The healing of the blind man in John 9 is not simply about the restoration of natural sight. Rather, the Evangelist uses this healing story to portray the process of spiritual decision-making. Light and darkness are no longer merely concepts, but are embodied by the characters portrayed in John 9:1–41 and 10:22–42. In the blind man's journey from physical blindness to spiritual sight, readers are able to watch as someone comes to the light and is given new life. In the Jewish authorities' passage from physical sight to spiritual blindness, readers are able to watch as the religious authorities close themselves to the light and place themselves under judgment. The dramatic structure of these passages intensifies what may be their most profound theological irony: the authorities, who position themselves as judges of others, finally bring themselves under judgment as sinners. Throughout John 9, the Jewish authorities insist on their right to judge both the healed man and Jesus as sinners (9:16, 24, 34). However, when the healed man confesses his faith in Jesus as the Son of Man, he acknowledges Jesus as the only judge, whose judgment renders impotent the authorities' judgment. Because of the obvious attention of John 9 to sight and blindness, knowledge and ignorance, its focus on sin is often overlooked. This is a serious omission, because the presentation of sin in John 9 is pivotal to the understanding of sin in John.

The theme of sin is introduced in the opening verses of chapter 9, when the disciples attempt to link the man's blindness to sin (see also 9:34). The theme of sin reappears in the Pharisees' response to Jesus' miracle. To many of them, Jesus' violation of the Sabbath marks him as a sinner (9:16, 24, 31). To both the disciples and the Pharisees, sin is a moral category, primarily defined in relation to actions. John 9 redefines sin by demonstrating its theological, not moral, nature. The key to this redefinition is found in Jesus' words in 9:41 ("If you were blind, you would not have sin. But now that you say, 'We see,' your sin remains"), where the Pharisees' assertion of self-righteousness is the basis for Jesus' judgment of them as sinners. The Pharisees have physical sight, but they are spiritually blind in their inability to see God revealed in Jesus (cf. 9:3). From the perspective of the Fourth Evangelist, their refusal to acknowledge this "blindness" proves that they are sinners, for "sin is defined not by what one does, but almost exclusively by one's relationship to Jesus, and more specifically, by whether one believes that God is present in Jesus."[1]

This view of sin and salvation can be difficult for contemporary Christians to grasp, because the linkage of salvation with Jesus' death is so dominant within the church. The Gospel of John invites believers to reevaluate the criteria by which sin is defined and by which people are judged. The Fourth Gospel reduces sin to its Christological and hence its theological essence. Sin is fundamentally about one's relationship with God, and for John, the decisive measure of one's relationship with God is

---

1. O'Day, *John*, 664.

one's faith in Jesus. The Gospel is unequivocally clear: Jesus' incarnation, not the expiation of his death, brings salvation from sin. John's Gospel invites believers to recognize the transformative power of the love of God made manifest in the incarnation and to shape their lives accordingly. To reject Jesus is to reject the love of God in Jesus and so to pass from the possibility of salvation to judgment (3:16–17). The blind man's words in John 9:25 offer eloquent testimony to the transforming power of God's grace in the hymn "Amazing Grace": "I once was blind, but now I see."

Analysis of John 9:1—10:42

This passage contains two blocks of material that are frequently viewed as distinct: the healing of the man born blind (9:1–41) and the discourse on the good shepherd (10:1–21). But this distinction owes more to chapter division than it does to the text itself, which displays no break between 9:41 and 10:1; both belong to the same speech of Jesus. The absence of a clear break suggests that Jesus' words in 10:1–18 should be read as a continuation of the discourse to the Pharisees of 9:40–41.

A distinct literary feature—the principle of duality—marks the story in chapter 9 and gives it dramatic quality. The principle of duality, taken from classical Greek drama, allows no more than two characters (or character groups) to speak on stage at the same time. The use of this technique by John heightens the sense of drama as the events of the chapter unfold.

The care with which the Evangelist has drawn his portraits of increasing insight and hardening blindness is masterful. The blind man emerges as one of the most attractive figures in the Gospel. Chapter 9 is a delightful short story by itself, but one with links to the rest of the Gospel. Having revealed himself as "the light of the world," Jesus now gives sight to a blind man. John 9 may contain reminiscence of the experience of the Johannine community, because it describes the blind man's expulsion from the synagogue, an act viewed by scholars as anachronistic to historical conditions during the life of Jesus. Expulsions from the synagogue, if they occurred at all, reflect conditions at the end of the first century or later.

By way of background, it is important to note that there is in the Old Testament no story of giving sight to the blind. In the Hebrew scriptures, the giving of sight to the blind is associated with God's own activity (Exod. 4:11; Ps. 146:8) or with the messianic era (Isa. 29:18; 35:5; 42:7).

It is quite likely that by recording this miracle the Evangelist is saying something special about Jesus' status. While stories of Jesus' giving sight to a blind man are found in every gospel, John's account seems to come from an independent tradition rather than any of the Synoptic traditions. The story is in many ways an apt exegesis of John 1:4–9: "In him was life, and the life was the light of all people."

One of the surprising aspects of the whole discussion of light in John 8—9 is that it is interwoven with the theme of judgment. This emphasis, however, has less to do with condemnation than with illumination. Light's effect, for anyone who has stepped directly from darkness into light, without adjusting to its presence, is to be momentarily blinded, which is what happens to Jesus' opponents in this story.

The Healing of the Blind Man (Chapter 9:1–12)

In telling this miracle story, the Evangelist follows a distinct literary pattern, describing (a) the situation of need (9:1–5), (b) the miracle (9:6–7) and (c) the attestation to the miracle (9:8–12). The disciples reappear for the first time since John 6, and their appearance here is perfunctory. Their question in 9:2, "Who sinned, this man or his parents, that he was born blind?" reflects Jewish speculation on the relationship of illness and sin. Like the story in John 5, this issue arises again (see 5:14), as does the issue of work on the Sabbath (9:14). The connection between sin and death was common in Judaism at the time of Jesus (see Ezek. 18:20), as was the notion that a parent's sins are visited on the children in cases of suffering (see Exod. 20:5). The words of Jesus in 9:3, translated "he was born blind so that God's works might be revealed in him," can have two meanings: either (a) the man was born blind for the *purpose* of revealing God's work in his life, or (b) he was born blind and the *result* of this is that God has chosen to reveal his work in this man's life. Both are grammatically possible and the latter is preferable, in which case we are not being told that God caused a person to be blind so that he could be used as an illustration of divine power, but rather that the man's blindness could be made to serve God's larger purposes (see 11:4).

Verses 4 and 5 speak of the light Jesus sheds in the world, by contrast with coming darkness, which stifles revelation. Dark/light imagery permeates the Gospel, particularly here. The miracle is not said to have occurred when Jesus spread clay and spittle on the man's eyes, but rather when he went and washed in the pool of Siloam. Like the similar account in John 5, nothing is said in the miracle story about the man in question having faith in Jesus, or of faith being a prerequisite for such a miracle. The miracle itself is not the focus, for it is told with surprising brevity. Verses 8–12 complete the third element of the miracle story, the attestation to the miracle. However, though the neighbors confirm the healing, their questions about the healing require the healed man to serve as his own witness and thus to provide his own attestation to the miracle. This sets the stage for the interrogation of the blind man by the Pharisees.

The Pharisees Interrogate the Blind Man and His Parents (Chapter 9:13–34)

John 9:13–41 divides into five scenes, three scenes in which the Jewish authorities have the lead role (13–17, 18–23, and 24–34) and two in which Jesus has the lead (35–38 and 39–41). The three scenes that feature the Jewish authorities are scenes of interrogation.

In the first scene the Pharisees interrogate the blind man. As in 5:1–18, the concern with Sabbath violation reflects an issue current in Jesus' time. To violate the Sabbath law was to challenge the laws that bound the Jewish community and the authority of the Pharisees as interpreters of those laws. The Pharisees are portrayed as divided, as was the original crowd, only this time over whether Jesus could have been sent by God. Some Pharisees view Jesus' violation of a Sabbath prohibition as proof of his distance from God (in this context the violation of the Sabbath seems to have been Jesus' act of kneading, which he did when he mixed mud and saliva, an activity forbidden on the Sabbath; see 9:15–16a). Their assumption is ironic (as the blind man points out in 9:33), because the correct interpretation of the healing is revelatory: "so that God's works might be revealed in him" (9:3). Other Pharisees link this healing with other miraculous acts Jesus has performed and remain open (9:16b; cf. 3:2); the double meaning of receiving sight emerges.

In verses 18–23 the Pharisees (called "the Jews" in this scene) continue their search for a solution to the dilemma by interrogating the man's parents, hoping to show that he was never blind and thereby dismissing the miracle altogether. The parents confirm that their son was born blind, but fearing reprisals, direct the inquiry back to their son. In verse 22 the narrator introduces the fear of excommunication from the synagogue as a pretext for family fear.

The authorities again question the man born blind, this time hoping to get him to repudiate Jesus (9:24) by "giving glory to God," an expression meaning by "swearing to tell the truth." Jesus is called a sinner, doubtless due to his action on the Sabbath, and the man, now exasperated, mocks them, asking if they want to become Jesus' disciples (9:27). Their response is to revile him by labeling him a disciple of Jesus, unlike themselves, who remain disciples of Moses. Then, speaking more truth than they realize, they say that they do not know where Jesus comes from, while the origins of Moses are clear (9:29). This, of course, is precisely the problem: not knowing Jesus' origins and destiny leads to inevitable misunderstanding of Jesus and his work. The man born blind, with obvious sarcasm, says in effect that though the officials remain ignorant about Jesus and are ready to condemn him, yet it was he who had opened his eyes, and surely God does not grant miracle-working ability to people who are sinners. Verse 32 indicates that no one had ever restored sight before, and surely this must mean that if Jesus were not from God, he would be unable to perform such a miracle. The authorities, unable to stomach such threats to their authority, expel the man from their presence, thereby exposing their blindness.

If we read this account as reflecting late first-century Jewish-Christian debates, the question at issue between the Jews and Christians concerned the authority of Jesus, which is based on his origin, home, and parentage. The Jews asserted that Jesus' home was the unclean district of Galilee (7:27, 41, 52), that his parentage was obscure (8:41), and that as an ordinary sinner, he possessed no divine authority. He was not the Messiah, not even a prophet. The Christians countered by asserting that he came from heaven (3:13, 31; 6:33), that God was his Father, that he was sent by the Father for the salvation of the world, and that his authority was the authority of God (6:38; 8:14, 18, 28; 16:28).

Jesus Questions the Blind Man (Chapter 9:35–41)

Thus far the story has progressed like a detective story: an alleged crime has been committed and the Pharisees, the defenders of the law, have questioned the witnesses. In this final scene, Jesus comes to the expelled man to test how clearly he can "see." Fourteen questions are asked in this chapter, none more important than "Do you believe in the Son of Man?" (9:35). In marked contrast to the man at the pool of Bethesda (John 5:1-18), the man born blind replies, "Lord, I believe" (9:38), followed by prostration: "And he worshipped him." In terms of the larger narrative, this conclusion jumps the gun, since the Son of Man has yet to be exalted. Nevertheless, it is an important preview of what the Evangelist discloses to be the outcome of the journey of faith: adequate confession and worship of Jesus (20:28). John views the blind man (in late first-century terms, one who has passed from Judaism to Christianity) as the prototypical believer. This is the climax of the narrative and the purpose for which it is told.

Ben Witherington suggests that this final scene in chapter 9 "may be meant to instruct Johannine Christians in how to bring about closure, how to lead a religious seeker to a more adequate faith in Jesus.... The story then could be used as a paradigm to reveal the progress of a soul and so lead others in the same direction. It is also a negative paradigm about how *not* to respond to Jesus and his deeds, and the Pharisees play the negative role."[2] Jesus' response to the man's prostration is to explain the meaning of judgment: that Jesus' coming into the world promotes sight to the blind or provokes blindness to those who falsely claim to see (9:39; cf. Matt. 13:13; Mark 4:12; Luke 8:10).

The story serves as a powerful appeal for faith, but also as a powerful indictment of willful disobedience. The Pharisees have enough spiritual information to be held responsible for rejecting Jesus. They demonstrate their own blindness and hence judge themselves (9:41). Their sin remains, for they act like the blind rather than in accordance with God's revealed truth. They have chosen darkness rather than light. The blind man, not the religious Pharisee, becomes a model for humanity. In John's view, all humans are born blind and all are called to believe. Sin consists not in being born unbelieving but in refusing to believe when one has seen the power of God at work.

The Parable of the Good Shepherd (Chapter 10:1-21)

John 10:1-18 continues the words of Jesus begun at 9:41 and is positioned in the narrative as Jesus' reflection on what has taken place with the religious authorities. This combination of miracle (9:1-12), dialogue

---

2. Witherington, *John's Wisdom*, 184-85.

(9:13–41), and discourse (10:1–18) is common in the Fourth Gospel. This discourse has a transitional function in the Gospel, as the last full discourse of Jesus' public ministry. Jesus next major discourse is the Farewell Discourse of 14:1—16:33, which is directed to his disciples.

While some categorize this text as an allegory, the Evangelist describes it as a "figure of speech" (*paroimia*; 10:6; see also 16:25, 29), a difficult word to translate precisely. In the Septuagint, this word translates the Hebrew word that means "proverb" (*mashal*). The only New Testament usage of the Greek word *paroimia* outside John is 2 Peter 2:22, where it clearly means "proverb," since it introduces a quotation from the book of Proverbs. The translation "figure of speech" for this term at 10:6 is accurate, for images of sheep and shepherd were frequently used with metaphorical significance in the Old Testament. Traditionally God is understood as shepherd and God's people as sheep (Ps. 23:1; 74:1; 79:13; 80:1; 95:7; 100:3). Of particular importance for the background of John's use of pastoral imagery here is Ezekiel 34, where the kings of Israel are bad shepherds who endanger and exploit the flock (34:1–10). God is the good shepherd who rescues the sheep and places them in the care of the restored monarchy, described as "my servant David" in Ezekiel 34:23.

To the reader of John's Gospel, the imagery in 9:1–5 goes beyond Old Testament pastoral imagery, for it carries echoes of Johannine themes such as "his own" (9:3–4) and "hear his voice" (9:3). These references open up to more explicitly Christological uses of the same pastoral imagery in 9:7–18 and 26–29. In early Jewish Wisdom literature there was a sliding scale between parable and allegory. Parables often had more than one point and could have allegorical elements, as we find here. When Jesus' figure of speech is read in the context of chapter 9, it seems clear that Jesus is positioning the Pharisees in the role of thief, bandit, and stranger. Their conduct toward the blind man (see 9:34) has demonstrated that they do not have the flock's best interest at heart, whereas Jesus' conduct toward the man born blind has shown Jesus to be the shepherd who comes to the sheep (see 9:35) and to whom the sheep respond (see 9:36–38).

John 10:1–18 combines two parabolic images, one having to do with Jesus as the good shepherd and the other with Jesus as the door, or gate, for the sheep. Verse 1 contrasts the true shepherd with thieves and robbers. The sheep know the shepherd when they hear his voice. They cannot be fooled by strangers, who climb in by another way. Verse 7 summarizes the theme of the second parable, presenting Jesus as "the gate for the sheep" and thereby introducing the third "I am" saying, whereas verse 11 summarizes the theme of the first parable with the fourth "I am" saying, presenting Jesus as "the good shepherd." The reference to those who come before Jesus in 10:8 must be to the religious leaders of Jesus' day, including possibly the many pretenders to the messianic role who abounded in the first century. Jesus' reference is clearly not to the prophets or patriarchs.

Under duress, hired hands care only about their own safety, rather than about what happens to the sheep. In contrast to false shepherds, who come to destroy life, the good shepherd is willing to die for the sheep to protect them from harm. His desire is to give his sheep (his followers) life in abundance (10:10). The issue in the second parable is not just good leadership versus poor leadership but salvation or, as verse 10 puts it, abundant life. A person who is "saved" (10:9) is one who has life, and in John's Gospel true life comes from a relationship with God. Verses 9 and 10 record the supreme Christian truth that salvation is by faith in Jesus alone and that salvation means Life, characterized as abundant. Such life is not different in degree from ordinary life, but different in kind; abundant life, an extension of God's love, is measureless and unlimited.

Verses 14–18 provide further commentary on Jesus' role as the good shepherd. Recognition and relationship are again the key elements. Jesus knows his sheep and they know him; furthermore, his relationship to them reflects his relationship with the Father. The "other sheep" (9:16) include Gentiles, Jewish Christians who are not part of the Johannine community, or persons who in the future will come to believe in Jesus. These shall comprise one flock (10:16). The idea of one flock is paramount in John (see 11:52). In his prayer in 17:22, Jesus prays that his followers be one; there, as elsewhere in the New Testament, unity and harmony among believers are vital (see Eph. 4:1–16).

John 10:17 contains the Gospel's first linkage of love with Jesus' death. In John, the core commandment that Jesus gives his disciples is that they love one another as he has loved them (13:34). Jesus' death is the ultimate expression of the love relationship that defines his identity, his relationship with God, and his enactment of God's will for the world. An additional claim is made in 10:17c, that Jesus has the power to retake his life. This is part of John's message that Jesus as a divine agent of God has eternal life in himself, the sort of life that cannot be halted by physical death. Verses 17–18 make clear that Jesus freely chooses to lay down his life as an expression of his obedience to God. Jesus is not a victim in death or a martyr against his will. His death is the culmination of his love and that of the Father.

The overall image here is of Jesus as a powerful and deeply caring shepherd who can provide for, protect, and even rescue his sheep. It is the image of a universal shepherd, whose ambition is to have one flock made up of Jewish and Gentile sheep.

Verses 19–21 are transitional, recalling the disagreement among the "Jews" in response to Jesus' teachings and deeds. Faith in Jesus' identity integrates his words and his works. These verses conclude this part of the discourse, effectively tying the discourse to the debate in chapter 8 and the healing of the blind man in chapter 9, ending the scenes depicted as occurring during the festival of Booths.

Jesus at the Festival of Dedication (Chapter 10:22–42)

John 10:22–42 bring the second cycle of Jesus' ministry to a close. John 7:1—10:21 occur at or around the festival of Booths. As John 10:22 indicates, Jesus is still in Jerusalem, but the time of year has changed. Booths was celebrated in the fall of the year, while the festival of Dedication, known in modern times as Hanukkah, in December. This latter festival commemorated the rededication of the temple in Jerusalem by the Maccabees in 164 BC, after it had been desecrated by the Greek Emperor Antiochus Epiphanes. While the liberators found only oil enough for one day, consecrated oil for the temple lights lasted for eight days; hence, the festival lasts eight days. It is thought that during New Testament times the celebration closely resembled that of the festival of Booths, since Jews viewed Dedication as another festival of Booths, only celebrated in the winter (see 2 Macc. 1:9; 10:6).

At the festival Jesus is confronted by the Jewish authorities and asked to indicate plainly if he is the Messiah (10:24); the word "plainly" presumes a contrast with Jesus' use of "figures" or "riddles" in 10:6. John 10:24 is the only place in John where Jesus is questioned directly on the topic of his messiahship. Earlier he had revealed himself as Messiah to the woman at the well (4:25–26), and he allows Martha to give him that title in 11:27, but here his answer is oblique. It may be that Jesus did not want to identify himself with the popular view that the Messiah would be a military leader who would free Jews from Roman domination. Perhaps the Jews pressed the question because they desired a political liberator (like the Maccabean warriors whose exemplary model they were commemorating during the festival of Dedication).

Jesus responds in 10:25-26 that he has already answered their question. Readers of John's Gospel know this to be true, for they interpret Jesus' "I am" sayings—titles such as "the light of the world," "the gate for the sheep," or "the good shepherd"—as referents to his messianic vocation. In addition, the Fourth Gospel describes the messiahship of Jesus in terms of Sonship: Jesus is the Son of God sent into the world as the Son of Man; his vocation cannot be measured by contemporary Jewish messianic expectation.

In the good shepherd discourse Jesus answered the question of his messiahship by speaking of the nature of leadership. That passage alludes to Ezekiel 34, where God is shown as having indicted the appointed leaders of Israel for failing to feed or care for the flock. Denouncing the evil shepherds, God says: "I myself will be the shepherd of my sheep" (Ezek. 34:15). In John 10 Jesus calls himself the good shepherd, thus identifying himself with the nature and work of the God of Israel. The same criticism that God leveled against the religious leaders of Ezekiel's day, Jesus as God's Messiah levels against the religious leaders of his own day.

John 10:28-29 indicate that the power Jesus uses to hold the flock is the very power of God; it is in that regard that we must understand Jesus' ensuing statement: "The Father and I are one" (10:30). The Greek numeral here is neuter, not masculine, implying that Jesus and the Father are one entity, but not one person. While the Evangelist never defines the precise nature of the union between the Father and the Son, it is clear from the Johannine context that Jesus' unity with the Father means one in intent, one in purpose, one in power, one in authority, and one in works (10:25). Jesus is God's true and faithful agent, carrying out the Father's will. While the statement in 10:30 has been called John's highest Christological claim,[3] it should not be viewed as moral, metaphysical, or mystical in nature. Rather, the author's intention is to accentuate that Jesus is the object of faith and the means of revelation and salvation, and that the honor that is paid to the Son is honor paid to the Father (see 14:9). The claims in this text became foundational for the church's creedal statements about the nature of the Trinity during the fourth and fifth centuries.

The authorities' response that Jesus is speaking blasphemy, claiming to actually make himself God while being only human (10:33), is a claim

---

3. Culpepper, *Gospel and Letters*, 182.

that is at once both true and false. The authorities are right that there is a divine claim in Jesus' words, but they are wrong that he is a mere human trying to make himself into a god. The reader of John will know that divinity was not something the Word must attain at some point, since the Word of God was God from before the foundation of the universe. The authorities want to distinguish between Jesus' good deeds as a human and his Christological claims, stoning him for the latter only (this is the same charge made in 5:18). The entire dialogue may also be read as suggesting that Johannine Christians had been in grave danger with Jewish synagogue officials because of the claims Christians were making about Jesus.[4]

Jesus' rebuttal in 10:34–36, quoting Psalm 82:6, is a form of rabbinic argument that argues from the lesser to the greater. If lesser beings than God can be called gods (the original context seems to make the Israelites the equals of the angels of the heavenly court, whereas in John the "gods" are ordinary Jews to whom God's word had come, presumably because they have knowledge of divine things revealed to them; see 10:35), how much more the one whom God sanctified and sent into the world, the one who is God's Son. The contrast here seems to be between the recipients of the former covenant (the theme of the Old Testament) and Jesus, the bearer of God's new covenant (the theme of the New Testament). The term translated "sanctified" here has its normal biblical sense of being set apart or dedicated to God, a reference to the Son's divine mission as God's agent on earth. In its literary and polemical context, this verse seems to be the strongest Old Testament citation John could find for attributing deity to humans, though John's Christological use of the text considerably extends its original meaning.

What is said of Jesus here and throughout this chapter is similar to what Wisdom of Solomon 7—9 attributes to Wisdom: (1) Wisdom is sent forth from the holy heavens (9:10) and is set apart in herself (7:22); (2) she understand and gives understanding of parables and riddles (8:8); (3) she rescues humanity, saving them (9:18); (4) she sits by the throne of God (9:4); (5) she is a partner in all God's works (8:4); (6) she has the qualities and character traits of God (7:22–30).[5]

In John 10:37–38 Jesus appeals to his opponents to believe in his works even if they cannot believe his words, urging them to use sign-faith as a stepping-stone to the true faith that sees in the works and words

---

4. Witherington, *John's Wisdom*, 191.

5. Wisdom of Solomon, a Jewish work published only decades before the birth of Jesus, was widely influential among Hellenistic Jews during the first century AD.

of Jesus the very nature of God. Yet the response to even this modest request is negative, for it is joined to his astounding claim, "that you may know and understand that the Father is in me and I am in the Father" (10:38). Verses 37 and 38 should not be read as isolated remarks but as part of the entire Johannine message. Though the ministry of Jesus is viewed as one coherent whole, the whole is contained in each part. Verses 40–42 give John the Baptist one final opportunity to witness to Jesus: "everything that John said about this man was true." With chapter 11 Jesus turns toward his death.

Essay 6: The Paradoxical Nature of Faith

One of the most pressing questions for biblical scholars and modern Christians is the question of salvation (the transition from unbelief to belief) and its relation to divine determinism and free will. To pose the question from John's perspective, we might ask: how does one make the transition from the realm of darkness to the realm of truth and light? How does one move from the realm of "the below" to "the above," from inauthentic to authentic existence, from autonomy and independence to creaturehood and dependence on God? Such questions lead to the concept of faith in the Fourth Gospel and to the related concepts of (1) divine determinism and the free will of individuals, (2) seeing and hearing, and (3) knowing and believing.

Jesus is presented in John as knowing not only what is in the hearts of humans but also who will receive or reject him. If this is so, why does John emphasize the priority of the human response to the divine initiative, and why does Jesus teach and act as though it might make a difference? The Fourth Gospel does not give a clear answer. The invitation to believe, the command to believe, and the testimony of others designed to evoke belief—these imply that the individual is responsible for his or her own faith or unbelief. One set of texts seems to favor human freedom (1:12; 3:14–17, 36; 4:47; 12:32; 20:31), and another set favors determinism (6:44, 64–65; 8:47; 12:37–40). How can we resolve the contradiction?[6]

One way to do so would be to prioritize one set of passages over the other, reading one set in the light of the other. Those who assume that the freedom passages are predominant would argue that the point of the Gospel is that everyone is selected by God for belief: all are drawn by

---

6. Material in this essay is adapted from Kysar, *Maverick Gospel*, 84–113.

God; all are granted the capacity for faith. It then becomes a matter of individual freedom whether one chooses to accept or reject the God-given capacity to believe. The other approach assumes that the deterministic passages control the Gospel. Hence, only those who are selected by God are given the capacity for faith. Others are ruled out by divine decree.

Another way allows the tension to stand: perhaps John's message supports a paradoxical dimension to religious belief. While human choice seems to be central in the acceptance of the truth, God has a hand in the origin of religious faith, meaning that without divine influence, faith cannot be present. For the Evangelist, both positions are valid, and he does not attempt to work out the relationship between them. Unlike modern theologians, who might attempt a logical determination of how both factors might contribute to produce belief, the Evangelist remains content in the knowledge that there is a mystery involved in the human capacity to believe.

Some scholars introduce a third explanation, which takes us to the Gospel's compositional history. Perhaps the Gospel contains two records, the author's views and communal traditions, both existing side by side, largely unreconciled. Perhaps the traditional material originated at a time when the Johannine Christians were optimistic about converting persons to their faith. If so, that material might have stressed the decisiveness of individual faith. By the time the Evangelist wrote, the missionary work of the church had encountered significant opposition. Fewer were willing to accept the teaching of the community, particularly among the Jews, where the earlier missionary efforts once flourished but now produced drastically fewer converts. Their recent experience has led them to conclude that it took a particular divine gift—God's "drawing" of the person (6:44)—in order for a person to believe.

Whatever the origin of the Gospel's teaching, it leaves us with a paradoxical view of faith. On the one hand, it insists that no one can take credit for belief, for faith is always at least in large part a gift from God. On the other hand, the Gospel persists in holding humans responsible for unbelief. The paradox remains: humans cannot boast of their faith, but neither can they excuse their lack of faith. Incidentally, the same paradox occurs in the Pauline literature (see Romans 10:9 and Eph. 2:8–9) and throughout the New Testament.

A similar tension occurs when we examine the term "sign" in John, a wondrous deed of Jesus that plays an ambiguous role in relation to belief. On the one hand, signs provide opportunities for insight into the true identity of Jesus. They are works of God, expressions of the power of God that produce faith. This is true of each of the seven (or eight) major signs performed by Christ in the Gospel (2:1–11; 4:46–54; 5:1–9; 6:1–14; 6:15–25; 9:1–8; 11:1–46; and 21:1–14). Of the first, the transformation of water into wine, the narrator tells us that it served to reveal Christ's glory, "and his disciples believed in him" (2:11). In 2:23 we read that the signs produced widespread faith in Christ. Likewise, 20:30–31 makes clear that the signs were intended to provoke faith on the part of the reader. The implication is that these signs are evidence that Jesus really is the Messiah (see 2:18).

However, John 6:26 suggests that to follow Jesus simply for the sake of his gifts or benefits is not enough. "Seeing signs" involves more than having one's needs met, more even than a visual perception. It is an insight into the identity of the performer of the sign, a comprehension of Jesus as more than a wonder-worker. He is the Christ, the heavenly revealer, the father's unique Son. As is often the case, the Evangelist has proposed two levels of thought, two ways of experiencing the signs of Jesus. At one level they present a perception of Jesus as one who fills human physical needs; at another level they nurture an awareness of Jesus as the divine revealer. In both cases, the signs are treated in a positive way.

Elsewhere the Fourth Gospel has serious reservations about the effectiveness of signs in producing genuine faith, such as in 12:37, where they seem powerless to arouse faith. In the case of the healing of the son of the royal official, Jesus does the healing only after complaining about belief based on signs (4:48). The Evangelist's own point of view seems to be implied in 20:29, where the text commends the kind of faith that blossoms independent of signs. Faith that builds on signs may be seen as the first level of faith, but it must grow into something more.

In the Gospel this understanding of faith is expanded by the Evangelist's use of the terms seeing, hearing, and knowing. In the case of *seeing*, readers must distinguish between two meanings: sensory perception and faith perception (faith-seeing). While the verb often indicates the first meaning, such as in 1:47, the second meaning is evident in 14:8, where Philip asks that Jesus show the disciples the Father. Jesus' reply, "Whoever has seen me has seen the Father" (14:9), refers to spiritual or faith perception, to the ability to discern in the person of Jesus the nature of God. The Gospel of John has a profound understanding of faith perception resulting from an encounter with Jesus. This interconnection is evident in 6:40; 11:45; and 12:45. In each of these passages, the act of believing seems to be an integral part of the process of faith. More specifically, the point is that the origin of faith is based on the contact with the earthly Jesus. Faith does not simply blossom out of the inner self but rather arises from contact with a material, physical object—in this case the man Jesus. In 9:39 we learn that while Jesus' mission might accomplish physical healing, it provides far more, granting the gift of perceiving the truth about life and existence.

The same applies when we turn to the Evangelist's use of words for *hearing* ("to hear" or "to listen"; see 5:24; 6:60; 8:43). As with faith-seeing, faith-hearing involves the apprehension of meaning in a believing way. Faith-hearing is not the sensory experience of sound but the act of discerning the presence of God in this man, Jesus. There is the same parallel between the disciples' hearing the Son and the Son's hearing the Father (8:26). Again, we have evidence that for the Fourth Evangelist, the origin of religious faith is in a peculiar discernment of an event or encounter. "Seeing" and "hearing" refer to something deeper than physical seeing or hearing. They represent the apprehension of truth or the comprehension of the presence of a divine agent. Thus John presents us with a profound relationship between experience and faith. The physical, the sensory, the material is the medium by which faith is born: "and the Word became flesh and lived among us, and we have seen his glory" (1:14). Direct encounter with God's incarnation as a human is the necessary prerequisite for believing. Thus we have in the Gospel of John a two-level experience that symbolizes the ground of faith. The base of this experience is an encounter with Jesus and his message.

We arrive finally at *knowing*, including the paradoxical relationship between faith and knowledge. Is there a requisite knowledge one must have before faith? Or is faith the foundation for knowing? Is one more important than the other? Are they synonymous? In 8:31 (also 10:38) the implication is that faith leads to knowledge, whereas 17:8 (also 16:30) suggests the opposite, that knowledge leads to faith. There is still further confusion, for some passages appear to use the Greek words for knowing and believing synonymously: "We have come to believe and know," confesses Peter (6:69). In 14:7 and 17:3 it appears we could substitute the word "believe" for the word "know" and have exactly the same meaning.

The solution may be quite simple, for it seems that the reason knowing and believing are used interchangeably in John is that they really were synonymous for the Johannine church. What it means "to know" may be no different from what is meant by "to believe." The Fourth Evangelist is not a philosopher concerned with epistemological subtlety. The author uses these concepts synonymously because he conceives of them in their Hebraic sense. In the Hebrew Bible the word for "knowing" had less of a sense of intellectual comprehension (as it did in the Greek language), and more of an interpersonal comprehension. "To know" in a Hebraic sense is to enter into a personal, intimate relationship. As a subject, one knows someone by entering into a personal and trusting relationship with another subject. Thus, there is no intent to suggest greater intellectual content when the text uses "know" rather than "believe." Both are personal; both are intimate; both have to do with the relationship between two subjects and not between a subject and an object. "In the Johannine sense of knowing, there is no detachment but just the opposite—involvement."[7] If the Gospel of John means by "knowing" something synonymous for faith, then one aspect of what John means by faith becomes clear: faith is the trusting personal relationship between two subjects. For Johannine Christians, belief is not confined to the intellectual acceptance of doctrine but rather includes a relationship with the living Word that involves the whole person: mind, body, emotions, and everything else.

There is one final feature of the Johannine concept of faith we should mention. The author of the Gospel never uses the noun ("faith" or "belief") but always the verb ("to believe"; the Greek has only one word that we translate either "belief" or "faith"). What this means is that for John, belief is always an active matter. It is not an inner disposition, not something one has, but something one does or has done on one's behalf. Faith as a noun is static, akin to a state of being; faith as a verb is active, dynamic, and relational. Faith as a verb means that believing is not a decision made once, that must be guarded lest it grow or change; such faith is progressive.

Questions to Ponder

1. Why might first-century Jews have thought that sin caused human suffering? How does Jesus address this issue?
2. Why did the Pharisees fault Jesus for doing good deeds on the Sabbath?
3. Can you give some examples of how God's truth is different from what the world sees as true?

---

7. Kysar, *Maverick Gospel*, 108.

4. What do you think Jesus means in 9:39? What does this tell you about Jesus' skills as a teacher?

5. In your estimation, what point is Jesus making in John 10:1–18?

6. What feelings toward Rome would the festival of Dedication be likely to produce? To whom would the Jews be looking for liberation? How might this prompt the question in 10:24? What influence would this have had on their rejection of Jesus' claims? Why?

7. In your estimation, what truth is Jesus stating in 10:30? Support your answer.

8. With regard to the matter of faith and salvation, how do you resolve the relation of divine determinism and free will? If both are important, which has priority? Why?

CHAPTER 7

Scenes Preparatory to the Glorification of Jesus
(John 11:1—12:50)

Summary: John 11 and 12 bring to a climax the mighty works of Jesus and set the stage for his death. In chapter 11 Jesus raises Lazarus to life—his final and greatest sign—a sign that seals his own death warrant. Jesus' discussion with Martha identifies him as the resurrection and as life. This great sign brings many to Jesus; some of the Jews believe, while others go to the authorities, who are plotting to kill Jesus. As the Passover draws near, the growing crowds wait to see whether Jesus will appear. In chapter 12 Mary anoints Jesus amid protests from Judas. Jesus enters Jerusalem for the final time, the crowds waving palm branches. Later, when some Greeks wish to see Jesus, he begins to speak openly about his impending death. The public ministry of Jesus ends at the conclusion of John 12.

Assignment: Read John 11–12

Key Passages: John 11:25–26; 12:26

Central Theme: Jesus is the Resurrection and the Life

Key Symbols/Concepts: glorify, resurrection and life, belief, Messiah (Son of God), Passover, the Greeks, Son of Man, lifted up, glory, judgment, salvation

Learning Objectives
Participants will examine:

1. The account of the raising of Lazarus in its Johannine setting

2. The relation between Jesus and Mary and Martha in John and in the Synoptic Gospels

3. The metaphorical meaning of Jesus as "the resurrection and the life" in John 11:25

4. The relation between the raising of Lazarus and the decision to kill Jesus

5. The meaning of Jesus' anointing by Mary at Bethany

6. The Johannine version of Jesus' triumphal entry into Jerusalem

7. The reference to Greeks who wish to see Jesus in 12:20–26

8. Jesus' interpretation of his death in John 12:27–36

9. Jesus' summary of his ministry in John 12:44–50

10. The Johannine emphasis on "realized eschatology"

Outline to John 11:1—12:50

I. The Raising of Lazarus 11:1—12:11

    A. The Death of Lazarus 11:1–16

    B. Jesus Comforts Martha and Mary 11:17–37

    C. Jesus Raises Lazarus to Life 11:38–44

    D. The Plot to Kill Jesus 11:45–57

    E. Mary Anoints Jesus 12:1–11

II. Jesus' Entry into Jerusalem 12:12–19

III. Jesus Interprets his Death 12:20–36

IV. The Epilogue to Jesus' Public Ministry 12:37–50

    A. The Narrator's Commentary on Jesus' Ministry 12:37–43

    B. Jesus' Summary Discourse 12:44–50

Light and Life in John

In John 1:4–9, light is the central image for the presence of the Word in the world. "Light" and "life" are identified in 1:4 as two ways in which the

Word expresses itself in the world. Light and life are signs of the Word's relationship to the world, two ways in which human beings experience the incarnate Word. In John, Jesus is both the light of the world (8:12; 9:5) and the giver of life everlasting (5:21-29; 10:27-28). These two themes belong together in the thought of the Evangelist, for whom there can be no eternal life apart from faith, knowledge, and sight.

John 9, where Jesus gave sight to a man born blind, prefigures the raising of Lazarus from the grave in chapter 11, as this account prefigures the resurrection of Jesus in chapter 20. From the beginning, the Evangelist has been preparing us for this moment, the climactic and most miraculous episode in the series of signs in Jesus' public ministry: "the hour is coming when all who are in the tombs will hear his voice" (5:28-29). The story of the raising of Lazarus, while a complete literary unit, is Johannine throughout, unintelligible apart from its relation to the whole Gospel. It underscores the theme of Jesus as the giver of life while at the same time declaring that those who believe already have life (5:24).

In many ways this story parallels the first sign, in John 2, thus bringing together and reemphasizing basic Johannine themes. In both scenes the hope is held that Jesus will act despite the seeming impossibility of the situation. The theme of "glory" is found in both stories. In John 11, as in chapters 2 and 7, Jesus acts only as the Father wills, not at the request of his mother, brothers, or friends. As the best wine is saved for last in John 2:10, so the best "sign" is saved for the close of Jesus' public ministry. In John 2 Jesus brought new life and joy to the wedding celebration, while in John 11 he brings new life to a family he dearly loved. Both narratives also portray women in the process of learning Jesus' true nature and thus becoming his true disciples. Mary and Martha, like Jesus' mother, believe in Jesus' power, but in both cases this faith and knowledge is inadequate. They do not yet realize that Jesus can bring life because he is the resurrection and the life.

Chapters 11 and 12 are pivotal chapters that bring to a climax the mighty works of Jesus and set the stage for his death and resurrection. In the Synoptic Gospels, the cleansing of the temple led to the arrest of Jesus, but in John, it is the raising of Lazarus that sets in motion the events that lead to Jesus' death. As the Word comes into the world to give life to those who receive him, so Jesus returns to Jerusalem to give life to Lazarus, knowing that it will cost him his own life (cf. 11:16). The giving of life, paradoxically, becomes the impetus for Jesus' death: "from that day they planned to put him to death" (11:53; cf. 12:10-11).

Analysis of John 11:1—12:50

The Raising of Lazarus (Chapter 11:1—12:11)

The story of the raising of Lazarus (11:1–44) is incomplete without its aftermath in 11:45—12:11, and thus this interrelated material will be addressed as a single unit. This unit has a complex structure and does not follow the common Johannine pattern of miracle, dialogue, discourse. The miracle concludes rather than begins the story and represents only a fraction of the story, which focuses on Jesus' conversations with his disciples, with Martha and Mary, and with the "Jews." There is no concluding discourse. Instead, narrative and discourse are tightly interwoven.

While the Synoptic Gospels recount the story of the raising of Jairus's daughter (Matt. 9:18–26; Mark 5:21–43; Luke 8:40–56), a story not found in John, the raising of Lazarus is unique to John. There is no question that John has shaped this story to fit his theological purposes. It serves as a catalyst for Jesus' death, a role played in the Synoptic Gospels by the cleansing of the temple.

The story takes place in Bethany, a Judean town close to Jerusalem (11:18). The Synoptics mention Bethany as the place where Jesus stayed during his passion week, but John alone identifies this village with Mary and Martha. The two sisters appear in Luke 10:38–42, but without reference to Lazarus (the name does appear in Luke 16:19–31, in a parable about a poor man, but these are different characters). The characterization of Martha and Mary in John closely matches the portrayal in Luke—of Martha as the outgoing and vocal sister and Mary as the quieter but more devout one, always found at Jesus' feet (compare John 12:3 to Luke 10:39).

John 11:2 introduces Mary as the one who anoints Jesus and wipes his feet with her hair (12:1–8), an act that is attributed to a harlot in Luke 7:37–38. It is conventional to read John 11:2 as an editorial gloss inserted to clarify which of the many Marys known in Christian tradition is meant here, but it is not necessary to attribute this verse to a later editor. By pointing forward to Mary's role in this anointing, the Evangelist connects the Lazarus story with Jesus' death, something made explicit throughout the account.

The sisters refer to Lazarus as "he whom you love" (11:3), prompting some scholars to wonder if Lazarus is the unnamed Beloved Disciple of later chapters of John. That identification, however, should be rejected, as I argue in the Introduction. The message sent by the sisters is meant to hasten Jesus' visit, but it seems to have the opposite effect. It is clear from the context that Jesus' response does not reflect a callous disregard for the sisters' concern, but rather follows a pattern in John's Gospel to act only as the Father wills, for he is God's agent.

The term "glory" in 11:4 and elsewhere in John means not "praise," as if illness brings God's praise, but rather is a means of disclosure. This gift of life will be revelatory of Jesus' relationship with God. As in 9:3, the point is not to turn terminal illness into an object lesson of divine praise, but rather to make it serve God's larger purpose. The "glorification" of Jesus in John always refers to his death, resurrection, and ascension (12:16, 23, 28; 13:31; 17:1, 4). There is an irony to Jesus' words in 11:4, because while the illness will not end in Lazarus's death, it will end in his. In 11:15 Jesus gives his delay and Lazarus' death a theological interpretation. Not only is Lazarus's death an occasion for revelation, but it also is an occasion for the disciples to come to faith.

Jesus' sudden resolve to return to Judea at 11:7 is met with concern by the disciples because of the imminent danger, but Jesus replies that he must continue his work while there is still time. Jesus has the light within him, and he knows in advance when the darkness will enfold him. The response of Thomas in 11:16 ("Let us also go, that we may die with him") reads as an expression of courage, but it sounds more like fatalistic resignation to what seemed inevitable. This conclusion is supported by the later depiction of Thomas in John 20 as skeptical and doubting, as well as by the seeming lack of comprehension of the disciples in general, as 11:11–14 indicates.

When Jesus finally arrives in Bethany, Lazarus had been in the grave for four days, an expression of some significance, since according to Jewish traditions the spirit of the deceased remained near the corpse for three days before it departed. After three days, then, there was no hope of resuscitation. Martha is understandably upset with Jesus for his delay, though she is seen to demonstrate faith in Jesus, particularly in his healing power and messianic character, but she does not yet understand that Jesus is the resurrection and the life, who can give life even in the present. Her objection to Jesus' command to roll away the stone at the tomb's entrance clearly reflects a lack of adequate faith and understanding, earning somewhat of an exasperated response by Jesus (11:39–40). This story, like earlier stories in John, portrays the progress of individuals in their journey to a more adequate faith in Jesus.

In response to Jesus' promise, "Your brother will rise again" (11:23), Martha recites the belief in the resurrection of the dead common among the Pharisees and many other first-century Jews. Her answer in 11:24 ("I know that he will rise again in the resurrection on the last day") is the fullest pre-resurrection confession of faith she could make. She believes that Jesus is the Messiah, the Son of God. She believes truly, yet still inadequately.

Jesus goes beyond this eschatological hope by announcing: "I am the resurrection and the life" (11:25). For those who believe in Jesus, eternal life need not wait until the final resurrection, but rather begins here and now. Consistently in John there is eschatological tension between the "already and the not yet." To follow Jesus is to have eternal life now, we are told, a reality that continues in the life to come.[1] John presents here the ultimate witness to God's power over life and death, and it is this power that marks the new age. The saying in 11:26, "everyone who lives and believes in me will never die" is difficult and requires explanation. The original Greek states that those who believe in Jesus "will never die into the age [to come]," meaning they will not be cut off from "the age to come."[2] This statement, then, reassures believers that Jesus' being "the life" means that "he gives eternal life, which begins in the present life and continues beyond death, while Jesus being the resurrection means that . . . a person who believes in him will never die (i.e., go on to experience eternal death), for he or she will be raised."[3]

Jesus is not here saying that the faithful will not die physically, but rather speaks of life and death in a theological and relational way. The Fourth Gospel maintains that people enter a right relationship with God through faith, and that faith brings eternal life because it brings people into relationship with the eternal God. Since faith is the way that people relate to God in the present, eternal life is the relationship with God that begins in the present and endures beyond the grave.

Mary is summoned as well and goes to meet Jesus, offering much the same complaint as Martha. She too does not understand that Jesus is already the resurrection and the life. She kneels at Jesus' feet in devotion (11:32) and moves Jesus to tears. Verse 33 is crucial for understanding this passage: "When Jesus saw her weeping . . . he was greatly disturbed

---

1. For additional information, see essay 7: "John's Realized Eschatology."

2. Schnakenburg translates John 11:26a: "and whoever lives and believes in me shall not die to eternity," *St. John*, 1:331.

3. Witherington, *John's Wisdom*, 203.

in spirit and deeply moved." Seeing both Mary and the consoling Jews weeping produces a strong emotional reaction in Jesus. The Greek word used here encompasses grief and weeping, but also conveys the sense of anger or outrage. While the crowd interprets Jesus' response as a sign of love, Jesus' indignation seems to be caused by their lack of faith, for they mourned as people without hope although in the presence of one who was both resurrection and life. There is a certain irony in their words, for while they were right that Jesus loved Lazarus, they were wrong to interpret his tears as an expression of that affection. Verse 38 indicates that he was deeply disturbed. He is approaching the close of his ministry and yet no one adequately understands and believes. Jesus' response to Martha in 11:40 seems to support this impression, as does Jesus' prayer in 11:42: "that they may believe that you sent me."

When Jesus calls Lazarus by name, he comes forth bound in burial clothes. This miracle is a preliminary fulfillment that the dead would respond to the Son's voice and come forth from their graves (5:25–29), confirming that Jesus has the power of life. Because of this power, death disappears as darkness disappears before light (see 1 Cor. 15:54b–57). The response to Jesus' miracle was mixed. Many Jews believed in his sign, while others went to report him to the Pharisees. The authorities are concerned with the political implications, for believing in Jesus is not simply a matter of religious faith. As the Evangelist makes clear during the upcoming trial of Jesus, belief in Jesus comes to mean accepting his authority as God's agent and therefore as the leader and ruler of his people (18:37–38). This comes to mean rejecting the present religious leadership as invalid, and thus also implies rejection of the Roman imperial power that sanctioned the current Jewish authorities, in particular the high priest. In short, Caiaphas and the Sadducees as well as other members of the governing Sanhedrin had the most to lose if Jesus were recognized as messianic leader of the Jews. The words in 11:47–48 must be evaluated in this light. The mention of the word "Romans" here is important, this being the first and only time in all four gospels where this term is used. Its use in this context is significant, for the Romans caused much of the anxiety of the Jews in Jesus' day, both of ordinary Jews and their Jewish leaders.

Caiaphas responds with his own solution, one that will guarantee the ruling authorities' mutual survival: "It is better for you to have one man die for the people than to have the whole nation destroyed" (11:50). Jesus is declared public enemy number one, suggesting that if the crowds get out of hand, if the leaders are unable to control the people, Rome will surely do it for them. A simple solution presents itself: sacrifice Jesus for the security of the nation. At John 11:50 we reach the height of irony: Jesus would indeed be the one who died so that the nation and also the dispersed children of God might be saved. By the time John's Gospel was written, the irony of Caiaphas's statement had compounded: Rome had destroyed Jerusalem and sent the Jews into exile. Crucifying Jesus had not saved them from that fate.

Until this point Jesus had been subject to informal trial by his peers, but now the Jerusalem authorities are also prepared to act against him. Jesus responds by going to Ephraim, a remote town near the Judean wilderness, remaining there for an undisclosed length of time. The Passover is mentioned as being at hand (11:55), the third Passover cited by John. People had to purify themselves ritually before they could participate, something that required a week. Again, the crowds speculated about whether Jesus might appear at the festival, because of the danger involved. Verse 57 presents a concerted effort on the part of the Sadducees and Pharisees to arrest and try Jesus, which suggests that he was seen as a considerable political threat, since these two groups rarely saw eye to eye.

John 12:1-11 records a second episode at Bethany, this time at a dinner given in Jesus' honor. There we are told that Mary took costly perfume and anointed Jesus' feet, wiping them with her hair. The story of Jesus' anointing by a woman also appears in the Synoptics (Mark 14:3-9; Matt. 26:6-13; Luke 7:36-50). Luke's version reflects a different tradition altogether, while John's version presents unique details differing from the other Synoptic tradition. In the Johannine version, the anointing of the feet symbolizes Jesus' kingly burial, while in the Markan and Matthean accounts the anointing on the head indicates his kingly character. The Johannine setting is ironic, in that the place where Jesus gave life to Lazarus (12:1) becomes the very place where he is anointed as one would anoint a corpse. Mary's perfume was used in small quantities for cosmetic purposes, but could also be used for burial rites, as Jesus indicates (12:7).

Jesus' response to the objection of Judas that this was a waste of money ("She bought it so that she might keep it for the day of my burial") has been much debated. If the meaning of the Johannine explanation is that Mary should take advantage of the opportunity to prepare Jesus for burial now, since she will not be able to do so later, this agrees with the explanation in Mark 14:8. The saying in 12:8 ("You always have the poor with you, but you do not always have me") is found in the Synoptic accounts of this story and should not be taken out of context or used as an excuse to avoid helping the poor simply because the problem of poverty seems to be insurmountable. What Jesus is talking about is a matter of priorities. For the time being, acts of devotion for Jesus are in order, but they should not minimize or replace concern for the plight of the poor (cf. Matt. 25:31–46). The narrator notes that the objector was Judas, whose objection was far from altruistic.

The narrative closes in 12:9–11 with a reference to the crowd and the authorities. While the crowds are curious to see Jesus and Lazarus, the authorities determine to execute Lazarus as well, since many Jews are forsaking traditional Judaism to follow Jesus. There is a certain feeling of desperation in this passage, which provides a transition from the anointing story to the account of the passion.

Jesus' Entry into Jerusalem (Chapter 12:12–19)

The Johannine account of the events leading up to the passion of Jesus is notably different from the Synoptic accounts, though they hold certain events in common, such as the entrance into Jerusalem. All four gospels depict the crowd waving branches and shouting the words: "Blessed is the one who comes in the name of the Lord," taken from Psalm 118:25. Likewise, all note that Jesus rides a donkey during his entry. However, John's version is considerably briefer than those of the other three gospels and is bracketed by references to Lazarus (12:9–10 and 17), whereas in the Synoptics the entry is tied to the cursing of the fig tree and the cleansing of the temple. Given the numerous differences between John's version and that of the Synoptics, a theory of Johannine dependence on Mark seems untenable. John's account represents an independent testimony of early Christian traditions about Jesus.

John alone among the gospels identifies the branches waved by the crowd as palm branches, important because of their association with the triumph of the Maccabees and their triumphal entry into Jerusalem, celebrated at the festival of Dedication (1 Macc. 13:51). Furthermore, the Hallel psalms (Ps. 113—118) were associated with the festival of Booths, sung to pilgrims entering Jerusalem during a feast, and there is evidence that by the first century they had come to be associated with the Messiah's coming to the city. If one connects the phrase "the King of Israel" in John 12:13 with the earlier account of the attempt by the Galileans to make Jesus their king (6:15), there can be little doubt that the Evangelist is depicting the crowds as proclaiming Jesus their long-awaited political Messiah. The portrayal of Jesus riding on a young donkey rather than on a warhorse suggests a different sort of Messiah than commonly envisioned—the humble and peaceful ruler described in Zechariah 9:9–10. John, like the Synoptics, makes clear that Jesus did not come to be a political Messiah but rather a universal Savior who would bring peace to all nations. The crowds do not understand this perspective of the Messiah, nor do the disciples, whose enlightenment awaits Jesus' death and resurrection (12:16; see also 2:17, 22).

Of the four gospels, only John depicts the crowds taking the initiative in going to meet Jesus (12:13, 18), testifying to his power and his person, eliciting an ironic remark from the Pharisees: "The world has gone after him," for in due course, this would prove to be true.

Jesus Interprets his Death (Chapter 12:20–36)

The desire of the Greeks to see Jesus marks the beginning of a new section. Some have suggested that these are Greek-speaking Diaspora Jews, but it is more likely that they are devout Gentiles (characterized as proselytes or as "God-fearers" in Acts 10:2, 22, 35; 13:16, 26, 43, 50; 16:14; 17:4, 17; 18:7). The Greeks target Philip and Andrew as intermediaries with Jesus because these disciples come from Galilee and alone among the disciples preserved Greek names. The Greeks cannot speak with Jesus directly because as Gentiles they were limited to the outer court of the temple. The Evangelist is not interesting in narrating the outcome of this particular quest (the Greeks disappear entirely from the discussion after 12:21) because he is using their quest to stress the universal scope of Jesus' work (see 4:42). As the raising of Lazarus and Jesus' anointing prefigured Jesus' glorification, the arrival of the Greeks prefigures the church's future mission to the Gentiles. Readers will detect here a reference to the future of the Jesus movement, particularly in light of the rejection of Jesus by many fellow Jews.

John 12:24–26 introduces teachings about Jesus' death. The parabolic saying in 12:24 indicates that Jesus' life will bear significant fruit after his death. It is his death that will "bear much fruit" (cause significant growth). The saying in 12:25 ("Those who love their life lose it, and those who hate their life in this world will keep it for eternal life") is one of the best-attested sayings of Jesus, having much in common with sayings found in the Synoptic tradition, particularly Mark 8:35 (cf. Matt. 10:39; 16:25; Mark 10:39; Luke 9:24; 17:33). The saying in 12:26 ("Whoever serves me must follow me, and where I am, there will my servant be also") has parallels in the Synoptics as well (see Matt. 10:38; Mark 8:34; Luke 14:27), but whereas the Synoptic versions establish a condition for following Jesus ("taking up one's cross"), the Johannine version adds a promise: "Whoever serves me, the Father will honor." This is the only time in the Gospel that God is said to honor someone, and it anticipates the mutuality of relationship among God, Jesus, and the believer promised in the Farewell Discourse, to the effect that Jesus and his followers will remain together (14:2-4, 18-20; 17:23-24).[4]

John 12:27-28 has been called the Johannine version of Jesus' hour of anguish, said in the Synoptics to occur in Gethsemane. However, unlike the Synoptic Jesus, the Johannine Jesus would never pray "not what I want, but what you want" (Mark 14:36). Jesus, depicted by John as one with the Father (10:30), deeply desires to fulfill his mission in life, to have his "hour" on the cross, which will glorify his Father as much as himself. At 12:28, for the first and only time in John, a voice from heaven speaks, affirming Jesus' prayer: "I have glorified [your name], and I will glorify it again." God has already been glorified by the Son (through his life and signs), and God will be glorified again (through Jesus' death, resurrection, and exaltation). While the crowd could not understand what was said, Jesus indicates that it was spoken for the crowd's sake, to reveal to the crowd their spiritual state—that they stand in danger of judgment (12:31a).

John 12:31-32 depicts Jesus' death as the decisive eschatological event, described in sweeping terms as (a) the crucial point in the judgment of "this world" (meaning the key event in the war against the powers of darkness) and as (b) the universal offer of salvation available in Jesus' crucifixion. The urgency and immediacy of Jesus' "hour" are underscored by the repetition of the term "now" in 12:31. The expression "the ruler of this world" occurs only in John (see 14:30; 16:11), but similar imagery is used elsewhere in the New Testament and in the Dead Sea Scrolls to refer to the devil, the embodiment of opposition to God. Verse 31 predicts the defeat of the power of evil in the world (cf. 13:2, 27; 16:33).

The crowd's misunderstanding of Jesus' words in 12:34 ("We have heard from the law that the Messiah remains forever") recalls 7:26-27,

---

4. O'Day, *John*, 711.

41–42. They expect a Messiah who remains forever, as opposed to one who dies on a cross. The reference to "law" here and elsewhere in John is to scripture in general and not strictly to the Jewish Torah (see 10:34); the text alluded to here is probably Psalm 89:36, which states that the line of David will continue forever. The crowd's misunderstanding leads to 12:35–36, where Jesus turns from direct speech about his death to metaphorical depiction of his ministry. Because of the urgency of the hour, these verses function as the concluding appeal for faith in Jesus. Jesus' departure in 12:36b marks the end of his public teaching. He is said to hide from the crowd because the decisive moment has arrived.

The Epilogue to Jesus' Public Ministry (Chapter 12:37–50)

John 12:37–50 serves as the epilogue to Jesus' public ministry. It summarizes the state of unbelief Jesus found in Judaism, followed by a succinct summary of Jesus' teaching during his public ministry (12:44–50). In 12:37–43 the Evangelist struggles with the same dilemma as does Paul in Romans 9—11: why did the Jews reject Jesus? The problem is stated succinctly in verse 37 and the explanation follows. In 12:38–41 John fashions an argument built around two Old Testament quotations (Isaiah 53:1 and 6:10). These Isaiah passages are pivotal in the structure of the Gospel, as they are elsewhere in the New Testament. The former, used in Romans 10:16, played an important role in early Christian attempts to explain lack of faith in Jesus, and the latter was quoted frequently by New Testament writers, including in the Synoptics to explain the purpose of Jesus' parables (Matt. 13:14; Mark 4:12; Luke 8:10). In Romans 11:8 the text from Isaiah 6:10 serves as an explanation for the failure of the mission to the Jews, and it also stands at the conclusion of the book of Acts (28:26).

Far from catching God by surprise, John 12:38–41 indicates that Israel's disbelief in the Messiah had been incorporated into God's plan all along. The point is that just as Jesus' death was part of God's plan, so too was his rejection by many fellow Jews. Yet the Evangelist points out that this was not some blind predestination scheme that consigned Jews to temporary unbelief, much less permanent rejection of Jesus. This explanation clarifies the statement in 12:42 that many of the Jewish authorities believed in Jesus (we learn in John 19:38–42 that this includes Nicodemus and Joseph of Arimathea). From this passage we may conclude that Jewish unbelief at that time was the means by which Jesus fulfilled his plan for his Son to be glorified (by being lifted up on the cross), and so "they could not believe" (12:39) at that time.[5]

The theological conception that Jesus is the revelation of God's glory (12:41), which is emphasized throughout John's Gospel, seems to be based upon the book of Isaiah. The theme of God's glory is central to Isaiah, holding together the three major parts of the book (chapters 1—39; 40—59; and 60—66), as indicated by 6:3: "the whole earth is full of his glory" and by the opening statements of Second and Third Isaiah. In 40:5 we read: "Then the glory of the Lord shall be revealed, and all people shall see it together" (see also 42:8; 48:11), and in 60:1: "Arise, shine; for your light has come, and the glory of the Lord has risen upon you."

The summary in 12:44-50 stands as an overview of the dominant themes of Jesus' ministry. Verses 44-45 and 49-50 provide a frame for the discourse and proclaim the central theological claim of Jesus' ministry, that Jesus makes God known (1:18; 8:19). These verses add no new teaching, but rather present the reader with the theological issues necessary to make a decision about Jesus. Despite rejection, Jesus indicates that he is God's agent, and that belief in him entails belief in God, just as rejection of him implies rejection of the one who sent him. Jesus came into the world as light in the darkness, not to judge the world but to save it. Yet "on the last day" the very words of good news will witness against those who reject them.[6]

As John makes clear, Christian faith is not a Jesus cult, but rather faith in the Father who sent him and commissioned him (13:20). The author ends the discourse by declaring as forcefully as he can that the rejection of Jesus is the denial of God. More than a mere epilogue to the public ministry, this summary connects the account of the public ministry to the Farewell Discourse, the final private session between Jesus and his closest followers (compare 12:45 to 14:9 and 12:50 to 14:31).

Essay 7: John's Realized Eschatology

Eschatology is the study of final things. "Realized" eschatology speaks of final things as being here with us now. A life with God is possible in the

---

5. Witherington, *John's Wisdom*, 226-27.

6. The expression "on the last day," utilizing traditional eschatological teaching such as the idea of a final day of judgment, is found six times in John (at 6:39, 40, 44, 54; 11:24; and 12:48).

present even though that final life in all its fullness has not yet arrived. There is a tension in John's Gospel, and indeed throughout the New Testament, between "the already and the not yet." Passages such as John 3:17–21, 31–36, and 6:47 exemplify realized eschatology, meaning that God's long-awaited eschatological transformation of reality, including judgment of evil and reward of faith (eternal life), is underway in the present, initiated by Jesus' coming into the world. The very presence of Jesus in the world confronts the world with a decision, to believe or not to believe, and making that decision is the moment of judgment. If one's life is characterized by transformative belief, so that one's deeds are "done in God" (3:21), then one is saved; if one does not believe, one is already condemned. John's Gospel does include traditional understandings of eschatology and the final judgment (5:28–29; 12:48), but judgment and eternal life as present realities are at the theological heart of the Fourth Gospel.

It is crucial for the Evangelist that God's judgment of the world arises out of God's love for the world. When God sent Jesus, God presented the world with a critical moment of decision. In each person's decision whether to accept God's offer of salvation, the world judges itself. Decision and self-judgment define Johannine eschatology. In Bultmann's eloquent words, the Fourth Gospel expresses "a radical understanding of Jesus' appearance as the eschatological event. This event puts an end to the old course of the world. From now on there are only believers and unbelievers, only saved and lost, those who have life and who are in death. This is because the event is grounded in the love of God, that love which gives life to faith, but which must become judgment in the face of unbelief."[7]

As the Evangelist believed in eternal life as something already present for the followers of Jesus, so he also believed in realized wrath, that God's wrath is already present for those who reject and disobey God. For John, there are always moral consequences to one's actions, both sooner and later.

"Eternal life," the term John uses instead of "the Kingdom of God," is not something believers possess only after death. It begins as soon as one places trust in Jesus as God's Son. Contemporary Christians have become so used to associating eternal life with going to heaven that the idea of realized eschatology, which views the future as somehow present now, seems perplexing. The notion of "eternal life," like the "Kingdom of

---

7. Bultmann, *John*, 159.

SCENES PREPARATORY TO THE GLORIFICATION OF JESUS

God," is paradoxical at its core. In the Synoptic Gospels, the paradoxical nature of the Kingdom is manifested in several ways: (a) it is present (Matt. 12:28; Luke 17:21), yet not fully present (Matt. 8:29; 13:30); (b) it is a gift (Matt. 25:34; Luke 12:32), yet it also involves human effort (Luke 12:31); (c) it is an internal reality (Luke 17:20–21), yet it has external implications for the world (Matt. 6:10).

Eternal life, like the Kingdom of God, (a) is already present, yet not fully so. This becomes clearer when we understand that "eternal life" has as much to do with the quality and direction of life as with the length of one's existence. A better term might be "everlasting life," meaning a life that begins for believers in this lifetime but continues on forever; (b) eternal life is a gift of God, yet it requires belief and is validated by bearing good fruit; (c) such life has a spiritual nature, yet is related to physical existence.[8]

If there will be a new heaven and a new earth, as the book of Revelation indicates, if God's Kingdom will one day fully manifest itself on earth, as Matthew indicates, and if there will be a future resurrection, as 1 Corinthians 15 declares, then Christians must be concerned not only about heavenly things but also about earthly things—for all creation shall one day be redeemed (Rom. 8:19–20). No one should be more concerned about caring for the earth and matters of global import than Christians, since they are evidently God's concern as well. God not only made creation, God loves all of creation, and is already in the process of redeeming it. It is an impoverished vision of the Gospel "that cares for the souls of the unsaved but not their bodies or minds, that cares for heaven but not the conditions on earth, that cares for spiritual things but not also material things."[9]

Questions to Ponder

1. How many different stages of grief do you detect in John 11:1–44? Was Jesus' response to Lazarus's death at all normal? Explain your answer.

2. How does Martha's response to Jesus in John differ from her response in Luke 10:38–42?

---

8. According to Pauline expectation, human existence will continue in bodily form ("further clothed"; 2 Cor. 5:4) after death.

9. Witherington, *John's Wisdom*, 113.

3. In your own words, state what you believe Jesus meant in John 11:25 when he told Martha: "I am the resurrection and the life. . . . Everyone who lives and believes in me will never die"?

4. Did Mary or Martha believe that Jesus could raise Lazarus? Explain your answer.

5. What principle underlies Jesus attitude about the poor in John 12:8?

6. Does John's account of Jesus' entry into Jerusalem overlook any features found in the Synoptics that you consider important to understanding the meaning of this event for Christians?

7. How is the message of John 12:25 similar and dissimilar to Jesus' death and resurrection?

8. How might the notion of "realized eschatology" impact the way you live your life in the present?

PART IV

The Private Ministry of Jesus

(JOHN 13–17)

CHAPTER 8

Jesus' Farewell: Part One
(John 13:1—14:31)

Summary: In chapters 13—17 Jesus turns toward his disciples and the future in which they will live. Chapter 13 is John's version of the Last Supper. It differs radically from the Synoptics in that the institution of the Eucharist is not recounted. Instead, there is the foot washing, unique to John. The chapter reports what Jesus knows and the actions following from that knowledge. The disciples, especially Peter and Judas, do not share Jesus' knowledge, and their ignorance leads to denial and betrayal. The first farewell discourse (13:31—14:31) continues in chapter 14 as Jesus prepares his gathered disciples for his death and resurrection. He is interrupted four times by disciples: Peter (13:36), Thomas (14:5), Philip (14:8), and Judas (not Iscariot; 14:22). In his discourse, Jesus reassures the disciples that he is going to prepare a place for them and that he will return for them. He gives them a "new commandment"—that they should love one another—promises to send the Paraclete (Advocate), and leaves them his peace.

Assignment: Read John 13–14

Key Passages: John 13:1, 34; 14:6, 16–17, 26

Central Theme: Jesus is the Way to the Father

Key Symbols/Concepts: foot washing, glorify, new commandment, believe, dwelling places, the way, the truth, the life, works, Advocate (Paraclete), peace

Learning Objectives

Participants will examine:

1. John's version of the Last Supper and compare it with the account in the Synoptic Gospels
2. The metaphorical meaning of the foot washing ritual in John's Gospel
3. The teaching about the nature of discipleship in John 13:12–35
4. The meaning of the commandment to "believe" in God and in Jesus in John 14:1
5. The metaphorical meaning of the phrase "I go to prepare a place for you" in John 14:2–4
6. The metaphorical meaning of "I am the way, and the truth, and the life" in John 14:6
7. The meaning of the exclusivist phrase "no one comes to the Father except through me" in John 14:6
8. The meaning of Jesus' teaching that his disciples will do "greater works than these" in John 14:12
9. John's doctrine of the Holy Spirit in 14:16–17, 26–27
10. The meaning of the expression "the ruler of this world" in John 14:30
11. John's sacramentality

Outline to John 13:1—14:31

I. The Farewell Meal 13:1–30

    A. The Foot Washing 13:1–20

    B. Jesus Foretells Judas's Betrayal 13:21–30

II. Farewell Discourse One: Jesus Prepares His Disciples for His Death and Resurrection 13:31—14:31

    A. The New Commandment 13:31–35

    B. Peter's Question 13:36—14:4

    C. Thomas's Question 14:5–7

D. Philip's Request 14:8–21

E. Judas's (not Iscariot's) Question 14:22–31

Farewell Discourses and a Farewell Meal

Commentators tend to divide John's Gospel into equal halves, contrasting "The Book of Glory" (chapters 13—21) with "The Book of Signs" (chapters 1—12). Chapters 13—17 might fittingly be called "The Book of Jesus' Hour," since a good portion is a reflective prelude to that "hour." John 13:1 is probably intended as a preface to the entire "Book of Glory," not just to chapter 13.

There are good reasons to divide chapters 13—17 into several discourses as follows: Discourse One (13:31—14:31; the statement in John 14:31, "Rise, let us be on our way," indicates that the discourse is over); Discourse Two (15:1-17); Discourse Three (15:18—16:15); Discourse Four (16:16-33); and a Closing Prayer (17:1-26). In addition to the clear break at 14:31, the material in John 15—16 contains considerable repetition of various major themes also found in 13:31—14:31. Even more significant is the fact that in 13:36-38 Peter raises the very question about where Jesus is going that Jesus reprimands the disciples for not raising in 16:4-6. The simplest solution is that 13:31—14:31 makes up one discourse, while 15:1—16:33 seems to be a composite of several discourses, all followed by the prayer in chapter 17.[1]

Readers familiar with the Synoptic account of Jesus' passion will be surprised to find that John has inserted a lengthy farewell discourse by Jesus after the Last Supper and before his arrest, beginning with 13:31 and not ending until 17:26. In addition, the Fourth Gospel gives no indication that Jesus is celebrating a Passover meal. Rather, we are told that the meal takes place before the festival of the Passover and therefore not necessarily on the eve of Passover (13:1). Perhaps this teaching, combined by John, was offered on successive nights leading up to Good Friday, indicating the sort of in-house teaching that Jesus offered to his disciples at the close of his ministry, when he was preparing them for his departure.[2]

If John's account does not present a Passover meal, what might he have had in mind in these chapters? The Fourth Evangelist seems to

---

1. This argument is made convincingly by Segovia, *Farewell of the Word*, 319–28.
2. This segment is adapted from Witherington, *John's Wisdom*, 231–34 and 244–45.

portray a farewell dinner with Jesus rather than a Passover meal. The time reference in 13:1 supports this interpretation, as does the lack of any mention of the Passover elements in these chapters. As John makes clear in 19:31, the crucifixion took place on the Day of Preparation for the Passover, at the same time as the lambs were being sacrificed in preparation for the Passover Seder meal later that night. Instead of a Passover meal, what we have in these chapters is the portrayal of a quasi-religious or philosophical banquet common in the Greco-Roman world, complete with closing symposium. John is portraying Jesus as a Jewish sage who provides discourses, with some dialogue, after the meal, as was common for a sage to do at such a banquet. Jesus' closing prayer would have been an appropriate closing act at such a meal. This pattern is not unlike what we find in 1 Corinthians 11–14, where Paul describes a Christian worship event that involves a meal, a symposium, and closing religious acts. The book of Proverbs provides instructive background as well, describing Wisdom as calling her disciples to a feast saying, "Come, eat of my bread and drink of the wine I have mixed . . . live and walk in the way of insight" (9:5-6). Jesus, in the manner of Wisdom, before his rejection and departure, calls his disciples to hear and heed the voice of Wisdom. The reason John portrays Jesus' last meal with his disciples in this manner, instead of bringing out its associations with the Jewish Passover meal, is that John is writing for an audience whose character, ministry, and mission is in a Greco-Roman world, with traits that would appeal to Diaspora Jews as well as to potential Gentile converts.

The material in these chapters also shares many traits with ancient farewell discourses in the Bible (cf. the farewell of Jacob in Gen. 49; Elijah's in 2 Kgs. 2:1-12; David's speech to Solomon in 1 Chr. 28-29; the entire book of Deuteronomy as Moses' farewell; and Paul's farewell address to the Ephesian elders in Acts 20:17-38). The function of such speeches is the preservation and handing on of wisdom to the next generation shortly before one's death or departure.[3]

---

3. Segovia provides a summary of analyses of scenes and discourses in the farewell testament of a dying hero in *Farewell of the Word*, 2-19.

Analysis of John 13:1—14:31

The Farewell Meal (Chapter 13:1–30)

If we are correct that John is not interested in speaking about Jesus' Last Supper as a specifically Jewish celebration of Passover, but rather as portraying a banquet that leads to discourses after the meal, then all speculation attempting to relate the account in the Fourth Gospel to the accounts of the Last Supper in the Synoptics is pointless. If John's Last Supper had any bearings on baptism or the Lord's Supper, we would hardly expect the washing of feet to be the prime object of attention. The foot washing rite points to the actual cleansing work of Christ on the cross, not to later sacraments such as baptism.

The account of the foot washing begins in 13:1 with an indication that Jesus knew that the hour to culminate his ministry had come. The Evangelist wishes to portray Jesus as being in control every step of the way, even to the point that he orders Judas to get on with his treachery (13:26), a feature not found in the Synoptic accounts of the Last Supper. The events of the Last Supper are enacted against the backdrop of a cosmic struggle between the powers of good and evil to be manifested in Judas's betrayal of Jesus (cf. 12:31; 14:30). While Christians traditionally personify evil, equating it with the devil, the main idea here is to identify that which is the opposite of God: dark instead of light, lies instead of truth, hatred instead of love. The love Jesus has for his disciples is contrasted with the evil the devil has put within the heart of Judas to betray Jesus (13:2). Judas's act of betrayal at a meal is more than an act of treachery; it violates a basic rule of ancient hospitality that one does not break fellowship with one's host while one is sharing in a meal.

In John 13:3 Jesus chooses to perform a dramatic act during the meal, enacting a task reserved for servants or slaves. This act should not be interpreted as Middle-Eastern hospitality shown by servants at the behest of the host, a ritual occurring before food is served. Here, in the middle of the meal, Jesus disrobes, ties a towel around himself, and proceeds to wash the feet of the disciples, apparently including Judas. Peter questions and then rejects this shocking behavior of his master, this role reversal with which he cannot comply. The statement by Jesus in 13:7 ("You do not know now what I am doing, but later you will understand") creates important context, for it points ahead to Peter's denials of Jesus (18:15–18, 25–27) and perhaps to Peter's eventual restoration as well

(John 21:15–19). When Peter asserts, "You will never wash my feet," Jesus replies: "Unless I wash you, you have no share with me." Peter needs to understand that to have fellowship with Jesus is to participate intimately and fully in his life and through him, with the Father. Peter's responds in 13:9, "Lord, not my feet only but also my hands and my head!" suggests that he locates the value of the foot washing in the cleansing power of the water and not in Jesus' offer of relationship. Jesus' reply in 13:10 ("One who has bathed does not need to wash, except for the feet") is sometimes taken as a reference to baptism and to the later Christian ritual of foot washing, but the focus here is Christological, not sacramental. "It is Jesus, not some rite, that cleanses in particular by his death, as is symbolized in this act of foot washing."[4]

The narrator inserts his comment in verse 11, "Not all of you are clean," to ensure that readers recognize Jesus' disclaimer at 13:10b as an allusion to the betrayal. The fact that the one who is not clean is the one who will betray Jesus confirms that cleanliness has to do with one's relationship to Jesus, not with the cleansing power of the water itself. To be unclean is not to be unwashed but to turn away from union and intimacy with Jesus. Earlier references to Judas' betrayal (6:70–71), then at 13:2, 11, and again in 13:21, could be warnings of Johannine Christians apostatizing and returning to the world, events transpiring when the Gospel and the letters of John were being written.

Having washed the feet of his disciples, Jesus then proceeds to interpret his act. As their Teacher and Lord (13:13), this act teaches something about their need and his provision of cleansing. He then suggests that they ought to wash one another's feet. Given the Gospel's lack of interest in sacraments in general,[5] John's Jesus is not alluding to a ritual that his followers should perpetuate, but rather to the practice of forgiveness and cleansing that he had symbolically depicted. Here as elsewhere in our reading of John's Gospel, we should look beyond the literal. Jesus sees his followers as his agents sent into the world to do what he has done, offering the same sort of loving and forgiving acts as he has performed. They, like Jesus, are called to perform self-sacrificial deeds, to exercise their authority in mutual humility. The following chapters reinforce this teaching, introducing a new commandment—mutual love based on Christ's love (13:34; 15:12–13; see 1 John 2:7–11; 4:7–12; 2 John 4–6). The expres-

---

4. Witherington, *John's Wisdom*, 236.
5. For additional discussion, see essay 8, "John's Sacramental Language."

sion *egō eimi* in 13:19 is correctly translated as "I am he," meaning the one about whom scripture spoke, rather than in the absolute sense of "I am," which implies a claim to deity or eternity.

This episode should not be simplified to a detached action containing a merely ethical lesson on humility. The foot washing is a symbolic depiction of the whole life of the Church, a manifestation of the love of God in the death of his Son. Purification from sin and the resultant love that binds the community together are grounded upon the complete obedience of Jesus to the will of the Father, including his humiliation unto death. This much, at least, is implied in 13:1–20.

John 13:21–30 is tied to the preceding scene with the words, "After saying this" in verse 21. As we noted earlier, the narrative of the foot washing places Jesus' act of service and love in the inescapable context of his betrayal. The notation that Jesus was "troubled" describes an emotional state of anger or indignation (see 11:33). Again, this reference must be placed against the context of his imminent betrayal by a disciple who is rejecting Jesus' offer of forgiveness and renewal; unbelief deeply upsets Jesus.

John 13:23 introduces a new character into the narrative, "the disciple whom Jesus loved." He is described as "reclining next to Jesus," likely an allusion to 1:18, where Jesus as God's Word is said to be "close to the Father's heart." Some commentators take the location of the Beloved Disciple next to Jesus as an indication of his role as host at the banquet, but surely this is incorrect, not because that designation exaggerates John's depiction of the Beloved Disciple, but rather because it minimizes John's intent. The Evangelist introduces the Beloved Disciple as standing in analogous relation to Jesus as Jesus to the Father. Elsewhere the Beloved Disciple stands as witness to Jesus much as Jesus is witness to the Father (21:24). These statements make exalted claims about the authenticity of the witness of the Beloved Disciple—he understood the mind and meaning of the Word of God.

In the betrayal scene, although Peter and Judas are the featured disciples, it is the Beloved Disciple who is depicted as sitting closest to Jesus, as is shown when Peter inquires through the Beloved Disciple whom Jesus had in mind as the betrayer. In view of 13:24, Peter seems to have been ranked next to the Beloved Disciple. The side to the right of the host was the most favored side at such meals, while the left-hand side was less favored and sometimes even had negative associations. Judas seems to have been seated on Jesus' left side. Satan enters Judas after Judas receives the bread from Jesus (cf. Ps. 41:9), and then at Jesus' command ("Do quickly what you are going to do") Judas immediately leaves the room. The story returns to the theme of knowing: "Now no one at the table knew why he said this to him" (13:28). The reference to Satan reminds the reader of the cosmic dimensions of the betrayal: the critical players in the betrayal are Jesus and Satan, not Jesus and Judas. Here, as elsewhere, Jesus is in charge, for Satan's work is framed by Jesus' initiative.

The scene ends abruptly with the revealing phrase: "And it was night" (13:30). This notation underscores the truth of Judas's identity. By removing himself from Jesus, who is the light of the world, Judas has demonstrated that he prefers the darkness. This verse brings home the truth in John's prologue: "The light shines in the darkness, and the darkness did not overcome it" (1:5).

Farewell Discourse One: Jesus Prepares His Disciples for His Death and Resurrection (Chapter 13:31—14:31)

This section reports further instruction, including the new commandment to love one another and the second conversation with Peter, both of which have significant connections with the foot washing account and with the Farewell Discourse that follows. In 13:31 Jesus' death is characterized as his "glorification," his glory veiled by the cross. The eschatological import of the announcement is underscored by the use of the title Son of Man. In this passage Jesus' and God's mutual glorification is depicted as a reality underway even as Jesus speaks. The arrival of Jesus' "hour" is now the governing theological reality. Past, present, and future are redefined in the light of the advent of the hour. Verse 31 thus heralds the eschatological hour (see 4:23; 5:24).

In John 13:33 Jesus repeats the riddle he has used twice before concerning his departure: "Where I am going, you cannot come" (see 7:33–36; 8:21–22). Earlier, when Jesus spoke to the "Jews," he pointed to his return to God as a moment of judgment. Here, his departure is presented to his disciples as the seal of their new relationship with God, with Jesus, and with one another (this is the only place in the Gospel where Jesus' followers are addressed as "little children," a term of intimacy; see 1 John 2:1, 12, 28; 3:7, 18; 4:4; 5:21).

Jesus then leaves the disciples with a new commandment: "Just as I have loved you, you also should love one another" (13:34). At first glance, it appears that Jesus is asking them to imitate his loving by their love for one another. Of course, his loving is indeed a model, but as Raymond Brown points out, more than that is intended here: "love is more than a commandment; it is a gift."[6] It is a commandment Christ's followers are unable to observe except for the fact that they are recreated to share the very life of God, which is love. This commandment sums up all previous ones. It is old (Lev. 19:18) yet also new in that it models the self-giving love of Christ and of God (3:16; 1 John 3:16). The "new" aspect of this commandment is that those who belong to Jesus are asked to enter into the love that denotes the relationship of the Father and Jesus. The demonstration of that love will be the primary witness to the world that they are Jesus' disciples.

The first part of the Farewell Discourse is interrupted four times by the disciples: Peter (13:36), Thomas (14:5), Philip (14:8), and Judas (not Iscariot, 14:22). The first discourse is structured around their questions. Their inquiries will allow Jesus to open their minds to the meaning of his death. Notice that the questions are asked by different disciples, indicating that it was not just one but all of the disciples who fail to understand Jesus. The disciples are not portrayed here as any more spiritually perceptive than previously, but at least a partial rationale for their obtuseness is provided in these discourses—they had not yet received the Paraclete who would lead them into all truth.

1. Peter's Question – *"Where are you going?"* (13:36—14:4). The Farewell Discourse really begins at 13:36 with Peter's question about where Jesus is going. Because verses 36 and 37 indicate that the disciples are troubled by Jesus' talk of leaving them, Jesus in this discourse wishes to relieve their fears and show that his leaving will work to their advantage. The "meaning" of the departure and its consequences for the disciples can be seen as the overarching theme of the unit. As in earlier chapters of John, the clue to understanding where Jesus came from and where he is going is to know his identity, namely, the perfect image and revelation of the Father, one who has come from God and will return to God. Peter, like the "Jews" before him, does not understand Jesus' words about his departure. Jesus' response in verse 36 ("Where I am going, you cannot follow me now; but you will follow afterward") anticipates the prophecy of Peter's future in 21:18–19, but Jesus' comments also correct Peter's misperception of the nature of Jesus' departure. Jesus is leaving his disciples in order to complete God's work and to make a new life

---

6. Brown, *John*, 2:612.

with God possible for them (14:2–3); they will not be able to follow him into that life until his exaltation (the sequence of death, resurrection, and ascension) is completed.

The dialogue between Jesus and Peter serves notice to the disciples (and the reader) that in significant ways Judas's betrayal is not an isolated case. The irony of Peter's pledging loyalty to Jesus, even unto his death ("I will lay down my life for you"; 13:37), is illustrated by Peter's misunderstanding the meaning of Jesus death. His pledge is ironic because Peter does not understand that Jesus is going to the Father by means of his death, or that eventually Peter would indeed lay down his life (21:19). Jesus confronts Peter with reality: Peter's shallow pledge will be followed by his denying Jesus three times (13:38). The contrast is clear between knowledge and ignorance of the truth conveyed by Jesus' death. This contrast is fundamental to the plot of the entire Gospel, and will be developed further in the events leading to Jesus' death.[7]

Faith rather than fear is the called-for response in 14:1: "Do not let your hearts be troubled. Believe in God, believe also in me." In all likelihood "believe in" here is in the imperative and means "Trust in God, trust also in me." In 14:2 Jesus assures the disciples that there is room for them in his Father's house. The term "house" reflects the Greek *oikia* (rather than *oikos*, the building), meaning "household" or "family" (cf. 14:23, where the same noun is used). By having Jesus tell the disciples that there are many "dwelling places" (lit. "abiding places"), the Evangelist prepares readers for the discussion about "abiding" in 15:4–11. William Tyndale, a Reformation scholar, translated the term "rooms," leading to the well-known mistranslation in the King James Bible: "In my Father's house are many mansions."

John 14:2–3 is often interpreted as a promise that Jesus is going to prepare a place in heaven for the disciples, but that is not Johannine theology. Jewish traditions did identify the "Father's house" with a heavenly dwelling place (Ps. 2:4; 66:1; 113:5–6; Isa. 66:1), but it is critical to the interpretation of Jesus' words here that the reference to "my father's house" not be taken as a synonym for heaven.[8] Instead, this reference needs to be read in the context of the mutual indwelling of God and Jesus, a form of "residence" stressed in the prologue (1:1, 18). Throughout the Gospel, location has consistently been a symbol for relationship (cf. 1:18). Jesus'

---

7. Culpepper, *Gospel and Letters*, 209.
8. O'Day, *John*, 740.

description as one who comes from heaven (3:31; 6:41, 51; cf. 3:12–13) confirms his origins with God. To know Jesus' origin (where he is from) is to know his relationship with God. By the end of the chapter John has brought his own "realized eschatology" to bear on the hope of being with Jesus in this life (14:23, 28). The disciples are not concerned about where they will go after they die, but how they will relate to Jesus since he is going away.

Jesus assures the disciples that he is going to prepare a place for them, and that he will come again to be with them (14:2–3). Because the reference is ambiguous, three options are generally suggested: that Jesus is referring (a) to his return from death on Easter, (b) to his Second Coming, or (c) to a more individual coming for believers at their death, ushering them into the eternal home. Given John's eschatological perspective, the first option seems preferable. To turn Jesus' promise here into language about Jesus' coming to individual believers at their death or at some time in the distant future is to misconstrue the eschatological significance of the promise. His return enacts the eschatological announcement of the Lazarus story: "I am the resurrection and the life" (11:25). That assertion is the ultimate witness to the power of God over life and death, and this power is the mark of the new age. Jesus' promised return to his disciples thus functions as "the seal of the new eschatological reality ushered in by the events of his hour."[9] We must bear in mind that in a sense Jesus *is* the dwelling place of the believer, who dwells or abides in him. Earlier in the Gospel Jesus spoke of the temple as his body (2:21), reflecting on the concept of the temple as the place where one meets God. But as Jesus will explain in 14:6, he is the way to the Father; he is God's agent—on earth and in heaven.

Because Jesus, as divine Word, goes to the Father through his death, resurrection, and ascension, like the Father, he will be everywhere at once. Johannine Christians viewed themselves as already in heaven in the sense that they were already abiding in the Son and experiencing even in this life the fruit of that abiding—eternal life. According to Johannine theology, heaven begins on earth for believers (much as for the author of Revelation, eternal life is on earth; Rev. 21:2–7).

2. Thomas's Question – *"How can we know the way?"* (14:5–7). In 14:1–4 Jesus reassures the disciples that he is going to prepare a place for them and that he will return to them. When he adds that the disciples

9. Ibid., 741.

already know how to reach this wonderful destination, Thomas objects, pointing out that they know neither the place where he is going nor the way. Jesus responds with his sixth "I am" saying: "I am the way, and the truth, and the life" (14:6). It has been suggested that the three terms in that phrase are related in that "the way" is the process, "the truth" is the means or goal, and "the life" is the result. While that approach is attractive, it is misleading, for John is presenting one clear solution here, stating what Jesus had said earlier, that he is "the gate for the sheep" (10:7). "The way" is not a geographical term, as Thomas perceived it, but is instead a description of the revelatory work of Jesus. To "know the way" is thus synonymous with knowing Jesus himself. Interestingly, the term "way" is used of the Christian movement in Acts (9:2; 19:9, 23; 22:4; 24:14, 22), as it seems to have been used earlier by Jewish sectaries in the communities that wrote the Dead Sea Scrolls (1QS 9:16–21). In the Greco-Roman world, the term "way" was widely used symbolically to refer to a way of life or a philosophical practice. John also uses the term to speak of following Jesus. For John, the journey into the reality of God is both inward and outward, a way of living whereby one discovers the freedom of giving oneself away. One of the names of this journey is *martyria* (cf. Acts 1:8, where *martyres* is translated "witnesses" but literally means "martyrs"); another is "embodied faith."

Since God is the source of all truth and life, and Jesus is the way to God and the one who embodies God's gifts, Jesus is also the truth and the life. These two nouns are concrete terms whose specific Christological content has been demonstrated throughout Jesus' life and ministry. If "life" may be said to be the key term in the first half of John (thirty-one times in John 1—12 and only four thereafter), "truth" is the characteristic theme in John 13—21 (twelve instances).[10]

The irony of Jesus' statement in 14:6b is its exclusivity: "No one comes to the Father except through me." This claim is central to the faith of many Christians, for Christianity is a missionary religion, but it poses an insurmountable obstacle to faith for believers and unbelievers alike in today's pluralistic climate. Japanese Christian Dickson Kazuo Yagi, a third-generation Japanese American convert from Buddhism, writes of his struggle with a Christian gospel that presents two centers: faith (epitomized by Paul) and love (epitomized by John). A gospel with two polarities presents modern people with tensions that cannot be reduced to only

---

10. Witherington, *John's Wisdom*, 249–50.

one center. "Just as Christians who do not love are solidly rejected by one center, non-Christians who do love are affirmed by the other center."[11]

Properly interpreted, the statement in 14:6b should be placed in historical and cultural context, for it presupposes a bitter polemic between Christ-confessing and Christ-denying Jews, whereby confessors are being expelled from synagogues for their belief (9:22). According to D. Moody Smith, "the assumption that there is no way to the Father, and that Jesus has opened one (Heb. 10:20) and has become himself that way, is probably a more accurate reading of this statement than the assumption that there are many ways to the Father and that the Johannine Jesus is closing off all save one, himself"[12] (cf. 1:18, where the classical Jewish belief that humans cannot see God is reflected).

John's Gospel presents a symbol of cosmic power and universal hope. According to John 1:9, Christ is the true light that enlightens everyone. As Wisdom, the Logos was the creative agent, manifesting God's design and power in all the creation. Describing the work of the Logos by drawing from the Jewish Wisdom tradition, the Evangelist utilizes the universal phenomenon of Wisdom to highlight how inadequate exclusivist religious belief systems are in light of our contemporary pluralistic world. The exclusivist claims of the Fourth Gospel, such as that cited above, must therefore be understood in the context of John's opening claim that the revelation that came through Jesus Christ is the same as that which is universally present in the Logos. In this respect the Fourth Gospel undercuts the triumphalism of claims that Christendom has a monopoly on the revelation of Christ. Such an understanding of Logos Christology "allows Christians to affirm that adherents of other religious traditions may come to know God through the work of the Cosmic Christ."[13]

3. Philip's Request – "*Show us the Father*" (14:8-21). Philip's request reflects a misunderstanding of Jesus' function as the Logos and the fundamental reality of the incarnation. Jesus' answer is emphatic: "Whoever has seen me has seen the Father" (14:9). While Philip's request seems astounding, he gets an equally amazing response—the one who has seen Jesus *has* seen the Father. While the union between Jesus and the Father has been described as mystical, moral, or metaphysical, viewed independently each is misleading, for none capture John's essential understanding

---

11. Cited in Culpepper, *Gospel and Letters*, 301.
12. Smith, *John*, 269.
13. Ibid., 302.

of agency. Once again the point is not that Jesus *is* the Father but that he is the expression of the very mind and character of God.

As in John 5:30–42, Jesus appeals to his words and his works as witnesses to the truth of his claims (14:10–11). Because God is revealed in Jesus, knowledge of God through faith is the supreme calling of the believer (note that 14:11–12 returns to the exhortation in 14:1). The one who believes can then be part of the "greater works" that Jesus will do after his resurrection: "the one who believes in me will also do the works that I do and, in fact, will do greater works than these, because I am going to the Father" (14:12). What John has in mind here is akin to Matthew's Great Commission (Matt. 28:19–20). The future works will be greater not because they will be better or more spectacular, but because they will be more extensive (the mission and spread of the church) and because they will be executed through the agency of the Paraclete. Unless Jesus dies and returns to the Father, there can be no sending of the Spirit, nor can Jesus respond to the believers' prayers unless he is in heaven. In 14:13 ("I will do whatever you ask in my name") the phrase "ask in my name" involves asking in accord with the character and will of Jesus. Such asking rules out mundane things and focuses on Jesus' mission to glorify the Father (14:14). John 14:15–16 ("If you love me, you will keep my commandments. And I will ask the Father, and he will give you another Advocate, to be with you forever") utilizes a conditional statement to underscore that all depends on the believer's loving Jesus. Notice the juxtaposition of loving and keeping Jesus' commandments, which leads to his sending the Advocate (Paraclete). If one does the former, Jesus will send the latter, and the Spirit will remain a permanent possession, as it was for Jesus, who, unlike the Old Testament prophets, is said to possess the Spirit continually (1:32; 14:16).

The Spirit is a major player in the Fourth Gospel, unlike in Matthew or Mark, where mention of the Spirit is infrequent. John 14:16 is the first occurrence of the term Paraclete in the Fourth Gospel. This is the only New Testament document that uses the noun Paraclete to describe the Holy Spirit. Paraclete is not simply another name for the Spirit, but is a particular way of describing the functions of the Spirit, functions held in common with Jesus. What the Paraclete does is not new, but is a continuation of the work of Jesus. This can be seen clearly in the description of the Paraclete as the "Spirit of truth" in 14:17a. As the Spirit of truth, the Paraclete shares in the work of Jesus, because Jesus is the truth (14:6).

The work of the Paraclete is thus to keep the truth of Jesus present in the world after Jesus' departure (16:7–11).

Knowledge of the Paraclete is defined as the Paraclete's abiding with the believing community: "You know him, because he abides with you, and he will be in you" (14:17b). The Paraclete is repeatedly described in ways that emphasize its presence in and relationship with the faith community. Since this section of the Gospel is especially directed to disciples, it follows that the Spirit's role must have a great deal to do with the essential condition and function of disciples after Jesus' lifetime. The promise of continuing presence made by Jesus in 14:18–20 is the first in a series of promises in the Farewell Discourse that finds fulfillment in Jesus' Easter appearances (see also 14:27; 16:16, 20, 22). The language in 14:18–20 also highlights the eschatological dimension of the promise, recalling the traditional language of the *parousia* (Second Coming): "I am coming to you" (14:18). The notion of the *parousia* is transformed, however, for the events of Jesus' hour are said to usher in a new age of intimacy with God: "On that day you will know that I am in my Father, and you in me, and I in you" (14:20).

The Greek term *paraklētos* (Paraclete) conveys a variety of translational nuances. The most common translation is Advocate, a concept that connotes someone's defense attorney or judicial agent. In John 14:16 the Spirit is Jesus' representative, who enables believers to confront whatever trials they may face, as well as equipping them for effective witness. In addition, the Spirit's presence comforts and consoles the disciples, bringing them peace and joy despite Jesus' physical absence. Hence the translation "Comforter" found in the King James translation. In Romans 12:8 a similar word is translated "proclaim or exhort," meaning that the term Paraclete can also be translated "Proclaimer." The Fourth Evangelist seems to draw on the entire range of meanings in the five Paraclete passages of the Farewell Discourse (see also 14:26; 15:26; 16:8–11, 12–15), combining rich and varied meanings to create a new concept.[14]

When Jesus says that the Father will give "another" Paraclete (14:16), John evidently intends for readers to understand Jesus as having been a Paraclete also. The Spirit's role as Paraclete is to continue doing what Jesus began. The language of agency is particularly appropriate here; as Jesus was the Father's agent, so the Spirit is Jesus' earthly agent (see 16:13–15). The Spirit will equip the disciples with the presence of Jesus

---

14. For additional information on the Johannine view of the Spirit see the discussion in the Epilogue as well as Kysar, *Maverick Gospel*, 126–32 and Brown, *John*, 2:1135–44.

and the understanding of Jesus' teaching, as well as with the power to convict others when witnessing to the world. The Spirit is the surrogate of Jesus when he leaves the earth. The Spirit is basically not an innovator, but by reminding them of Jesus' teaching leads the disciples into the truth already conveyed by the Son (14:26). The Spirit is seen as a source of continuing revelation for the disciples, a revelation ultimately going back to the exalted Jesus.

An intriguing correspondence exists between the promised work of the Paraclete and the functions that John attributes to the Beloved Disciple. Like the Paraclete, the Beloved Disciple guides the community, bears witness to Jesus, reminds members of all that Jesus had said, and possibly defends the community in times of conflict. Naturally, he did not remain with them forever (see 21:23), but "the parallels in function are sufficiently strong to suggest that the Johannine community recognized that the Paraclete was at work in the Beloved Disciple."[15]

The rudiments of a doctrine of the Trinity are present in John's Gospel, for Father, Son, and Spirit act as divinity; all bear the divine presence and power and all are deeply personal. Even the Spirit is seen as personal—the term *paraklētos* is masculine, not neuter. Yet there is a functional subordination of the Son to the Father and of the Spirit to the Son. A controversial point arises at 14:16, with profound historical implications for eastern and western branches of Christianity. In that verse, the Father is invoked as giver of the Paraclete, whereas in other Paraclete passages, the relationship is nuanced differently. While John 14:26 most closely resembles 14:16, at 15:26 and 16:7 Jesus speaks of himself as the one who sends the Paraclete. This interchange of the roles of the Father and Jesus in the description of the Paraclete's origin is not a theological inconsistency in the discourse, but rather is a further demonstration of a vital theological perspective in this Gospel, that the Father and Jesus are united and share fully in the work that they do (5:17, 19; 10:30, 37–38).

One of the early achievements of the church was the attainment of broad agreement on the text of the Nicene Creed (325). For some time, this document provided stability to the church, both Eastern and Western. The agreed text referred to the Holy Spirit as "proceeding from the Father." By the ninth century, however, the Western (Latin-speaking) church routinely altered this phrase, speaking of the Holy Spirit "proceeding from the Father and the Son." This Latin term, *filioque*, which means

---

15. Culpepper, *Gospel and Letters*, 212.

"and from the Son," came to represent the idea of a "double procession" of the Holy Spirit, thereby raising serious theological difficulties for Eastern (Greek-speaking) Christians. The basic issue at stake is whether the Spirit may be said to proceed from the Father alone or from the Father and the Son. The former position is associated with the Eastern church, the latter with the Western. The Greek patristic writers insisted on only one source of being within the Trinity, meaning that the Father alone was the cause of all things. For them, the Son is begotten of the Father, while the Spirit proceeds from the Father. Failure to distinguish between these modes of proceeding would lead to God having two sons, which raised insurmountable problems. The Greek fathers argued that by introducing the term *filioque*, the West had depersonalized the Spirit and thereby reduced the Godhead to an impersonal principle. Their intention was to safeguard the individuality of the three persons of the Trinity, while maintaining the unique position of the Father as the sole source of divinity. The Latin intention, however, was to safeguard the unity of God, ensuring that the Son and Spirit were adequately distinguished from one another, yet mutually related to one another. The ill will that resulted from this disagreement contributed to the split between the Eastern and Western churches, which took place in 1054.

4. Judas's (not Iscariot's) Question – *"How is it that you will reveal yourself to us, and not to the world?"* (14:22-31). The interrelatedness in the life of the believing community of the love of Jesus, the keeping of Jesus' commandments, and the indwelling of the divine presence is evident in the promise of presence in 14:23: "Those who love me will keep my word, and my Father will love them, and we will come to them and make our home with them." In 14:21 Jesus links his love for those who love him with his self-revelation ("and I will love them and reveal myself to them"), but Judas's question in verse 22 ("How is it that you will reveal yourself to us, and not to the world?") shows that he misunderstands this linkage. In looking for a messianic sign that will impress the world, Judas does not recognize Jesus' love as the manifestation he seeks.

Readers who attempt to harmonize this second Judas with any Synoptic lists of the Twelve will be frustrated, for the name of this Judas does not appear elsewhere. On the whole, John does not restrict the disciples to the Twelve. As is typical of Jesus' teaching (cf. 3:4-8; 4:12-14; 14:5-7), he does not directly address Judas's misunderstanding, but instead restates his words about love and revelation (14:23). When the disciples live in love, and thereby obey Jesus, they experience the love of God, through which they will also experience the indwelling of God and Jesus. The word translated as "home" in 14:23 is the same noun translated as "dwelling place" in 14:2. In 14:2–3 faith in Jesus leads to the disciples' communion with God and Jesus, whereas at 14:23 love of Jesus leads to the same end. To love Jesus is to live with God and Jesus—that is, to enter into relationship with them (15:9–10, 12).

John 14:25–31 concludes the first farewell discourse by recapitulating themes of 14:1–24 (see verse 25). The discourse ends with the affirmation both that Jesus is going away and that in another sense he is coming to them: "You heard me say to you, 'I am going away, and I am coming to you.' If you love me, you would rejoice that I am going to the Father, because the Father is greater than I" (14:28). He tells this to the disciples in advance so they will be prepared when it happens (14:29). The "ruler of this world" is about to come and do his worst with Jesus, but he really has no ultimate power over Jesus, who has chosen to act in this manner, in accordance with the will of his Father, not with the demands of temporal powers (14:30–31). On one level, the "ruler of this world" coming to arrest Jesus is Caesar, whose soldiers will take Jesus to his death not many hours later. At another level, it is the dark power that stands behind tyrannical rulers, the spiritual force of wickedness called Satan. The phrase "the world" gets its negative force in John's Gospel from Jewish apocalyptic thought, which finds few "gray areas" in life's spiritual (and therefore social, political, and economic) struggles. Jesus' approaching death and resurrection will inflict a lethal wound on "the world's" rule, though opposition will remain potent and imposing (see 16:18–26).

When Jesus states that "the Father is greater than I" in John 14:28, "greater" should be interpreted to mean greater in power and authority (4:12; 8:53; 10:29; 13:16; 1 John 3:20). In the fourth century, at the time of the Council of Nicaea, Arius and his followers detached this phrase from its context (14:28), locating a counterpart in the Septuagint translation of Proverbs 8:22, "The Lord created me." The Athanasian Creed reflects more accurately John's intention as applying to the incarnation: "Equal to the Father, as touching his Godhead; and inferior to the Father, as touching his Manhood." Athanasius's argument at the Council of Nicaea still persuades: "if Jesus is not God, his worship is idolatry, and humans remain in their sin." Of course, the Nicene debate is foreign to the Fourth Gospel, which is less concerned with the relation between the Father and the Son than with the relation between the Father, the Son, and the disciples. John's Gospel promotes salvation through the worship of God, not the revelation of an independent Jesus.

In his first farewell discourse, Jesus reveals his legacy to the disciples. He has commanded them to love one another (13:34–35; 14:21, 23). Now he leaves them his peace, "Peace I leave with you; my peace I give to you. I do not give to you as the world gives. Do not let your hearts be troubled, and do not let them be afraid" (14:27). This peace is not the absence of conflict but inner peace in the face of conflict because the Spirit dwells in them. In the next chapter Jesus adds joy to this legacy of love and peace.

Essay 8: John's Sacramental Language

The first thing one notes about John's Gospel is that the author avoids talking about the sacraments of the Lord's Supper (the Eucharist) or baptism.[16] Nowhere does he mention or discuss Jesus' baptism by John the Baptist. While he does mention John's baptismal activity in general, he does so only as a precursor and foil for the baptism with the Spirit that will come from Jesus (1:30–34). Further, when the Evangelist discusses the Last Supper, he avoids saying anything substantive about the meal aspect of the supper, omitting any comment about the significance or symbolic interpretation of the wine or bread (13:1–12).

However, some scholars find implicit reference to the sacraments in the following passages: 2:1–11; 3:5; 6:1–13, 51–59; 13:1–17; 15:1–6; and 19:34. They argue that the transformation of water into wine in the story of the wedding at Cana implies the wine of the Eucharist. They view Jesus' statement that one must be born "of water and Spirit" in 3:5 as an allusion to baptism. They understand the feeding of the multitude in chapter 6 to be the Johannine institution of the Last Supper. In 6:11, when Jesus gives thanks and distributes the bread and fish, the Greek word translated "gave thanks," *eucharistēsas*, is the root of the word Eucharist. For these interpreters, the Eucharistic meaning of the feeding of the crowd is made explicit in the speech of Jesus in 6:51–58, particularly in the statement, "unless you eat the flesh of the Son of Man and drink his blood, you have no life in you" (6:53). Others find the washing of the disciples' feet in chapter 13 to be a symbolic representation of the meaning of the Eucharist. Some also interpret the allegory of the vine (15:1–6) as a reference to the Eucharistic wine, and find in 19:34, which speaks of blood and water

---

16. The following discussion is adapted from Kysar, *Maverick Gospel*, 143–47.

flowing from Jesus' side, a possible representation of the Eucharistic cup and baptism. According to this understanding, the Fourth Evangelist is a sacramentalist of the highest kind.

Other scholars propose a drastic alternative: the Fourth Gospel is antisacramental. While the Johannine community knows about the sacraments, its members are alarmed by their abuse in the larger church of the time. Perhaps this concern underlies the dismissive statement "the flesh is useless" in 6:63. Believing that the sacraments have come to take the place of Christ himself, the Evangelist ignores them altogether. According to this view, whatever sacramental presence may be found in John is due to a later editor, who inserted words such as "water and" in 3:5 and the entire discussion in 6:52–58. Furthermore, the latter passage follows verse 51, with its emphasis on the way of the cross rather than on cultic rite. John's point to the Jews in 6:52–58 is that if they wish to have eternal life, it is Jesus and his death that they are required to "swallow," and it is precisely Jesus' divine claims and his death that they can't stomach.[17] Hence the incarnate Word, Jesus, and particularly his death, not the Passover or the Lord's Supper, is central. The emphasis in John is upon solidarity with Jesus and his followers, not upon the Eucharistic rite, if one expects to receive eternal life.

A third view claims that the Johannine church was not acquainted with the tradition of the sacraments because Johannine Christians represented a movement out of the mainstream of early Christianity. In this assessment, John's followers were neither sacramental nor antisacramental but rather nonsacramental. If this last alternative was the case, then the references often argued to be sacramental must be read differently. In the "bread of life" discourse of John 6 that follows the loaves and fish miracle, references to "gave thanks" and "eat flesh" are not Eucharistic, for the miracle that prompted the discourse involved bread and fish, not bread and wine. In addition, the crowd is depicted as receiving "as much as they wanted" (6:11), not sacramental-sized portions. Such an understanding must also be borne in mind when reading texts like John 3:1–12 or 1 John 5:6–8. Thus, without intending sacramental meaning, the Gospel could well use words that elsewhere in the Christian movement were associated with the sacraments. Obviously, some sacramental-sounding passages could have been later additions.

---

17. Witherington, *John's Wisdom*, 149.

The problem may elude solution. Whether Johannine Christians were sacramental or not, the focus of John's Gospel is Jesus Christ, the person to whom all the signs and sayings point. The Gospel does not pause more than briefly to reflect on a sign's qualities, characteristics, or elements. In none of the seven sign miracles is there any interest in describing how such occurred, only that it did happen, thereby pointing to the power and glory of the one performing the sign. It is not accidental that neither Christian baptism nor the Lord's Supper is the subject of a single discourse in John, even under the guise of ritual washings, John's baptism, or the Passover meal. The Johannine community seemed interested in focusing on Christological, not sacramental matters.

However, this is not to say that the Gospel ignores the sacraments, for there is a fundamental sacramentality about Johannine theology, which is sensory. John's suggestion that faith grows from everyday physical experiences is precisely what the sacraments signify in Christian thought. When the Gospel asserts that seeing and hearing stimulate the growth of faith, it proposes sacramentality, for the sacraments are sensory experiences epitomizing God's presence in ordinary realities.

Johannine Christianity evidently maintained a primitive form of the fellowship meal, which emphasized faithfulness to Jesus and his community as a factor of costly discipleship. The primitive Christian Eucharist did not consist merely of partaking of the bread and wine. It was the occasion of formally recognizing the redemptive significance of the death of the Lord and of prophetic and didactic discourse. John 13—17 records such a setting, a tripartite pattern modeled by Jesus, where the Lord (a) purifies his guests (13:1–17), (b) delivers a Eucharistic discourse (14:1—16:33), and (c) offers the prayer of thanksgiving (17:1-26). Celebrating the Lord's ministry and sacrifice together in community through table fellowship, not formalized rite, is emphasized in passages such as John 6:53–58, 13:1-17, and 21:15-19. This celebration is because the Evangelist's sacramentology was *incarnational* rather than cultic.

If a sacrament can be described as a physical and outward expression of a spiritual and inward reality, a living person has a greater capacity to convey the saving love and presence of God than do inanimate means or objects—including rites, forms, and symbols. God's revealing work in John takes place most powerfully through persons: because God loved the world, the Father sent the Son; the Word became flesh; and that Word gave the Holy Spirit. In John baptism is not a hydraulic reality but a pneumatic one. John baptizes with water, but Jesus baptizes with the Holy Spirit.

Likewise, the essence of communion in John is true faith in Jesus, true discipleship, and the benefits thereof. For John, incarnational sacramentology finds expression in Jesus, the embodied expression of God's love in the world, and in authentic discipleship, characterized by love for another. Authentic followers of Jesus demonstrate the same love that the Father and the Son shared from the beginning of time until the present day (13:35; 17:26). John's incarnational sacramentology deepens our understanding of how God's love is encountered and conveyed in the world.[18]

The Fourth Gospel, then, is neither sacramental nor anti-sacramental; those categories are misleading. By careful use of language, John drives people to the reality of Christ, refusing to focus instead on pointers to that reality.

Questions to Ponder

1. What does Jesus' act of foot washing symbolize about his ministry? How does this relate to Jesus' words in 13:8?

2. What was the essence of the charge Jesus gave his disciples in John 13:12–17? How is this related to the sentiment expressed in 13:1b?

3. How do Jesus' actions and words in John 13:1–17 demonstrate his purpose as Messiah? How do they compare with the popular view of the Messiah's vocation and strategy?

4. What does the account of the betrayal by Judas tell us about the nature of evil? Do you find John's explanation adequate?

5. In your own words, decipher Jesus' teaching about glorification in 13:31–32. How do these verses compare with John 12:23–28?

6. How would you explain the meaning of John 14:6 to a person of another religious faith?

7. How are love and obedience connected in John 14:15–31?

8. What roles are given to the Paraclete in John 14:15–17 and 26–27?

9. How would your life be different if Jesus had not given his followers the Holy Spirit?

10. What role do the sacraments play in John's Gospel? If you are a Christian, what role do they play in your life?

18. Anderson, *Riddles*, 229–31.

CHAPTER 9

Jesus' Farewell: Part Two
(John 15:1—17:26)

Summary: John 13:31—16:33 contain four discourses of Jesus. Discourse One (John 13:36—14:31) contains teachings of Jesus punctuated by questions from his disciples, whereas Discourse Two (15:1-17) and Three (15:18—16:4a) consist exclusively of Jesus' teachings. Chapter 15 contains the extended metaphor of the vine and the branches (15:1-11), as well as a restatement of the love commandment (15:12-17). Together these two sections articulate the theme of abiding love. Discourse Three (15:18—16:4a) warns about persecution and mentions the role of the Paraclete in the experience of persecution. Discourse Four (16:4b-33) returns to the themes of consolation and assurance in the face of Jesus' departure, but with a particular focus on the role of the Paraclete in offering that consolation (16:7-15). The farewell discourses are followed by Jesus' closing prayer in 17:1-26, which brings to a climax this subsection of the Gospel.

Assignment: Read John 15-17

Key Passages: John 15:5; 16:13, 33; 17:3, 17-18, 22-23

Central Theme: Abiding in Jesus

Key Symbols/Concepts: vine, branches, abiding in Jesus, persecution, Advocate (Paraclete), testify, judgment, asking and receiving, peace, glorification, eternal life, truth, unity, glory

Learning Objectives

Participants will examine:

1. The metaphorical meaning of the vine and the branches in John 15:1–17
2. John's teaching about the nature of discipleship in John 15:1–17
3. The metaphorical meaning of "abide" in John 15:1–17
4. The warning about persecution in John 15:18—16:4a
5. The extended role of the Paraclete in John 15—17
6. The role of the Paraclete in John 16:8–11
7. The meaning of "Spirit of truth" in John 15:26 and 16:13 (see also 14:17)
8. The meaning of "a little while" in John 16:16–19
9. The meaning of "asking and receiving" in John 16:23–24, 26
10. The main themes of Jesus' prayer in John 17
11. The meaning of "sanctify" in John 17:17 and 19
12. John's use or irony and misunderstanding as literary techniques

Outline to John 15:1—17:26

I. Farewell Discourse Two: Abiding Love 15:1–17

    A. Metaphor of the Vine and the Branches 15:1–11

    B. Restatement of the Love Commandment 15:12–17

II. Farewell Discourse Three: Warning about Persecution 15:18—16:4a

III. Farewell Discourse Four: The Consequences of Jesus' Departure for His Disciples 16:4b–33

    A. The Work of the Paraclete 16:4b–15

    B. Sorrow and Joy 16:16–24

    C. Speaking Plainly 16:25–33

IV. Jesus Prayer of Consecration 17:1–26

    A. Jesus' Prayer for Himself 17:1–5

    B. Jesus' Prayer for His Disciples 17:6–19

C. Jesus' Prayer for All Believers 17:20–26

Jewish Parallelism

In his commentary on John, C. K. Barrett stresses the parallels between the first farewell discourse (13:31—14:31) and the extended one in John 15—17. In both places we have discussion of some of the same matters: Jesus' relation to the Father; his departure to the Father; his coming again; his revelation of the Father; prayer in his name; keeping his commandments; the Paraclete; the peace Jesus gives; and judgment, whether of the world or devil.

Barrett's explanation, that we have here alternate versions of the same discourse, is quite likely incorrect. Repetition is a common feature in Jewish teaching, especially sapiential teaching, and frequently involves looking at one subject from numerous angles (the speeches in the book of Job exemplify clearly this literary element). Repetition is also a feature of Johannine style. The best explanation is that the Farewell Address consists of successive discourses given in a short span of time on related themes. The first discourse (13:31—14:31) is the most unified and reveals the clearest logical progression.

As previously mentioned, 14:31 includes a distinct break in the discourse: "Rise, let us be on our way." These words, taken at face value, seem to end the discourse and to set in motion some other event, perhaps the passion itself (one can imagine 14:31 followed by 18:1). But the discourse continues and the passion event is still three chapters away. Scholars are accustomed to seeing here an editorial seam, evidence of various sources spliced together by the final editor of the Gospel, who simply overlooked the statement in 14:31. L. William Countryman disagrees, finding evidence here of a Jewish way of transitioning from a preliminary reading to a mystical reading. "This division is important for the reader precisely because the second discourse will rework material from the first and the reader needs a sense of a new beginning in order not to become disoriented. Mystically, the words ["Rise, let us be on our way"] can be read as an announcement that Jesus is about to move to a new level of speech."[1] While his explanation is unconvincing, it serves to remind us that the worlds of ancient Judaism and early Christianity are exceedingly complex

---

1. Countryman, *Mystical Way*, 105.

and that we should approach scripture with awe and respect, never rushing to conclusions or assuming certainty.

Analysis of 15:1—17:26

Farewell Discourse Two: Abiding Love (Chapter 15:1–17)

Despite words of departure in 14:31, the background is still the Last Supper, and the Farewell Discourse continues. Chapters 15 and 16 represent the epitome of the Christian experience. While 15:1—17 focuses mainly on the inward life of the Christian community and 15:18—16:4a on the community's outward relationship to the world, there is a relationship between the two sections. If John 14 presents Jesus as the way (the means) to relationship with the Father, John 15 focuses on the end product of such a relationship, the abiding results of relating to Jesus in that way. Nevertheless, the issue here is not only abiding in Christ but also in bearing fruit for Christ. The apostasy of "the Jews," of Judas, and of the unbelieving disciples (see 6:41, 52, 60, 66, 70, 71) here reappears in the figure of useless branches contrasted with those that are fruitful (see 6:68).

The basic structure of 15:1–8 is that verses 1–4 identify Jesus in relationship to the Father and verses 5–8 in relationship to the disciples. At 15:1 we find John's seventh and final "I am" sayings, "I am the true vine"; as in previous examples, the announcement is made twice for emphasis (15:1 and 4). While the other "I am" sayings focus on coming to Jesus, this one speaks to those who have already come and thus emphasizes remaining or "abiding" (this word occurs ten times in verses 4–10), as well as bearing fruit.

Like the true light (1:9) and the true bread from heaven (6:32), Jesus is said to be the "true" vine because he comes from the Father (see "the only true God" in 17:3). In addition to origin, the word "true" in 15:1 emphasizes dependability; those who abide in Jesus can trust in him, for he is trustworthy. The background for this imagery is the Old Testament, where one finds vineyard symbolism consonant with its use in John 15. The song of the vineyard (Isa. 5:1–7) offers an example of "vine" as a symbol for Israel. The failure of Judah to live in justice and righteousness is expressed through the metaphor of not yielding fruit: God, the planter, expected grapes, but Judah produced only wild grapes (Isa. 5:2, 4). These verses also use the language of pruning to describe God's actions toward the vineyard (Isa. 5:5–6). Similar imagery appears in Jeremiah 2:21,

Ezekiel 15:1-8; 19:10-14, Hosea 10:1, and Psalm 80:8-19. These and other passages conclude with a description of the corruption of the vine: faithless Israel is compared to the burned branch.

In John's version Jesus is the vine, the Father is the gardener in the vineyard, and the disciples are the branches on the vine. The vine is God's, for Jesus is the Son of God. The Father takes away the unprofitable branches and prunes those that bear fruit; the result of pruning is much fruit (15:5). The passage should not be misconstrued as a text on predestination or eternal security. The focus is not on believers losing salvation or being eternally secure, but on bearing fruit. The intent of the passage is not to frighten believers into thinking they can be cut off ("removed") from the vine (15:2; cf. 15:6). Rather, those that are unproductive are pruned ("cleansed"), as 15:3 makes clear. The Greek verb *kathairō* has the double meaning of "to prune" and "to cleanse." In verse 2 the translation of *kathairō* ("to prune") evokes agricultural realism, whereas its use in verse 3 ("to cleanse") suggests theological truth. The idea "You have already been cleansed" in 15:3 was used earlier, in the foot washing episode, where Jesus described all but one of his disciples as clean (13:10-11). Despite their cleansing, the disciples should expect to be further pruned, just as Peter after his denial of Jesus would experience the restorative pruning that followed (21:15-19).

John 15:7-10 is an example of the interweaving of themes that characterizes the Farewell Discourse. In these verses the themes of the first farewell discourse (13:31—14:31) are revisited in the context of the vineyard imagery of 15:1-6. For example, verse 7 echoes the promises of 14:13-14. Verse 8 reaffirms the claim of 14:12-14 that the community's works continue the glorification of God that characterizes Jesus' works. To bear fruit—that is, to do works of love—is the tangible sign of discipleship (see 13:34-35). Verses 9 and 10 make the connections between John 14 and 15 explicit; the ground of the community's abiding with Jesus is the love that God and Jesus share with each other and that the community is called to enact (14:20-24, 31). Jesus words about joy in 15:11 complement 14:28.

The request to "ask for whatever you wish" in Jesus's name (15:7) presupposes that one will ask only for things that are consonant with Jesus' will and with abiding in Christ and in his word (in verse 10 abiding is said to be contingent upon obedience to Jesus' word). Clearly, "abiding" requires ongoing effort on the part of the believer as well as on the part of Christ and the Spirit (note the emphasis on mutual abiding in 15:4, 5, and

10). Here as elsewhere in this Gospel we find a close relationship between love and obedience. Whereas in 15:10 the reference is to commandments (plural), in verse 12 the word becomes singular, meaning that love of God and of others belong together. The love commandment, therefore, encapsulates the whole of God's demands on the disciple.

John 15:12–17 focuses even more directly than verses 1–11 on what it means for the disciples to live out Jesus' love. Verse 13 ("No one has greater love than this, to lay down one's life for one's friends") is the most explicit statement in the Gospel of what it means to love as Jesus loves. That Jesus' death is the ultimate demonstration of his love has been implied in 10:17–18, in the foot washing story of John 13, and in the love commandment in verse 12, a restatement of 13:34. The reference to "friend" in 15:13–15 goes beyond the noble idea of friendship to application grounded in Jesus' particular love. As 15:14 emphasizes, to be Jesus' friend and to love Jesus are synonymous, because both involve keeping Jesus' commandments.

The language of friendship is contextualized by language of election in 15:16. To say that believers are chosen is to emphasize that the initiative belongs to Jesus, and that relationship with him is ultimately a result of God's grace (6:37–39, 44). This does not minimize free will, since followers must respond to God's call to discipleship, but if they do not continue bearing fruit, they can be broken off, meaning they are left to wither (15:6). Believers have been chosen, not for "salvation" or for some other such ultimate end, but in order that they might bear much fruit, thereby contributing to the life and mission of the Christian community. In this regard, the narrative of fishing in chapter 21 can be instructive: on their own initiative the disciples catch nothing, but under the guidance and in the presence of the Lord they catch many fish (21:6; see 15:5). However, this bearing of fruit cannot be confined to loving only fellow Christians. As Christ died for the world, so his disciples serve other disciples, both actual and potential.

Farewell Discourse Three: Warning about Persecution (Chapter 15:18—16:4a)

For the first time in the Farewell Discourse, Jesus addresses the believing community's relationship to those outside. This picture of the community's relationship to the world stands in stark contrast to the picture of its internal relationships. While internal relationships are governed by love, the community's relationship with the world will be governed by hate (15:18–19, 23–25), persecution (15:20; 16:2), and death (16:2). The call to love as Jesus loves receives its most crucial test when the community meets the world's hatred.[2]

Talk of laying down one's life is evidently not idle posturing. In view of the evangelistic overtones of the previous discourse, it is not surprising that John turns now to a warning about the cost of discipleship when one is a member of a witnessing community. There is a strong contrast here between "the world," which hates Jesus and his followers, and the community of faithful followers. The disciples, and by extension the Johannine community, would experience the hostility of "the world" firsthand. If love is to be the mark of the church, "the world" is distinguished by its hatred of this love (15:18; 1 John 3:11–15). Unlike its neutral sense in 3:16, the term "world" here epitomizes all that is opposed to God. Because Jesus was persecuted, the disciples should expect to be persecuted also. As Jesus is not of this world (8:23), neither are his disciples (though they remain in it).

The saying in 15:20, "Servants are not to be greater than their master," seems to have been drawn from early Christian tradition (see 13:16 and Matt. 10:24–25). According to John's dualistic perspective, those who hate the Son hate the Father, and those who hate the disciples hate both the Son and the Father (15:23–24). This reaction is without a justifiable cause and amounts to inexcusable sin, grounded in enmity against God: "It was to fulfill the word that is written in their law, 'They hated me without a cause'" (15:25). In fact, the apostasy of the world amounts to a fulfillment of scripture (Ps. 35:19; 69:4). The fact that this condemnation is said to come from "their Law" makes clear that "the world" is to be understood as the Jewish leaders who oppose Jesus and his followers, as becomes clear by the reference to the synagogue in 16:2.

John 15:26–27 refer once again to the advent of the Paraclete (see also 14:16–17, 26), also called "the Spirit of truth" (15:26; 16:13; see 14:17). The Paraclete and the disciples are said to have the same function: to witness on behalf of Jesus (15:26). The dependability of the Paraclete derives from the fact that he is sent by Jesus; of the disciples, because they have been eyewitnesses "from the beginning" (15:27). The fact that the Spirit is sent by Jesus has nothing to do with the "procession" of the Spirit debated in the

---

2. O'Day, *John*, 762.

Trinitarian councils of the church. John 15:26 serves not to describe the metaphysical unity of God and the Spirit, but rather to affirm that God is the source of the Paraclete's presence with the believing community.

The final paragraph of this discourse (16:1–4a) attests to the experience of the Johannine community, which continued to witness in synagogue settings long after its separation from traditional Judaism. Earlier, the expression "put out of the synagogue" (9:22 and 12:42) was part of the narrator's comments; at 16:2 the expression is placed for the only time in the mouth of Jesus, indicating the probability that before his death Jesus did warn his disciples in this fashion. If the language of 16:2 seems extreme when it argues that those who kill the disciples will view their behavior as an act of worship, keep in mind that before his conversion Paul himself seems to have seen such actions as religious duty (Gal. 1:13–14). The ultimate reason given for such behavior is that the persecutors know neither God nor God's Son (16:3). Here as elsewhere the ultimate issue is the proper reception of revelation, that is, "knowing" Jesus and the Father. From John's perspective, to know neither the Father nor Jesus is to be ignorant of the meaning of the incarnation, because it is in the incarnation that one comes to know the Father (14:7). The very identity of God is at stake in the persecution and martyrdom of Christian believers.

The expressions "the hour" and "the hour is coming" (16:4) point beyond Jesus' prediction of the persecution of the faith community to the prediction of Jesus' death. These terms are Johannine metaphors for Jesus' death, resurrection, and ascension, which represent the completion of God's work (12:23; 13:1; 17:1–5).

Farewell Discourse Four: The Consequences of Jesus' Departure for His Disciples (Chapter 16:4b–33)

The fourth discourse returns to various themes of the first (13:31—14:31). Yet it is no mere duplicate of that discourse, as the triumphant climax and conclusion in 16:33 make clear. The best explanation for certain redundancies and perplexities (such as the conflicting sequence of events suggested by the remark of Jesus in 16:5 and the question in 13:36) is that the Evangelist has grouped a collection of discourses together in the farewell ones. Though the basic themes of the first discourse reappear in this final one, here the emphasis differs. In 16:4b–15 the discussion of the consequences of Jesus' departure focuses on the Paraclete, while in 16:16–33 the discussion of consequences focuses on Jesus himself.

The contrast between the disciples and the world continues in this discourse, as does the focus on teaching and the provision of consolation. What is noticeably different now is the increased emphasis on Jesus' approaching hour, coupled with the increased failure of the disciples to understand what Jesus is saying. The disciples have more to say in this farewell discourse than in previous ones. While Jesus speaks more plainly here than previously, the disciples still do not fully understanding what Jesus is saying. Full and clear knowledge, as the Evangelist stresses, is not possible before Easter.

The discourse begins with Jesus affirming his imminent departure, something he had not disclosed previously, since he had planned to be with his disciples for a while. The language of agency recurs in 16:5: "I am going to him who sent me." Knowing that his disciples are sorrowful over his departure, Jesus explains to them the advantage if he departs. The first advantage is the coming of the Paraclete (16:7); the second is that he will speak to them plainly and no longer figuratively (16:25).

The coming of the Paraclete is dependent on Jesus' departure. In his absence, the Paraclete's ministry is to make Jesus and his work present and available for the community. Verses 8–11 paint a vivid picture of the Paraclete's ensuing activity in the world; the Spirit's work in the disciples is described as convicting (the Greek verb *elencho* has legal overtones, including accuse, cross-examine, and put to shame) the world concerning sin, righteousness, and judgment. These activities of the Spirit are selected by the author of the book of Acts to have been central themes of the apostolic preaching (Acts 24:25). They are Jewish themes, developed in a new tonality because they are described and related to Jesus. (a) Of *sin*: For John sin is the result of unbelief in Jesus. Because belief in Jesus cleanses and purifies, by rejecting Jesus, the world deprives itself of hope and the newness of rebirth. (b) Of *righteousness*: righteousness is a gift of God, ratified by the Father in the resurrection of Jesus. The righteousness of God is not only manifested in the life and death of Jesus, but is also made available to humans through his departure. As sin is grounded in unbelief, so faith in Jesus' death and departure produces righteousness and virtue. (c) Of *judgment*: the victory of Jesus over the world (16:33) involves judgment of the "ruler of this world" (12:31; 14:30; 16:11). Though the world still lies in the power of this evil ruler (1 John 5:19), yet he is fallen from power (1 John 3:8). The dethronement of Satan is central to the apostolic preaching (Rom. 16:20). Following John, Christians view Christ's death as indeed a judgment, not on Jesus and the validity of his ministry, but rather on sin, the world, and the prince of this world.

In 16:12-15 the focus shifts from the role of the Paraclete in the world to the functions of the Paraclete within the faith community. Verse 12 sets the context for the final Paraclete teaching in the Farewell Discourse (16:13-15). As the disciples face the future, there are things they cannot understand prior to Jesus' death and resurrection. These they would understand later through the work of the Paraclete, who would guide them into all the truth. As at 14:17 and 15:26, the title "Spirit of truth" underscores the reliability of the Paraclete and points to his link with Jesus, who is the truth (14:6). The Paraclete, as Christ's agent, speaks for Jesus: "When the Spirit of truth comes, he will guide you into all the truth; for he will not speak on his own, but will speak whatever he hears, and he will declare to you the things that are to come" (16:13). The verb "to declare" here means to proclaim what has been heard. It does not refer to prophecy or prediction, and thus does not describe the Spirit as one who foretells the future. Rather, John highlights the proclamatory function of the Paraclete within the community. "The things that are to come" may refer specifically to the events of Jesus' hour, but they may also include events for which Jesus cannot prepare them now. These words point to the Johannine perspective that the Spirit's role in the community after Easter would be to convey the words of the exalted Jesus to believers, applying the teachings of Jesus in the new and changing circumstances of their lives. The entire Gospel may be said to be a reflection of this understanding (see 2:22; 12:16; 20:9), the result of the work of the Spirit through the Beloved Disciple and the Johannine community.[3]

Verse 16 presents a typical Johannine riddle: "A little while, and you will no longer see me, and again a little while, and you will see me." There is considerable debate in regard to the phrase "a little while," which appears twice in this verse. The first use seems to refer to the interval until Jesus' death and the second to the interval between Jesus' death and Easter. Neither reference applies to the interval between Jesus' death and the Second Coming, however, for John says very little about the return of Christ and shows no interest in speculating about the timing of the Second Coming. The hour or time of gladness and joy described in 16:20: "your pain will turn into joy" (cf. 16:22) refers to the time of the

---

3. Culpepper, *Gospel and Letters*, 218.

Johannine community as well as to the present time of the church; again, John is not pondering the final eschatological joy.

Jesus freely admits that during the first "little while" the world will rejoice as the disciples experience pain. But this too will pass. Their pain will turn to joy at Easter. Drawing from the prophets, the analogy is made in 16:21 to a woman in labor who is temporarily in anguish but whose travail turns to joy (Isa. 21:3; Jer. 13:21; 22:23). Jesus' separation from the disciples, from his death until his post-resurrection appearances, can be an object lesson for the community that its travail also is temporary. John 16:22-23 speaks then of the reunion at Easter, when the disciples will see Jesus again: "but I will see you again, and your hearts will rejoice, and no one will take your joy away from you. On that day you will ask nothing of me. Very truly, I tell you, if you ask anything of the Father in my name, he will give it to you." On "that day," they will have no more questions, no more confused and anxious thoughts that marked their relationship to Jesus during his ministry and especially during the Farewell Discourse. In addition, disciples will be able to pray, like Jesus, in the full confidence that God hears their prayers. This confidence in prayer will be enacted for the disciples in Jesus' prayer in 17:1-16.

John 16:25-33 bring the Farewell Discourse to and end by saying that the time is coming when Jesus will no longer speak in "figures of speech" (10:6; 16:25, 29) but "plainly" (7:26; 10:24-25; 11:14; 18:20). The real emphasis of John 16:25 is not on Jesus' mode of speaking but on the changes that will be accomplished by "the hour." Jesus' promise here is not a general promise about direct speech, but is a very particular promise about his revelation of the Father: "The hour is coming when I will no longer speak to you in figures, but will tell you plainly of the Father" (16:25). Jesus' hour—death, resurrection, and ascension—completes his revelation of God, marking a decisive change in the believer's access to God. Jesus' promise in 16:25 must also be read alongside his promises of the Paraclete in 14:25 and 16:12-15. As this passage unfolds, Jesus' meaning becomes apparent: once he has returned to the Father, clear understanding will come through the Spirit and through prayer in Jesus' name.

John 16:26-28 affirm that the Father loves the disciples because they properly recognize that Jesus came from God and because they have loved Jesus. Readers will recognize in 16:28 a summary of the Johannine gospel, hinted at in 1:51 and first stated fully at 3:13. Both parts of this verse are essential to the Evangelist's theology: "I came from the Father and have come into the world; again, I am leaving the world and am going to the Father." Verse 28a is the key to understanding the incarnation and Jesus' revelation from God, and verse 28b is the key to John's eschatological vision, because Jesus' return completes his revelation of God, making possible the gift of the Paraclete, which in turn opens up the community to the possibility of a new relationship with God and with one another.

Although the disciples claim they believe that Jesus knows all things and that he came from God (16:30), it is clear from Jesus' reply that they do not yet understand well enough: "The hour is coming, indeed it has come, when you will be scattered, each to his own home, and you will leave me alone" (16:32). The reference to Jesus remaining "alone" is taken by some to refer to the "cry of dereliction" found in the Synoptic tradition (Mark 15:34), but that connection seems forced, particularly in light of the ensuing affirmation: "Yet I am not alone because the Father is with me." The allusion may be to Psalm 22:1–5, which affirms that God does not desert his own. The disciples' relationship with Jesus enables them to experience peace even in the face of the world's persecution (16:33; see 14:27). How and why that is so is declared in the ringing announcement with which the Farewell Discourse closes: "But take courage; I have overcome the world!" Here—and only here—John employs a motif prominent in 1 John and Revelation, that Jesus is the conqueror who has overcome the hostile world (1 John 2:13–14; 4:4; 5:4–5; Rev. 2:7, 11, 17, 26; 3:5, 12, 21; 5:5). The promise in 16:33 is directed to the original disciples but also to the later disciples in the Johannine community and to all who face persecution for their faith. John's language of victory here is similar to Paul's in 1 Corinthians 15:57, though the eschatological perspective is different. For Paul, the victory is future, but for John, it is present.

Jesus Prayer of Consecration (Chapter 17:1–26)

Theologically, John 17 is one of the most important chapters in John's Gospel. In this sublime prayer the writer captures the inner self of Jesus. The verb tenses here as in the Farewell Discourse alternate between the future and the past, "as though it were the prayer of the risen Lord looking back on Jesus' public ministry and looking forward to the next generation of believers."[4] In 17:1–5 Jesus prays for himself, in 17:6–19 for the disciples, and in 17:20–26 for future believers.

---

4. Ibid., 219.

In the Synoptic tradition the prayers of Jesus are stated alone and are handled with great reserve (Mark 1:35; 6:46; 14:32–34). In John's Gospel, Jesus' prayer life is focused on this one prayer, known traditionally as the High Priestly Prayer, a title that dates to the Reformation period. Hoskyns suggests that it be called the Consecration Prayer, for it is a prayer of consecration for Jesus at his death, for his disciples in their mission to the world, and for all future believers, that they may be blessed to the service of God, behold the glory of the Son, and dwell in the perfect love of the Father and the Son.

The Evangelist has crafted and positioned this prayer to stand as "the theological climax of the Fourth Gospel."[5] Within this prayer the reader hears echoes of themes from the farewell discourses as well as of John's prologue. The prayer also represents the pivotal turn into the events of the hour and needs to be read in the context of Jesus' announcement in 16:33: "I have overcome the world." This prayer, therefore, is not an ideal or timeless prayer of Jesus, but one shaped and grounded by the moment at hand. The shifting temporal perspective of the prayer can be daunting, for Jesus speaks of his departure in ways that bring past, present, and future into one narrative moment. Dodd's comment that the prayer "in some sort is the ascent of the Son to the Father" overstates the case, yet captures the prayer's theological and narrative significance for the Johannine story of Jesus.[6]

Some scholars view this prayer as replacing the Gethsemane prayer in the Synoptics, but as previously noted, 12:27–28 seems a closer parallel. Certainly there is nothing here to suggest that Jesus is troubled or in agony. Rather this prayer is best understood in the context of a Greco-Roman symposium, at which Jesus concludes the banquet discourse and discussion period with a prayer, as a sage leaving his legacy with his disciples, entrusting them to God's care. A similar format appears in Sirach 51, which closes with a prayer of the sage in 51:1–12, followed by concluding words on behalf of his disciples (51:13–30), and ending with a benediction in 51:29. What John 17 provides is not a "high priestly prayer" but a prayer consecrating both Jesus and his followers.

1. *Jesus prays for himself* (17:1–5). This passage is framed by the concept of glorification, which in the Bible refers to the external manifestation of a person's deeper, hidden nature. When Jesus asks his Father

---

5. O'Day, *John*, 787.
6. Dodd, *Interpretation*, 419.

to glorify him (17:1), he is affirming his role in the drama of salvation, namely, to make evident to the world the true, hidden nature of God, and he is asking that the drama be brought to its climax. Jesus' glorification is not a self-glorification but rather a self-giving, a demonstration of God's love for the whole world.[7] John 17:3 ("And this is eternal life, that they may know you, the only true God, and Jesus Christ whom you have sent") is best viewed as an editorial comment of the Evangelist, inserted to clarify the meaning of "eternal life," the reference to the "only true God" serving a confessional purpose. In typical Johannine language, Christ is confessed as God's agent (God's apostle, his sent one), a particularly Johannine way of confessing Jesus (cf. 1 John 5:20). "Eternal life" is God's own life, and because God loves us, God wants to share it with us. Eternal life for John, a present reality and not merely a future hope, consists essentially in knowing God through Jesus Christ and living in response to that knowledge.

John 17:4 ("I glorified you on earth by finishing the work that you gave me to do") could be said to look back on the finished work of Christ on the cross (cf. 19:30), especially in view of the phrase "on earth," and thus we note ambivalence about the one praying this prayer, who seems at one moment to be the exalted Jesus and at another moment the Jesus about to be lifted up. Verse 5, however, makes clear that the point of view of Jesus throughout this passage is of one about to die: "So now, Father, glorify me in your presence with the glory that I had in your presence before the world existed." This verse acknowledges that Jesus gave up a significant portion of his glory when he became incarnate, and that he looks to reassume it when he returns to heaven.

2. *Jesus' prays for the disciples* (17:6–19). After praying for himself, Jesus prays for his disciples. His first request is for their protection—not so much physical but protection of their unity (17:11). The second request is for the disciples' consecration in a world that does not value their witness. They do, however, have a pattern to follow, that of Jesus, who submitted completely to the will of God (17:19).

John 17:6–8 is best interpreted as having a double function, for Jesus' prayer for his disciples and their relationship to God refers at the same time to his relationship with God. The opening words, "I have made your name known" summarize Jesus' entire ministry (see 1:18b). As 17:9 makes clear, the prayer is specifically for the disciples, not directly for

---

7. Dumm, *Mystical Portrait*, 73.

the world ("I am asking on their behalf; I am not asking on behalf of the world, but on behalf of those whom you gave me, because they are yours"), though this is not because Jesus cares not about the world, as 17:18 indicates. Jesus is not promoting a sectarian model where Christians should withdraw and condemn their world from a safe distance. Indeed, the very reason the disciples need this prayer, including the consecrating and equipping of which it speaks, is so that they will continue to witness to God's love in word and deed.

In John 17:11 we see again indications of the dual perspective of the prayer: Jesus is no longer in the world (17:11), and yet he is (17:13). The way to make sense of the confusion is to recognize that Jesus is at the point of returning to the Father and speaks as if he had already gone. In this passage Jesus is entrusting the disciples into the care of the Father, praying that the Father will protect and keep them unified. Verse 12 alludes to Judas the betrayer, and uses scripture (Ps. 41:9) to warn of apostasy. John 17:14-15 affirm that though the disciples are in the world, they do not belong to it. Christ's prayer is not that the disciples be removed from the sphere of the world, but rather that they be guarded from evil while they remain therein.

John 17:17-19 represent a climactic moment in this final prayer, when Jesus asks his Father to sanctify the disciples in the truth, here identified as the Father's word. This is the truth to which Jesus refers in his dialogue with Pilate in the final moments of his life: "For this I was born, and for this I came into the world, to testify to the truth" (18:37). This truth is not esoteric, but rather is "the unveiling of the reality of God's unconditional love for us."[8] God's character is love; that is God's essence, God's truth: "Sanctify them in the truth; your word is truth" (17:17). But this love cannot be reduced to an idea, a formula, or an "essence" that one must believe or confess creedally. God's love cannot be reduced to romantic infatuation, but is authenticated when it is lived out, incarnated unselfishly for the sake of others. For this reason it would never have been sufficient for Jesus simply to tell us about the love of God; he felt compelled to live it. This love was expressed in his whole life of obedience to the Father's will, though most clearly in his dying. It is this way of living that the Evangelist earlier characterized as living abundantly (10:10).

Because the Logos is God (1:1; 17:11, 21-22), the Spirit also is God; God's essence, manifested through God's two Paracletes (see 14:16), is

---

8. Ibid., 82.

truth. The use of the word translated "sanctify" in 17:17 and 19 can be confusing, particularly if we assume that the reference is to the Christian doctrine of sanctification. That this is not the case is made clear by the fact that Jesus is said to "sanctify" himself in 17:19: ("And for their sakes I sanctify myself, so that they also may be sanctified in truth"). The translation here, as with the related adjective "holy" (17:11), should be "set apart" or "consecrate" (Jer. 1:5; Exod. 28:41). The disciples are to be consecrated (set apart) for God's work, just as Jesus consecrates himself to that work. Christ's dedication in life and in death makes available God's transforming love to all who would be his followers in the world. The disciples, to be like Jesus, must also be sent into the world. To be sanctified "in truth" (17:19) means "in reality" or "truly," though it certainly includes the truth of revelation that Jesus offers.

3. *Jesus' prays for future believers* (17:20-26). Jesus had prayed for unity for his disciples, and now he prays for the unity of all believers. Their unity is to be patterned on the unity of the Father and the Son (17:21). Sharing in this relationship further unites them in the goal of bringing the world to "believe" in the Father and the Son.[9] In this section, Jesus' second prayer for future believers is that they will be reunited with him and be able to experience his full glory, which he did not reveal during his earthly ministry (17:24). To experience his glory is to experience the divine presence and life to the extent that they are spiritually united with one another and with God. One purpose of such unity is so "the world may know that you have sent me and have loved them" (17:23). The vision of 17:24, with reference to "where I am" ("Father, I desire that those also, whom you have given me, may be with me where I am, to see my glory"), is not a prayer for the union of the individual believer with Jesus after the believer's death, as many commentators maintain, but rather speaks "of the radical indwelling of God, Jesus, and believers that will be the sign of God's new age. It points to a hoped-for future that transcends and transforms human and divine community, but it is a communal future eschatological vision, not a private individualistic vision."[10]

The reference to the "Righteous Father" in 17:25: "Righteous Father, the world does not know you, but I know you; and these know that you have sent me" (see "Holy Father" in 17:10), consummates the language of

---

9. Readers must keep in mind that the verb "believe" in John is expansive. More than head knowledge, "believing" connotes experiencing God's liberating and transforming love.

10. O'Day, *John*, 796.

consecration: God's Son and God's people must be set apart because God the Father is distinct and set apart from all else in the universe. Verse 26, the closing thought of the prayer, summarizes the work of Jesus' ministry but also points to the future work of Jesus: "I made your name known to them, and I will make it known, so that the love with which you have loved me may be in them, and I in them." This verse confirms one of the central themes of the Farewell Discourse: Jesus' death and departure does not end his presence and activity with the faith community. Jesus' work continues through the work of the Paraclete and whenever the community incarnates God's love. Christ has made the Father's character known and, through the Spirit, will continue to do so, that the love shared by Father and Son may also be shared by the children of God. The goal of the knowledge of God is the love of God, enacted ultimately in Jesus' gift of his life. The words with which the prayer of John 17 ends are the perfect transition to the story of Jesus' hour.

Essay 9: John's Use of Misunderstanding and Irony as Literary Techniques

While many Christians read the gospels as repositories of revealed doctrine, since 1800 the most serious New Testament study has been historical. Lately, however, a new dimension has been added, one that approaches the Gospels as not primarily history but as story. Scholars who approach John's Gospel in this manner, such as Craig Koester, focus on John's rich symbolism and character portrayal.[11] Alan Culpepper, a pioneer in John's literary techniques, was the first to produce a thorough exploration of John as literary art.[12] This essay explores two aspects that John utilizes frequently, irony and misunderstanding, features that seem to have been welcomed and enjoyed by his audience.

Misunderstanding

One of the distinctive features of the Fourth Gospel is the frequency with which its characters misunderstand Jesus. The misunderstandings provide an opportunity to explain the meaning of Jesus' words and further develop significant themes. Their effect on the reader is greater than if

11. Koester, *Symbolism in the Fourth Gospel*.
12. Culpepper, *Anatomy of the Fourth Gospel*.

the meaning had merely been stated plainly from the beginning. The Johannine misunderstandings are well known: those of Nicodemus, the Samaritan woman, the crowd that experienced the miracle of the loaves, the disciples who mistook Lazarus' "sleep" for death, and Martha who confused resurrection on the last day with the "life" Jesus came to give. In all such cases, John's audience is summoned to an understanding superior to that of the characters, for they "know" the author's intent and are thereby drawn into a circle of enlightenment.

Misunderstandings display a typical pattern: (1) Jesus makes a statement that is ambiguous, metaphorical, or double in meaning; (2) his dialogue partner responds either in terms of a literal meaning of Jesus' statement or by a question or protest that shows he or she missed the intended meaning; (3) in most cases an explanation is offered by Jesus or the narrator. In the past, scholars approached the misunderstandings with the idea that they did not arise from a word's double meaning but rather that earthly matters were used to illuminate the divine, but this assumption proved too restrictive and excluded misunderstandings that fit the pattern in other ways.

Herbert Leroy, an early specialist in John's literary techniques, defined the Johannine misunderstandings as concealed riddles, all of which arose from double meanings peculiar to the vocabulary of the Johannine community. Readers within that community would have understood the special meaning of these terms, but outsiders found their special meaning enigmatic. Leroy identified eleven such passages, all in John 2—8. While this approach advanced the study of literary technique, the major weakness was in his effort to isolate a textual form and to force all examples to fit a single characterization. For instance, he dismissed passages such as John 11:11–15, 23–26; 12:32–34; and 13:7–11, 23–26 because they did not follow the normative form that his definition requires. Other scholars traced the misunderstanding to John's concept of revelation, while still others explored historical causes, such as inadequate Jewish reactions to Christ.

Culpepper's examination attempts to be exhaustive. He locates eighteen passages that exhibit a common pattern and several others that contain variations. Each of the eighteen passages contains an ambiguous statement, metaphor, or double-entendre in Jesus' conversations. Other passages, such as those where Jesus' signs are misunderstood, deviate from this pattern sufficiently to warrant being treated as variations,. The following list contains Culpepper's eighteen passages, together with their ambiguous phrases: 2:19–21 ("this temple"); 3:3–5 ("born anew");

4:10–15 ("living water"); 4:31–34 ("food"); 6:32–35 ("the bread from heaven"); 6:51–53 ("my flesh"); 7:33–36 ("I go . . . where I am you cannot come"); 8:21–22 ("I go away"); 8:31–35 ("make you free"); 8:51–53 ("death"); 8:56–58 ("to see my day"); 11:11–15 ("sleep"); 11:23–25 ("your brother will rise again"); 12:32–34 ("lifted up"); 13:36–38 ("I am going"); 14:4–6 ("Where I am going"); 14:7–9 ("you . . . have seen him"); and 16:16–19 ("a little while").

The densest concentration of misunderstandings occurs in Jesus' debate with "the Jews" in chapters 7—8. "The Jews" are the victims of misunderstanding in seven out of the eighteen passages. They repeatedly fail to comprehend Jesus' death and resurrection. Highlighted by these misunderstandings as most scandalous to the Jews is the death of the Messiah. In this respect, Nicodemus is the paradigm of the Jews' inability to grasp the meaning of Jesus' metaphorical discourses and symbolic actions. The disciples, who as a group represent all who attempt to follow Jesus, misunderstand essential aspects of Jesus' life and death. They fail to understand that his fulfillment of the Father's will gives him life and that death cannot take them from his love. In chapters 13—14 various disciples show misunderstanding: Peter does not understand Jesus' need to die (13:36–38); Thomas cannot understand Jesus exaltation and glorification (14:4–6); and Philip does not understand Jesus' revelation of the Father (14:7–9).

The theme that appears most frequently in Culpepper's list (eight times) is Jesus' glorification (which, as readers know, includes his death and resurrection). Another set of misunderstandings revolve around the identity and nature of the children of God, including their birth (3:3–5), their "bread" (6:32–35; 6:51–53; see 4:31–34) and "water" (4:10–15), their "freedom" (8:31–35), their passage through death (8:51–53; 11:11–15; 11:23–25), their vision of the Father (14:7–9), and Jesus' continuing presence with them (16:16–19; see 12:32–34; 14:4–6).

One obvious function of the misunderstanding is to teach readers how to interpret the Gospel. Misunderstandings guide the reader by interpreting some of the metaphors and double-entendres and by ruling out literal, material, worldly, or general meanings of such references. Readers are therefore oriented to the level on which the Gospel's language is to be understood and warned that failure to understand identifies them with "the Jews" and others who cannot interpret the Gospel's language correctly. Indeed, those who fail to understand Jesus' riddles (10:6; 16:25, 29) will eventually be "scattered" (16:32). In this respect, the misunderstandings are related to the use of irony in the Gospel (e.g.

7:33–36; 8:21–22), pointing the reader to the detection of the multiple meanings on which irony is based.

Irony

The Fourth Evangelist has been characterized as a master of irony and drama. John's use of irony, where two levels of meaning are set in opposition, is another means of engaging readers. In such cases, the ability to perceive the author's intention underlying the double meaning is the key to the passage or story. While the use of irony does not generally advance the hearers' knowledge beyond what they learned earlier in the Gospel, the use of irony enhances the underlying message and facilitates the "silent communication" between author and reader.[13]

Irony has been described as a "two-story" phenomenon in which "below" is the appearance or apparent meaning and "above" is the implied meaning. In order to make the leap from one level to the other, the reader must take four steps: (a) reject the literal meaning, (b) recognize alternative interpretations, (c) decide about the author's knowledge or beliefs, and (d) choose a new meaning in harmony with the author's position. The following components are essential to the use of irony, adequately distinguishing this technique from metaphor, symbol, or mockery: (1) a contrast of appearance and reality; (2) a confident unawareness by the victim that the appearance is only an appearance; (3) the comic effect of this unawareness of a contrast between appearance and reality; and (4) detachment.

Everyone familiar with the Fourth Gospel is struck by the profound spatial dualism: there are earthly matters and heavenly matters; Jesus is from above and his opponents are from below or from the earth; the higher plane is associated with truth and the lower with falsehood, deception, and error. The lower level is the plane of appearances, the higher level the perception of right judgment (7:24). This distinction leads to the basic feature of irony: a contrast between reality and appearance. Passages such as the prologue invite readers to the upper level, which as we have seen serves the crucial function of elevating the reader to the author's vantage point before the drama begins. "Omniscient prologues" serving just such a purpose had been developed by tragic poets such as Sophocles to exploit dramatic irony based on hidden identities. In like manner the revelation of Jesus' identity

---

13. The following examples and explanations are adapted from Culpepper, *Anatomy*, 152–80.

in John's prologue provides firm footing for the reader's reconstruction of hidden meanings and reception of suppressed signals unknowable or undetectable to the Evangelist's characters.

The following topics underscore John's prolific use of irony: (1) *The rejection of Jesus*. The foundational irony is that the Jews rejected their eagerly awaited Messiah: "he came to what was his own, and his own people did not accept him (1:11); (2) *The origin of Jesus*. The debate between Jesus and his opponents often returns to the question of his origin, whether he is or is not from God. Although this is Jesus' true origin (1:1–2), the Jews do not see it; (3) *The identity of Jesus*. The Samaritan woman's blunders and evasions are ironic, since the reader knows that Jesus speaks of living water figuratively. The irony of events by which Jesus asks for water as he is dying (19:29) is evident to those who know Jesus as the bearer of living water (4:14; cf. 7:38). When the sick man at the pool of Bethesda complains that he has no one to help him (5:7), the reader sees the irony, for he is speaking to the only person who can provide help. This motif reaches its climax at the trial, when Pilate says to the crowd: "Here is the man!" (19:5). They beheld a man, but he was not simply a man, he was the Son of Man; (4) *The ministry of Jesus*. Dramatic irony is used to highlight Jesus' first sign, changing water to wine. The story provides a "third day" view of Jesus' ministry. In all that follows, Jesus will replace the water of the Jewish institutions, festivals, and Law with the wine of the Spirit and truth. In this sense, the good wine has been held "until now," and Jesus can be likened to the bridegroom (3:29). In 12:19 the Pharisees utter a truth of which they are unaware: "the world has gone after him." The Evangelist smiles, and so do the readers; (5) *The death of Jesus*. All along Jesus knows what is coming, as does the informed reader. The Jews quarrel over the enigma of Jesus' giving his flesh for the life of the world (6:51–52), but the reader who knows in advance the end of the story knows the meaning. So thoroughly ironical is the Evangelist's view of Jesus' death that each step along the way discloses fresh ironies. Judas is an object of the Evangelist's irony, for while he protests the waste of precious ointment on Jesus, Judas bears a heavy share of responsibility for that burial. Jesus is tried on false charges, but the charges are ironically true: he was equal to God (5:18) and he was the king of the Jews (19:19–22). Life triumphs through death; that is the fundamental irony of the Evangelist's faith and the foundational irony of Christianity; (6) *Discipleship*. Most of the ironic passages that fall into this category concern Peter. When the Twelve are asked if they would leave Jesus also, Peter speaks on their behalf: "Lord, to whom can we go?" (6:68). The irony is that Peter is later the one who denies Jesus so outspokenly.

There are many examples of dramatic irony in John, situations where the reader smugly enjoys knowing what the character has yet to discover. The most common device is the unanswered question, often based on a false assumption, in which a character suggests or prophesies the truth without knowing it (1:46; 4:12; 6:42, 52; 7:20, 26, 35, 42, 48; 8:22, 53; 9:40; 18:38). For each of these questions the character assumes an answer the reader knows to be wrong, so readers can congratulate themselves on having such a superior grasp of the situation. On other occasions the characters naively make statements that convey meanings they do not suspect (5:7; 7:4; 11:50; 12:19; 19:14). Each naively spoken truth spurs the reader on to detect yet other truths half hidden in the dialogue of John's characters. "In a world in which people get what they want to avoid, lose what they want to protect, and cannot find what they are looking for, it is understandable that the Christ would not be recognized by those who were looking for him. John's narrative world is therefore an ironic one, one which lends plausibility and verisimilitude to the ironic story he has to tell."[14]

The Gospel of John gains from repeated readings, since it depends more on dramatic irony than on mystery for its effect. Never is the reader the victim, for inclusion is the strongest effect of John's irony. The Evangelist's purposes require implicit trust by the reader, and when that trust is given, the Gospel achieves its intention. Culpepper concludes his examination of John's use of irony by suggesting that irony "sweetens and spices the fellowship between reader and narrator . . . In the hands of others irony becomes a sword, but in the hands of our author it is more like a net in which readers are caught and drawn to the Evangelist's theology and faith."[15]

Questions to Ponder

1. What does pruning represent in John 15? How would this help to produce more fruit?
2. In John 15:4–7, what is the meaning of abiding in Christ?
3. Why does the world "hate" Jesus (see John 15:18–19)? How does the world "hate" the followers of Jesus?

---

14. Culpepper, *Anatomy*, 177.
15. Ibid., 180.

4. How will the Paraclete convict the world "about sin and righteousness and judgment" (see John 16:8–11)? What part do Christians play in this?

5. What did Jesus mean in John 16:16 by "A little while, and you will no longer see me, and again a little while, and you will see me"? Why might the disciples have difficulty understanding this?

6. How does John 17:3 define "eternal life"? Does this explanation surprise you?

7. In your own words, explain Jesus' request in John 17:5?

8. What is Jesus' primary focus in John 17:6–19? What specific things does Jesus ask the Father to do for his disciples?

9. What one word summarizes what Jesus wanted for all believers in John 17:20–26?

10. In your estimation, how does John's use of irony or misunderstanding enhance his overall message and his literary intention?

PART V

The Glorification of Jesus

(JOHN 18–20)

CHAPTER 10

Jesus' Passion
(John 18:1—19:42)

Summary: Chapters 18 and 19 tell of Jesus' final hours, beginning with his arrest and questioning before the Jewish and Roman authorities and ending with the crucifixion, death, and burial of Jesus. The story of Peter's denials of Jesus is interwoven with the high priest's questioning of Jesus. In John there is no actual trial by the Jewish authorities, but Jesus' dialogue with Pilate (the Roman procurator from AD 26–36) is longer than in the other gospels. In the seven scenes of the trial narrative, Pilate is depicted as moving between Jesus and his Jewish accusers, trying to broker a deal. When his attempts fail, Pilate issues a death sentence and writes a title to be put on the cross. Jesus' mother and the Beloved Disciple appear at the foot of the cross, while soldiers gamble for Jesus' clothes and offer him sour wine. Strangely, Jesus is seen as in control throughout these events. His final words, "It is finished!" are words of victory at the completion of his God-ordained task. Jesus' body is removed from the cross and buried by Joseph of Arimathea and by Nicodemus.

Assignment: Read John 18–19

Key Passages: John 18:37–38; 19:30

Central Theme: Jesus is King

Key Symbols/Concepts: King of the Jews, truth, crucifixion, Golgotha, Beloved Disciple, Day of Preparation

Learning Objectives

Participants will examine:

1. The similarities and differences between the Synoptic and Johannine versions of the passion of Jesus
2. The seven scenes of the Johannine trial narrative
3. The portrayal of Pilate in the Fourth Gospel
4. John's interpretation of Jesus' death as his exaltation and glorification
5. John's use of Old Testament quotations and allusions in the passion narrative
6. John's depiction of the role of Jewish and Roman authorities in the passion of Jesus
7. The role of Jesus' supporters at the foot of the cross
8. John's unique depiction of Jesus' crucifixion
9. The meaning of Jesus' words from the cross

Outline to John 18:1—19:42

I. The Betrayal and Arrest of Jesus 18:1–11

II. The Interrogation of Jesus by Jewish Authorities and Peter's Denials 18:13–27

III. The Trial before Pilate: Seven Scenes 18:28—19:16a

    A. Scene 1 18:28–32

    B. Scene 2 18:33–38a

    C. Scene 3 18:38b–40

    D. Scene 4 19:1–3

    E. Scene 5 19:4–7

    F. Scene 6 19:8–11

    G. Scene 7 19:12–16a

IV. The Crucifixion and Burial of Jesus: Seven Scenes 19:16b–42

    A. Scene 1: The Crucifixion 19:16b–18

    B. Scene 2: The Inscription 19:19–22

C. Scene 3: The Seamless Tunic 19:23–24

D. Scene 4: Jesus' Mother and the Beloved Disciple 19:25–27

E. Scene 5: Jesus' Last Words 19:28–30

F. Scene 6: The Piercing of Jesus' Side 19:31–37

G. Scene 7: The Burial 19:38–42

The Passion of Jesus: Two Versions

The Johannine narrative, together with the Synoptic version, provides the basic description of the passion of Jesus. Both versions include the arrest in the garden, trials before the Jewish authorities and before Pilate, the crucifixion and burial of Jesus, and the discovery of the empty tomb, and both accounts make extensive use of Old Testament allusions and quotations. In spite of these similarities, John's account develops the early Christian tradition in a distinctive way. He summarizes the early stages of the traditional passion story, but greatly expands the account of the trial of Jesus before Pilate, devoting twenty-nine verses to this subject. It is here that we will find the central theme governing John's perspective throughout the Gospel. Twice in this account, in the trial and again at the crucifixion, John produces a chiastic literary structure of seven scenes. This literary device, much appreciated in the ancient world, provides a sense of symmetry and creates an internal dynamism that highlights elements central to the narrative. Much of the delight and significance of the passion material in John is found in its interpretation of Johannine themes and its use of symbolism, irony, and double meanings.

While John's account follows the basic structure of the Synoptic narratives, there are numerous differences, many theologically motivated: (1) the Johannine chronology differs. Mark makes it clear that the Last Supper is a Passover meal, and in this the other Synoptics seem to agree. In John's account Jesus was crucified on the day when the paschal lambs were killed, namely, on the day before the Passover meal was eaten; (2) John does not give a Eucharistic character to the Last Supper; (3) John emphasizes the voluntary character of the sufferings of Jesus at various point (see 18:6–6; 19:28–30); (4) there is no Gethsemane story in John (but see 12:27); (5) in his account of the high priest's court, John says nothing of the charge of blasphemy against Jesus; (6) in John's version of Jesus' religious trial, the hearing is conducted by Annas and not by Caiaphas the high priest. When Jesus is sent to Caiaphas, we are not given an account of that hearing; (7) in his account of Jesus' trial before Pilate, John gives greater prominence to the inquisition there (18:28—19:16), skillfully presenting the trial as a dramatic tragedy; (8) in the Synoptics we learn that Jesus was condemned by Pilate as King of the Jews, but in John the focus is upon the kingship of Jesus (18: 37; 19:15); (9) the editorial remark at 18:32 (a clear reference to 12:32–33) notes the transfer of jurisdiction from a Jewish to a Roman court, assuring that instead of being stoned Jesus should be crucified and thus "lifted up," a symbol of crucifixion but also of exaltation; (10) while in the Synoptic account of the trial Jesus rarely speaks, in John he defends himself vigorously; (11) omitting Mark's report that the cross was carried by Simon of Cyrene, John appears to contradict it (19:17); (12) John omits numerous Synoptic details at the cross, including references to the mocking and reviling of Jesus and conversations with the penitent thief crucified at his side; (13) the crucifixion scene is told with economy, yet adding details unknown in the Synoptics like "I am thirsty" (19:28) and fulfilled prophecies such as "None of his bones shall be broken" (19:36) and "They will look on the one whom they have pierced" (19:37). According to Exodus 12:5 and 46, a paschal lamb was to be "without blemish" and none of its bones were to be broken; (14) the episode of Jesus' mother and the Beloved Disciple (19:26–27) is unique to John, as are (15) Jesus' final words at the cross, including the significant "It is finished" (19:30; cf. 17:4); (16) immediately after the death of Jesus the Evangelist records that a spear-thrust brought water and blood from his side (19:34), which leads to the editorial remark in 19:35 (cf. 7:38–39; 4:14; 6:55); (17) John asserts, finally, what the Synoptics implicitly deny, that the body of Jesus was anointed for burial (19:38–40).[1]

Analysis of John 18:1—19:42

The Betrayal and Arrest of Jesus (Chapter 18:1–11)

The many unique emphases in the Fourth Gospel point to source material very different from that of the Synoptic writers, and there are clear signs that suggest eyewitness accounts. On the other hand, there are also numerous features in the account of the arrest and trial that are hard

---

1. This list is adopted from Dodd, *Interpretation*, 423–29.

to accept as historical. Particularly difficult is the idea that hundreds of Roman soldiers came to arrest Jesus (the term *speiran* in 18:3 means a cohort, normally taken to refer to six hundred men, although occasionally the term refers to two hundred soldiers), when no Roman soldiers are mentioned in the Synoptics. Also difficult is the idea that the soldiers fell to the ground when Jesus said "I am" (18:5). The Evangelist's well-known flair for drama may in part explain such features. John may be trying to dramatize the cosmic conflict by focusing on the magnitude of the forces of darkness arrayed against Jesus. Notice that the soldiers carry torches in the darkness (18:3), something mentioned only in the Fourth Gospel. They are guided by Judas Iscariot, himself aligned with darkness (cf. 13:30). As it is, this cohort of darkness cannot defeat Jesus by force, for he is the "light of the world."

John 18:1–3 sets the scene for the arrest. Upon completion of the farewell prayer, Jesus leaves the upper room and goes to the olive grove across the Kidron valley known as the Garden of Gethsemane. While the Synoptic accounts mention Gethsemane, John alone speaks of a garden. Commentators note the possible connection with the Garden of Eden, indicating John's intention to contrast the symbolism of salvation with that of sin and victory with that of temptation and defeat. In John the forces of darkness—both Jewish and Roman—from the start are arrayed against the Son of God.

The overwhelming impression of the arrest scene is of Jesus the divine Word who with mere words overwhelms his supposedly powerful adversary. Jesus is not at the mercy of the Romans but is in control of his own destiny, and is even able to rescue his disciples from a similar fate by commanding that his foes "let these men go" (18:8). Without question, at this juncture the Fourth Evangelist has chosen to emphasize the divine Jesus, who willingly drinks "the cup" of death (18:11), while the Synoptics here reveal Jesus at his most human, asking for the cup to pass if possible (Matt. 26:39).

At 18:4 we are told that Jesus knew what was about to transpire (see 13:1, 3; 19:28). He is not caught by surprise but rather is depicted as actually taking the initiative at his arrest. He comes forward and asks, "Whom do you seek?" When they respond, he says, "*Egō eimi*," which means either "I am he" or "I am." The Evangelist clearly intends the latter, in light of the reaction of the soldiers (cf. Ps. 27:2). In 18:8 the same phrase is used, in this case meaning "I am he." The usage here is yet another example of Johannine double-entendre.

At 18:9 a formula quotation from the Old Testament is used to introduce the words of Jesus (see also 18:32). This usage indicates that by the time John's Gospel was being published, Jesus' words were already considered to be on a level with scripture. That possibility, while striking, confirms what we saw earlier in 1:17, where Jesus' words are said to surpass Torah (cf. 17:8).

Jesus' intention to surrender to his adversaries is misread by Peter, who cuts off the ear of the slave of the high priest. Only in John are we told that his name was Malchus. The addition of this name should not be seen as a scribal creation but as a sign that we may have here an eyewitness account of someone such as the Beloved Disciple, who, according to 18:16, was known to the high priest and thus could have known the servant's name. Jesus tells Peter to put his sword (most likely a dagger) back into its sheath. Jesus' behavior toward Romans here indicates that he respected the authority of rulers (see his response to Annas in 18:23) and did not condone violence against any authorities or their representatives.

The Interrogation of Jesus by Jewish Authorities and Peter's Denials (Chapter 18:13–27)

According to 18:12–13, Jesus was arrested, bound, and taken first to Annas, the father-in-law of Caiaphas the high priest, who was certainly the power behind the authority of Caiaphas (Caiaphas held the office from AD 18–36). Annas, who had been high priest between AD 6 and 15, remained powerful through his five sons, who all served eventually as high priests. According to Jewish thinking, a person was appointed high priest for life, although Romans could remove someone from office. This makes the statement "that year" in 18:13 (see also 11:49) ironic, since it reflects the subservience of Jewish power to Roman rule. The impression that the Evangelist is being ironic here is confirmed by the later cry of the crowd in 19:15, "We have no king but Caesar." In other words, for Jews to get their way with Rome meant they had to renounce their own control over the land and its people.

In John 18:15–27 we find a technique used regularly in Mark's Gospel called intercalation (or bookend), where a story—in this case the account of Peter's denial—is interrupted by intervening material. The reference to "another disciple" in 18:15 is made clear in 20:2, where the identification of the anonymous disciple is none other than the Beloved

Disciple. If the latter was a Judean or a Jerusalem disciple of Jesus, this might explain how he might have been known to the high priest and why he could be familiar with details such as the location of the family garden tomb of Joseph of Arimathea (20:3). His familiarity with this location helps explain Peter's following him to the tomb and going with him to the courtyard of the high priest. In fact, the text indicates that the other disciple went into the courtyard of the priest with Jesus, while Peter waited outside the gate. Verse 16 states that the other disciple was known to the woman who guarded the gate, since she agrees to allow Peter entrance to the courtyard. The phrase "also one of [Jesus'] disciples" in verse 17 suggests that the other disciple was known to be a follower of Jesus. Peter's first denial, "I am not" may be seen as the opposite of Jesus' "I am." Verse 18 groups Peter with the servants and the temple police; like them, he is in the dark and in the cold, denying his allegiance to Jesus.

From chapter 13 on, we get the impression that John's narrative is being told by an eyewitness with a Judean/Jerusalemite perspective, a notion confirmed by the introduction of the Beloved Disciple at that point in the text. From then on, the rest of the story until the epilogue is clearly situated in Jerusalem.

The second scene in this minidrama is found in 18:19–24 and consists of Jesus' dialogue with Annas. When Jesus is questioned about his disciples and his teaching, he responds that he has nothing to hide, for his teaching was given publicly. Jesus' reply is taken as disrespectful and he is slapped by one of the temple guards. Jesus replies that if he has spoken wrongly, then testimony should be presented to that effect. In a normal trial, witnesses would be questioned, not the defendant. The language of a Jewish trial is used here, though it is clear that this is a pretrial hearing. Jesus' response leads to his being bound and sent off to the de facto high priest, Caiaphas. Since we are not told anything about their meeting, the impression given by the Evangelist is that these proceedings with the Jews settled nothing.

This episode is followed by a return to Peter's denials, where he again denies being one of Jesus' followers, even when he is confronted by a relative of Malchus, who seems to have seen Peter in the garden. At this point we are told that the cock crowed.[2] Jesus confronts his opponents denying nothing, while Peter, still in the dark, denies everything.[3]

---

2. This may be either the crowing of a rooster before dawn, or at the end of the third watch (from 12:00 pm to 3:00 am), which was called "the cockcrow."

3. Witherington, *John's Wisdom*, 288–89.

The Trial before Pilate: Seven Scenes (Chapter 18:28—19:16a)

John's account of Jesus' trial before Pilate is told less from a historical and more from a theological perspective; the theological meaning of Jesus' passion is revealed in the interaction between Jesus and Pilate. As we have noted, this account forms part of a careful literary structure called a chiasmus, in which the order of scenes are related to each other through a reversal of structure, in order to make a larger point. When applied to the seven scenes of the trial before Pilate, this means that scenes one and seven are related, as are two and six and three and five. This structure also draws special attention to scene four, which functions as the hinge between the other scenes.

In the case of John's trial before Pilate, it seems evident that John modified the sequence of episodes to achieve this effect. The scourging and mocking of Jesus, an event the Synoptics insert immediately before the journey to the cross, is moved to an earlier stage so that it functions as the pivotal scene in the chiastic arrangement. The setting also supports the chiastic structure, so that scenes alternate between Pilate confronting the crowd outside and interrogating Jesus inside (scenes one and seven and three and five are outside Pilate's headquarters while scenes two and six are placed inside the headquarters). This structure serves both a literary and a theological purpose. The trial before Pilate ultimately has Christological focus, as both Pilate and "the Jews" are brought to judgment by Jesus the eschatological judge and king. Themes from John 5:19-31 and John 10:24-39 provide the theological backdrop.

Scene 1 (18:28-32): "What accusation do you bring?"

We are told that the encounter between Jesus and Pilate took place at Pilate's temporary residence (the praetorium). Pilate, as Roman governor (procurator), normally resided at Caesarea on the seacoast. He had come to Jerusalem for this major feast, not for religious reasons, but to take personal charge of a situation that was always volatile and could easily lead to rioting. It is the day of Preparation for the Passover (19:14), a day also of ritual purification. The narrator notes that the Jewish authorities remain outside the headquarters to avoid ritual defilement through contact with the secular authorities (18:28). This comment is not intended to give a note of sociological import but rather to establish theological irony. The trial narrative opens with "the Jews'" insistence on ritual purity and their meticulous attention to the demands of their faith, and it will end with their complete denial of the claims of that faith in 19:15: "We have no king but the emperor" (cf. the critique of ritual insincerity in Matt. 23:24, where hyperbole is used to the same end).

Having decided that Jesus must die, the Jewish authorities bring Jesus to Pilate so that the death penalty can be enacted and so that the blame can be placed on the Romans. The contest of wills between Pilate and the Jewish authorities begins in the first scene. Because they will not enter the praetorium, Pilate is forced to go out to them. Then, when he asks what the charge is, they declare the verdict, that the prisoner is guilty. When he tells them to deal with Jesus according to their law, they raise the stakes by demanding the death penalty. In 18:32 the narrator reminds readers that Jesus said that he would be "lifted up" (cf. 3:14; 8:28; 12:32), so that his death would be by Roman execution—crucifixion—and not by stoning.

We should note the correspondence of this scene to scene seven where, as we shall see, Pilate again comes outside to address the Jewish authorities, but at this point he is finally ready to accede to their demands for the death of Jesus. "From a self-confident and imperious Roman official he has become a fearful and irresponsible judge."[4]

Scene 2 (18:33–38a): "Are you the King of the Jews?"

Scene two, like the corresponding scene six in the chiastic scheme, occurs in the interior of the praetorium and also is concerned with power. Under Roman law there was no trial by jury, and because Jesus was not a Roman citizen, Pilate had unlimited authority to deal with the situation as he wished. Normally, the judge would interrogate the accuser, the accused, and any witnesses before declaring the verdict. Having questioned the accusers, Pilate moves inside the praetorium to interrogate Jesus. The fact that no witnesses are called by Pilate suggests that Jesus had already been officially condemned by the Jewish authorities and so stands before Pilate as a culprit. The course of Pilate's dialogue with Jesus seems to confirm this, for Pilate alludes to an earlier discussion before the Jewish authorities by raising what appears to be their accusation: "Are you the King of the Jews?"(18:33). If the answer to that question were affirmative, the charge would have political implications, allowing for Jesus to be charged with treason.

4. Dumm, *Mystical Portrait*, 15.

The question about Jesus' kingship with which Pilate begins his interrogation is found in every gospel account of the trial. The Fourth Evangelist, however, takes this traditional passion item and develops it into the governing motif of the trial, utilizing the term "king" nine times in his account of the trial of Jesus. While the issue of religion and politics is present in John's trial narrative, the kingship motif is theologically significant.

Notice that in 18:34–35 the inquisitor is put on trial. Jesus becomes the interrogator and things seem to get out of hand for Pilate. His response, "I am not a Jew, am I?" (18:35) sounds like the words of a person who thought he was in charge but may be losing his grip. Verse 36 is crucial in the story, for Jesus comes to the defense of his disciples, stressing that they are not revolutionaries: "My kingdom is not from this world. If my kingdom were from this world, my followers would be fighting to keep me from being handed over to the Jews. But as it is, my kingdom is not from here." Verse 36 is also important because it reveals something about Jesus' Kingdom. Jesus is not saying that his Kingdom is not in this world. Rather, he is speaking about the source and thus about the nature of his Kingdom. His Kingdom is not a worldly political kingdom in origin or character.

Jesus does not entirely reject the notion that he might be a king: "You say that I am a king" (18:37). Of course, Pilate has not said this, but John wants Jesus to claim some kind of kingship and some form of power, even if it is far different from the kind of kingship and power that Pilate has in mind. Of course, both John and his readers believe that he is king of heaven and earth. But he is not a king in any earthly political sense: "my kingdom is not from here" (18:36). Then Jesus states positively the sense in which he is a king: "For this I was born, and for this I came into the world, to testify to the truth" (18:37). This response, one of the most significant declarations in John's Gospel, is quite unexpected at this point.

Jesus is not speaking of philosophical or scientific truth here, but rather is expressing a truth that represents all his words and deeds, indeed his very being. The significance of the word "truth" in John's Gospel is seen in the fact that this noun occurs twenty-five times in this Gospel, yet only seven times in the rest of the gospels. The adjective "truthful" occurs fourteen times in John and only twice in the Synoptics. In each instance, the reference is to the power of God centered in the unselfish loving that Jesus offered throughout his life and which he now expresses perfectly in his death (cf. 13:1). Since the loving power of Jesus' kingship is inevitably directed toward others, it is not surprising that Jesus continues with the words "Everyone who belongs to the truth listens to my voice" (18:37).

At this juncture Pilate seems to assume that the conversation has turned philosophical and so he asks, "What is truth?" (18:38a). John leads us to believe that this turn in the dialogue has led Pilate to conclude that Jesus is certainly no threat to society and not worthy of execution. Pilate, however, is no truth-seeker; indeed, the statement is ironic, for Pilate's question does not perceive the Truth that is standing before him in the flesh. Pilate's question should have been, "Who is truth?" For John, "truth" is not academic or propositional; ultimately, it is personal. Truth is revealed in the incarnation.[5]

Scene 3 (18:38b-40): "Not this man, but Barabbas"

It takes Pilate less than a minute to conclude that Jesus is no threat. The fact that the Jewish authorities charge him with a crime is proof that he is not a threat, since there is nothing that those authorities would want more than to be rid of the Romans. Nevertheless, the growing tension at the time of Passover, coupled with the possibility of riots, may have convinced Pilate to calm the waters, so he offers the crowd a choice between Jesus and Barabbas (18:39). There is no evidence outside the gospels for this "custom" of releasing a prisoner at Passover, but it may be related to the Jewish practice of Jews buying fellow Jews out of bondage during Passover as a way of tangibly commemorating the Passover.[6] It also makes good sense in light of the Roman custom of dispensing amnesty at various sorts at feasts.

The people choose Barabbas instead, a bandit (18:40). In the Synoptics Barabbas is described as a political criminal, but the Fourth Evangelist seems to have something else in mind, inserting the same noun used in the shepherd discourse to describe those who threaten the sheep (10:1, 8). The choice between Jesus and the bandit continues a theme from that earlier scene. Some scholars question the historicity of the Roman custom of releasing a prisoner at the Passover, since in Roman or Jewish history there is no reference to such a practice. They point to the use of the name "Barabbas" of a murderer as ironic, for in Aramaic the name means "Son of the Father" or "Son of God." Some scholars wonder

5. Culpepper, *Gospel and Letters*, 225.
6. Witherington, *John's Wisdom*, 292.

whether Barabbas might be a subterfuge for the Jewish people, suggesting that references to Barabbas (the name is found in all four gospels) might function as a means of asking Christians to choose between Jesus and the Jews (the "people of God").[7]

Similar concerns have been raised about the figure of Judas in the gospels. Was he a person of history or a character "invented by the Christians as a way to place on the backs of the Jewish people the blame for the death of Jesus?"[8] The gospel tradition certainly added details to Judas's life as the legend got retold. According to John Shelby Spong, the name "Judas" was simply the Greek way of spelling "Judah," the nation whose members became designated "Jews." Early Christians eventually made a connection between Judas as betrayer of Jesus and the betrayal of the shepherd king of the Jews for "thirty pieces of silver" (Zech. 11:13). In the book of Zechariah, this silver was said to be hurled into the temple treasury, a theme that Matthew connects with the Judas money when Judas repented (Matt. 27:3-5). While conjecture about the portrayal of Barabbas and Judas abounds, if their roles in the gospels lead to placing the blame for the death of Jesus on all Jews (as implied by texts such as Matt. 27:25), they are clearly mistaken.

Scene 4 (19:1–3): "Hail, King of the Jews!"

In this crucial "hinge" section in the trial's chiastic structure, Pilate orders Jesus to be flogged and to be subjected to ridicule by the soldiers. A flogging, a severe beating that left some dead, normally came after the condemnation of a criminal and not during the trial, much less after the accused had been pronounced innocent. The severe scourging of Jesus, probably with a flagellum (a cat-o'-nine-tails), the hooks of which would rip the flesh off a person, surely contributed to his expiration on the cross.

The soldiers place a crown made of thorns on his head, clothing him in purple and hailing him as the Jewish king. While the Synoptics label this action as mockery (Matt. 27:29, 31; Mark 15:20), John leaves the interpretation to the reader. Nowhere does John record that the soldiers strip Jesus of the royal garb; instead, 19:5 makes clear that Jesus stays dressed in the royal garb for the remainder of the trial.

---

7. Spong, *Liberating the Gospels*, 271–72.
8. Ibid., 259.

It is noteworthy that this is the only scene where Pilate is not personally present. Since he refused to act as a just judge, his attitude changes after this scene as he is placed more and more on the defensive and even becomes fearful. Most commentators interpret the flogging as Pilate's means to placate the crowd, but that act is said to occur inside the praetorium and not where it could be witnessed by the crowd. The events narrated in John 19:1–3 are clearly told for the Gospel audience alone, highlighting the love of Jesus and his true kingship.

Scene 5 (19:4–7): "Here is the man!"

Scene five corresponds to scene three, and here again Pilate goes outside to tell the Jews that he finds Jesus innocent of the charges brought against him. If there was sarcasm and irony earlier, this increases in John 19. The irony is particularly thick when Pilate presents Jesus to his detractors regaled in purple and a crown of thorns, stating starkly, *Ecce homo*, "Here is the man" (19:5). From the Evangelist's point of view, Jesus' suffering is the means of his glorification. If there is any mockery in John's trial, the object of the mockery is not Jesus but the Jewish leadership.

Throughout this drama Pilate is depicted as a pawn, not merely manipulated by "the Jews" but ultimately by Jesus as well, for by his *Ecce homo* announcement Pilate proclaims Jesus the Son of Man, the representative human being who will die for all, including Gentiles such as Pilate and "the Jews" as well. Like Peter, Pilate three times denies the Jews their request, saying he finds no fault in Jesus (18:38; 19:4, 6). When his parody backfires, Pilate replies "Take him yourselves and crucify him" (19:6), forcing them to choose the Roman punishment and thereby wiping his hands clean of this affair. In 19:7 the real bone of contention comes to light. Jesus is accused of blasphemy "because he has claimed to be the Son of God" (see 5:18; 10:33–36). Jesus' claim to a unique relationship with the Father proves to be the real sticking point, as it continues to be in the ongoing dialogue among Christians, Jews, and Muslims.

Scene 6 (19:8–11): "You would have no power over me"

Scene six, corresponding to the second, where kingship and power were the topics of discussion, finds Pilate inside his headquarters. The reaction of Pilate to the charge of "the Jews" is surprising: "he was more afraid than ever" (19:8). In the Gentile world, a person called "son of the gods" was considered a messenger from the gods, and Pilate, having heard the Jewish authorities call Jesus "the Son of God," may have been superstitious enough to be fearful of getting on the wrong side of the gods.

At this point Pilate asks the question that John's Gospel sees as the right question, "Where are you from?" (19:9). To this question, important both politically and theologically, Jesus replies with stony silence. When Pilate appeals to his authority as ruler, Jesus reminds him that he would have no authority or power over him if it had not been given from above (19:11; cf. 5:19–29). Jesus' claim that those who delivered him to Pilate have the "greater sin" (19:11) is directed at the ruling authorities in general. We must recall that references to sin in John are not about moral or legal culpability but are theological statements about relationship to God. In the Fourth Gospel, "sin" is defined by whether one believes that God is fully present in Jesus. For the Jewish authorities to be guilty of the greater sin, then, is to have the greater blindness to the revelation of God in Jesus, especially because they claim to know God (5:39; 8:41; 9:29; 10:33; cf. 9:39–41). By the end of the trial, when Pilate hands Jesus over to be crucified, Pilate will share their sin, because he too will have rejected God's revelation in Jesus.[9] In the hour of decision, Jesus' hour, the Evangelist makes plain that one's reaction to Jesus will determine whether one is liberated or lost. At his trial, Jesus becomes the judge.

Scene 7 (19:12–16a): "Here is your King!"

This scene corresponds to the first, where Pilate also leaves the praetorium to speak to the Jewish authorities. He tries once again to release Jesus, but "the Jews" cry out that if Pilate releases Jesus, he is no "friend of Caesar" (18:12), a technical term for a loyal public servant. This appeal to self-interest finally works. The irony is again heavy. "Pilate fails the test in the presence of the real divine king in order to maintain his status with a merely human king who claimed divinity."[10] Verse 13 ("When Pilate heard these words, he brought Jesus outside and sat [or seated him] on the judge's bench at a place called The Stone Pavement") can be translated in one of two ways: either that Pilate places Jesus on the judge's seat, unknowingly placing him in his rightful place as judge, or more likely, that Pilate sat on

---

9. O'Day, *John*, 821.
10. Witherington, *John's Wisdom*, 294.

the judgment seat for his final verdict. This time, however, it is to grant the request "the Jews" made in scene one, to have Jesus put to death. Yet Pilate cannot resist adding a further insult to Jesus' accusers (and therefore unconsciously speaking the truth about Jesus): "Here is your King."

Pilate asks one last time, "Shall I crucify your King?" (19:15). To this the Jews respond that only Caesar is their king, thereby renouncing what is most precious to them, their independence and their very Jewishness, for only God and God's Messiah could truly be their ruler. Ironically, Pilate must renounce Jesus' innocence in order to retain what is most precious to him, his status as friend of Caesar.

In yet one more ironic twist, the text at 19:16 declares that Pilate delivered Jesus "to them" to be crucified. Although most likely this refers to the soldiers who are mentioned at 19:23–25, the Evangelist could be alluding to the Jewish officials who presumably accompanied the Roman soldiers and the temple police when Jesus was arrested. The scene has been set for the crucifixion of the King.

John notes that this took place at about the sixth hour on the day of Preparation, which according to Jewish reckoning of time would have been noon (cf. Mark 15:25, where the time of crucifixion is at the third hour— nine in the morning). It is important to note that Friday was normally called Preparation Day by the Jews, although the allusion was to preparation for the Sabbath. If on this year the Sabbath and the Passover coincided, then the day of Preparation for both events would have been the same.

The Crucifixion and Burial of Jesus: Seven Scenes (Chapter 19:16b–42)

If there is one thing that New Testament scholars agree on, it is that Jesus was crucified in Jerusalem during the rule of Pontius Pilate (AD 26–36). While Christians accept the crucifixion of Jesus without question, it is perplexing how a person like Jesus got himself executed by a form of punishment normally reserved for the extreme elements of society (rebels, bandits, runaway slaves). Crucifixion was not seen as a noble way to die, nor was it viewed as an acceptable means of death for a person who wanted martyrdom. In a Jewish context, crucifixion was seen as a sign that one was cursed by God (Deut. 21:22–23). Prior to Jesus, no one envisioned the Messiah as dying on a cross.[11]

---

11. A later case involves the story of Jesus bar Hana, a Jewish prophet in the

John gives little attention to the crucifixion itself, devoting his attention to describing, often in symbolic language, the spiritual implications of Jesus's death. Once again one detects a chiastic structure in seven scenes. As in the case of Jesus' trial before Pilate, this arrangement provides sets of comparisons while drawing attention to the fourth or pivotal scene, where Jesus speaks to his mother and the Beloved Disciple.

While John's account of the crucifixion has much material in common with the other gospel accounts, the Johannine account handles these traditions quite differently from the Synoptics, arranging them to highlight the dignity and self-control of Jesus at his death.

Scene 1: The Crucifixion (19:16b–18)

In this scene we learn that Jesus was taken (presumably by the Roman soldiers) and that he was forced to carry his own cross. Unlike the Synoptic Gospels, there is no mention of Simon of Cyrene, a bystander compelled by the soldiers to carry Jesus' cross. Needing no help, John's Jesus is clearly in command of the events of his "hour" (10:17–18; 18:5, 8, 20–21). The place of the crucifixion is identified as Golgotha, which in Aramaic means "skull." The location of this spot has been much debated by archaeologists, but the evidence strongly favors the traditional location somewhere within the precincts of the Church of the Holy Sepulchre, not at the so-called Garden Tomb (Gordon's Calvary). Jesus was crucified outside the city walls, but those walls were at a different spot than they are today. None of the customary details of this cruel form of death is recounted, and the fact that Jesus is crucified with two others is mentioned only in passing, merely to state that Jesus was placed between the two (19:18).

When one notes the correspondence of this scene with scene seven, the emphasis here is on the lifting up of Jesus in crucifixion (see 3:14–15), just as in scene seven, by contrast, he is taken down from the cross.

Scene 2: The Inscription (19:19–22)

Despite the brevity of John's depiction of the crucifixion itself, he highlights the account of the inscription that was put on the cross, which read

---

generation after Jesus of Nazareth, who also spoke messianically, predicting the fall of Jerusalem and the temple in AD 62. He too was scourged until his bones showed, but he was eventually released by the procurator Albinus during the festival of Booths.

that Jesus was "King of the Jews" (19:19). Public crucifixion was practiced by the Romans as a deterrent, and although the law did not require a *titulus*, the placard attached to the cross, the Romans did in notable cases display the supposed reason for execution. We are told that many Jews objected to the *titulus*, for the inscription was written in the three primary languages of that part of the Roman Empire: Aramaic, Latin, and Greek. The chief priest asked Pilate to change the inscription to read "This man said, I am King of the Jews," but Pilate refused (19:21-22).

While no passerby would have believed that Jesus, suffering the fate of a common criminal, was in fact a king, on a theological level this inscription provides the interpretive lens through which to view Jesus' crucifixion. In the "lifting" up of Jesus on the cross, he is "exalted" as universal king and as "the Savior of the world" (4:42). Many commentators follow Raymond Brown in his assessment that this episode represents the "enthronement" of Jesus, for in the lifting up of Jesus on the cross, the truth of Jesus' prediction about his death is confirmed: "And I, when I am lifted up from the earth, will draw all people to myself" (12:32-33; cf. 11:52).

Scene 3: The Seamless Tunic (19:23-24)

At a Roman execution, it was common practice for the executioner to assume possession of the victim's effects. Each of the gospels interprets the soldiers' division of Jesus' clothing as a fulfillment of Psalm 22:18, a psalm about the suffering of a just man who is ultimately rescued by God. The most probable reason for John's frequent emphasis on the fulfillment of scripture in Jesus' crucifixion scenes (19:24, 28, 36, 37) may be to interpret the scandalous nature of Jesus' death, showing that what happened was in accord with a divine plan revealed in scripture.

The account of the soldiers' actions, in which Jesus' clothing is disposed of in two stages, seems to represent a literal reading of Psalm 22:18, thereby showing a misunderstanding of the function of synonymous parallelism in the psalm. The two halves of Psalm 22:18 describe the same action twice, but the Evangelist interprets the verse as referring to two distinct acts.[12] In addition to Jesus' other clothing, mention is made of the seamless tunic he wore, and for which the soldiers cast lots. On the surface, it appears

---

12. A similar misunderstanding occurs at Matthew 21:9, where the Greek text of Matthew understands Zechariah 9:9 as referring to two animals, not one, thereby depicting Jesus as riding on two animals simultaneously.

that the tunic is mentioned to explain how the casting of the lots came about, and thus how the scripture was fulfilled. But many commentators find a deeper symbolism here, in which the seamless garment represents Christ's unity with the church or with humanity, which the pagan world cannot tear apart. The same case is made for the net containing the great catch of fish in 21:11, also untorn and symbolic of the church's unity in mission. Some find in the seamless tunic a symbolic allusion to the high priest in Exodus 39:27, who is said to have worn a garment woven of one piece. The correspondence of this scene with scene 5 lies in the fact that we see there the ultimate priestly act in which Jesus gives up his spirit to establish a permanent bond between God and humanity.

Scene 4: Jesus' Mother and the Beloved Disciple (19:25–27)

Not only in the chiastic arrangement of the crucifixion story in John, but perhaps in the passion narrative as a whole, scene four is pivotal. Here John reveals his concern with the spiritual and theological implications of this climactic moment in the ministry of Jesus, rather than with mundane aspects of the cross. While the other Evangelists mention the presence of faithful women at the crucifixion, they tell us that these observed Jesus' death from afar (see Mark 15:40–41). In John, the women stand near the cross. The Johannine list of women includes the mother of Jesus, but has only one name in common with the Synoptic list—Mary Magdalene. Curiously, Jesus' mother is not mentioned in the Synoptics as being present, despite the fact that Luke has a special interest in her (see Luke 2; Acts 1:14). Only John makes reference to the presence at the crucifixion of a male disciple, the unnamed Beloved Disciple (19:26), often seen as the theological mentor of the Johannine community and likely the author of the Fourth Gospel.

The scene at the base of the cross is interpreted differently by Catholics and Protestants. Catholic interpreters emphasize the role of Jesus' mother in this scene, seeing her as symbolic of the Mother of the Church, the New Eve, or the New Israel. Protestant interpreters emphasize the role of the Beloved Disciple as a symbol of the church and faithful discipleship. The two approaches can be harmonized if we interpret the scene as representing a sort of last will and testament by Jesus. True to his principles (see Mark 3:31–35) and perhaps especially since his brothers did not believe in him (John 7:5), Jesus apparently preferred to have his mother cared for by a member of the family of faith rather than by his own physical family, for "his own people did not accept him" (1:11). Even the sayings "Woman, here is your son" and "Here is your mother" (19:26–27) suit the language of Jewish family law, in which someone is legally entrusted to another.[13] Whatever the full historical meaning of this event, the Fourth Evangelist has transformed the scene into a powerful statement about the church, the new humanity of male and female disciples caring for one another at the foot of the cross. The fact that neither of these persons is named leads to the view that they are being presented as paradigmatic of the future family of God, Jesus' family reconciled with the family of faith.

Here, as in John 2:4, Jesus addresses his mother as "woman," not just because he had disengaged from his mother in her parental role, but because she represents women in their pilgrimage toward full faith in Jesus. As Mary loses Jesus in a parental sense, she gains a new family, the Beloved Disciple being her first "son" in the faith. Discipleship, then, is the larger context in which Mary's role must be defined. The dignity and equality of women and men is affirmed at the foot of the cross, in this new family of faith.

Scene 5: Jesus' Last Words (19:28–30)

Having achieved this reconciliation, the Evangelist suggests that Jesus had completed his work, for the story is followed by the words, "when Jesus knew that all was now finished" (19:28), meaning that he had accomplished the Father's will (see 19:30). Of the seven last "words" of Jesus, two are found in John's Gospel. The first of these, "I am thirsty" (19:28), is told by John as a fulfillment of scripture. This further confirms that the Johannine Jesus is conscious of having done everything in obedience to God's plan and will. Psalm 69:21 is the scripture, though the words are also reminiscent of Psalm 22:15. On a mundane level, the episode surely depicts Jesus' true humanity, his vulnerability and capacity for suffering. On a deeper level, his words recall his question to Peter at his arrest, "Am I not to drink the cup that the Father has given me?" (18:11). The reference to Jesus' thirst contains some irony, since in John 4 Jesus was portrayed as the one who could meet all human thirst.

---

13. Witherington, *John's Wisdom*, 309.

This scene corresponds to scene three, where we noted references to Jesus' priestly ministry. The priestly allusion there may explain why John here mentions a branch of hyssop (19:29). The short and fragile hyssop branch would not have been suitable for its intended purpose here, but on a symbolic level it could evoke a priestly function in ancient Israel in which the covenant was sealed with the hyssop branch, used to sprinkle the people with sacrificial blood, thereby consecrating the people of God (cf. Heb. 9:19–20).

Having completed the work entrusted to him, Jesus "bowed his head and gave up his spirit" (19:30), meaning that he handed over his life. Unlike in Mark's Gospel, which records the cry of God-forsakenness, here Jesus is calm and aware that he has completed the work given by his Father. In relinquishing his spirit (a reference to his human spirit), we see another reference to Jesus' humanity. He was truly human and truly died. But he died freely, of his own volition (see 10:18). Once more we find an indication that Jesus is not a victim but a victor, in charge even at death.

Scene 6: The Piercing of Jesus' Side (19:31–37)

We are told in 19:31 that this is the day of Preparation and that the coming Sabbath is a feast day. The Jews wished for the legs of the three bodies to be broken, so that corpses would not be left on the crosses to defile the Sabbath. Breaking the legs would cause almost immediate suffocation. In Jesus' case, this was not necessary because he was already dead, a fact said to be confirmed by scripture (Ps. 34:20).

To make certain that Jesus is dead, a soldier pierces his side, causing a flow of blood and water. This particular act is of great importance to the Beloved Disciple, who is said to witness to the humanity of Jesus by affirming his physical death (19:35). This event, too, is seen to confirm scripture (Zech. 12:10). Some commentators see in the mention of blood and water a reference to the two sacraments that spring forth from the death of Jesus, but this is unlikely, given that the Evangelist has shown no interest in describing the baptism of Jesus or in mentioning the elements in his description of the Last Supper. Furthermore, blood by itself is never a symbol for the Lord's Supper, any more than the bread and fish in chapter 6. Most likely the theological point is that Jesus' death results in new life. "The blood shed symbolizes Jesus' death; the water, as elsewhere in this Gospel, symbolizes the life that comes from Jesus to his followers.

Jesus had to die so others might have life and have it abundantly. Since this is the Gospel that has eternal life as a chief theme, and Jesus' death is seen as its indispensable source, it is not surprising that the author stresses that this act is witnessed and a fulfillment of scripture, in accord with God's plan."[14] Scene six corresponds to scene two in the chiastic arrangement. By giving his life for humanity, Jesus is "King of the Jews," King of the new humanity, God's New Israel.

There is no general medical agreement as to the actual cause of Jesus' death on the cross. It could perhaps have been suffocation, though traumatic shock or heart failure is also certainly possible. It is anatomically possible for blood and a clear fluid to spurt from a pierced dead person if the person has recently died. The gush of blood and water could have come from the piercing with the lance of the pleural cavity, where fluid collects after heart stoppage.[15]

Scene 7: The Burial (19:38–42)

This scene stands in contrast to scene one, where Jesus is lifted up on the cross, as here he is taken down from the cross and laid in a new tomb. The emphasis is on the regal care given to the dead body of Jesus. Here Joseph of Arimathea appears for the first time as a sort of secret follower of Jesus (cf. 12:42–43). At his request, he is given care of the body of Jesus. He is supported by Nicodemus, whose role in the burial of Jesus is recorded only in John (cf. 3:1; 7:50). Nicodemus, who had come to Jesus at night, now publicly shows his commitment to Jesus. The number of spices used amount to extreme extravagance, as was Mary's anointing of Jesus in John 12. The large quantity of spices, one hundred Roman pounds (seventy-five pounds in today's standard), could be read as an example of burial fit for a king.

They took his body and wrapped it linen cloth. Much conjecture and study has gone into the unsubstantiated claims that the Shroud of Turin is Jesus' original burial shroud. Though relics should not become items of primary focus, lest they become idols, the Shroud of Turin continues to fascinate. The Evangelist states that Jesus is buried in a nearby tomb, one never before used. Thus there would be no mistaking it for someone else's

---

14. Ibid., 311.

15. For a moving account of ancient crucifixion by an eminent surgeon, see Barbet, *Doctor at Calvary*.

tomb, nor was it likely that anyone would visit this one by accident. The sequel to this somber scene is as dramatic as this is melancholy.

Essay 10: John's Perspective on the Passion of Jesus

The Fourth Gospel was written for believers, but was forged in a context of disputes with the non-Christian world. The Christian proclamation of a crucified Messiah was difficult to substantiate in Roman times, as Paul indicates in 1 Corinthians: "For Jews demand signs and Greeks desire wisdom, but we proclaim Christ crucified, a stumbling block to Jews and foolishness to Gentiles, but to those who are called, both Jews and Greeks, Christ, the power of God and the wisdom of God. For God's foolishness is wiser than human wisdom, and God's weakness is stronger than human strength" (1:22–25).

Justin Martyr, who composed his *Dialogue with Trypho* in the second century, grappled with Jewish objections to the idea of a crucified Messiah, quoting Trypho as saying that "this so-called Christ of yours was dishonorable and inglorious, so much that the last curse contained in the law of God fell on him, for he was crucified."[16] The Latin author Minucius Felix concluded that only "abandoned wretches" could possibly center their worship on "a man put to death for his crime and on the fatal wood of the cross."[17] Against such objections, the Gospel of John seeks to create a frame of reference that can disclose the transcendent significance of Jesus' death.[18] In John's narrative the crucifixion functions as a core symbol. The Johannine passion narrative is complex, conveying several levels of meaning simultaneously, though we must not overlook its primary level as Christological. Penning some of his most ironic prose, the Evangelist seeks to show that the hearings before Pilate exonerated Jesus and revealed that his accusers were guilty of the charges they had made against him (see 19:4, 6, 11).

Theologians frequently divide the topic of Christology into two subtopics: the "person" of Jesus and the "work" of Jesus. For purposes of discussion, they distinguish between Jesus' identity and what he accomplished in his life and death. Such a distinction, of course, is arbitrary, since the two are interrelated. Like the view of Jesus' identity, the earliest Christians did

---

16. Justin, *Dialogue* 32.1.
17. Minucius Felix, *Octavius* 9.4.
18. Koester, *Symbolism*, 208.

not maintain a single view of the cross. Jesus' death on a cross was doubtless an embarrassment to Christians, as can be seen in the numerous interpretations of the cross found in the New Testament. Paul, for example, speaks at times of the cross as atonement or expiation, borrowing traditional Jewish sacrificial language (Rom. 3:25; cf. 1 John 4:10). The Synoptics portray Jesus dying a martyr's death, an innocent victim of Roman brutality (Luke 23:47; see Mark 15:39). The letter to the Hebrews presents Jesus as both high priest and the sacrifice for sin (7:26–27).

John presents a different view. Throughout his gospel, the Fourth Evangelist has been preparing his audience for the work Jesus accomplished on the cross. Four themes predominate in John's discussion of Jesus' passion: (1) *liberation* rather than expiation (substitutionary atonement); (2) *glorification* rather than crucifixion; (3) *exaltation* (epitomized in the frequent use of the expression "lifted up"); and (4) *coronation* or enthronement of Jesus as king.

An early title for Jesus, given by John the Baptist, is that Jesus is the Lamb of God (1:29, 36). While this title evokes numerous possible meanings, the most likely is that of the paschal lamb, associated with the Passover celebration and therefore with the exodus, the liberation of God's people from bondage. In John this image symbolizes the new Passover, the new liberation from bondage offered by God. What the Evangelist conveys by the claim that Jesus is the Lamb of God is that he is the agent of God whose life and death result in liberation. In the Fourth Gospel, the death of Jesus is not so much expiation for sin as an ironic means of exalting Jesus. It is likely that John wanted his readers to understand the liberating qualities of Christ in broader terms than that of sacrifice for sin: "you will know the truth, and the truth will make you free" (8:32). For John it is Christ himself who is the truth (14:6); to know him is to be freed. In this way, the Evangelist employs a traditional title but with a new and fresh meaning.

Throughout the Fourth Gospel we encounter the expression "lifted up," generally with reference to the Son of Man's ascent into heaven. As God's agent, the Son has been sent by the Father into the world of humans to accomplish his mission. When he has done so, he will ascend to the Father (3:13; 6:62; 16: 28; 20:17). Yet when Jesus speaks of his being "lifted up" (3:13–15; 8:28; 12:32), for John this term has a double meaning. As previously noted, the expression refers to the act of crucifying, though it also means exaltation (as in exalting a king to his throne). The theme of the lifting up of the Son of Man is the Johannine theology of the cross in a nutshell. Throughout the Gospel, Jesus' death is the revelation of his identity, for the passion story in John is not the account of a victim suffering disgrace and humiliation but the story of the king going to his coronation. The Johannine Christ cannot be humiliated; when he is subject to human influence, it is only as a means toward his glorification.

Many issues in the Johannine passion narrative are important, but we limit ourselves to the following generalizations about the unique emphases of this account: (1) first is the remarkable attention given to Pilate. In developing his character, the Evangelist seems to want readers to become aware of the dangers on trying to remain neutral with regard to Jesus; (2) the Jewish leaders are made to bear responsibility for Jesus' death, even to the extent of making it sound as if the chief priests do the crucifying (to whom does "they" refer in 19:16b–18?); (3) the third emphasis is the centrality of Jesus, who throughout the narrative comes across as in charge. Even at the moment of death, he is in charge, voluntarily surrendering his life (19:30). The Evangelist clearly avoids characterizing his leading actor as humiliated or victimized, instead maintaining dignity in his suffering and culminating in Pilate's remarkable introduction of the regal Jesus: "Here is the man" (19:5), framed by declarations that Jesus was innocent. Before and after presenting "the man" to the crowds, Pilate announced his verdict: "I find no case against him" (19:4, 6).

John Kysar summarizes the meaning of the death of Jesus for John in ways familiar to readers of the Fourth Gospel:

1. The cross is *the enthronement of Jesus as king*. This theme is suggested by the "lifted up" sayings (3:14; 8:28; 12:32–34) as well as by the sign Pilate places on the cross, written in three languages: "The King of the Jews." Pilate means the sign as a taunt to the Jewish authorities, but for John it is the ultimate irony, for Jesus is not only king of the Jewish people, he is the universal king. The Gospel views the cross as the means by which Christ takes his rightful place on the throne to rule as king of humanity and of the whole of creation.

2. The cross is *the ascension and glorification of Jesus*. This theme is part of the process by which Jesus "goes away" (16:7; 20:17). Coupled with the resurrection, the crucifixion is the Revealer's departure from this world; the one who descended now ascends to his heavenly home (3:13). The crucifixion and resurrection are the imagery of that ascension. Glorification ("to glorify" means basically to honor a person) achieves the ascension. In John the cross glorifies God by making God's presence known in the world (12:28; 17:1).

3. The cross is *the new Passover*. As we have indicated, the entire ministry of Jesus is framed by Passover festivals. In addition, John depicts Jesus' death as corresponding to the time of the death of Passover lambs being prepared for the commemorative meal that evening. The Passover sacrifice, unlike others, was not ordinarily considered to be an offering for sin but a sign of deliverance from death. Christ is the new Passover lamb by which God decisively liberates people for newness of life. Consequently, the cross is presented as a new exodus, a new beginning that frees humanity to become children of God (see 1:12).

4. The cross is *God's supreme act of love*. The theme is introduced in 3:16 and repeated throughout the Gospel. In 15:13 the death of Jesus changes the relationship of humans to God, from servants to friends (15:15). The cross is the supreme expression of God's love, the model for what it means to love one another. Divine love casts the parable of the seed in 12:24 in a new light, for Jesus' death, like a seed in the ground, is the sprouting of divine love in the world. This also has a bearing on Jesus' act of washing the feet of his disciples because it is an act that anticipates the supreme act of love in the cross (13:7).

5. The cross *creates a new family of God*. That theme, already announced in the prologue (1:12), is realized on the cross. Hanging on the cross, Jesus creates the new family of God, starting with his mother and the Beloved Disciple (19:26–27). Like a pair of bookends, the claim of the gift and the enactment of the power to become children of God encompass the whole Gospel.[19]

Questions to Ponder

1. What does the account of the arrest tell you about Jesus? About Peter?
2. Why do you think Peter's denial of Jesus is recorded in all of the gospels? Why do you think Peter denies Jesus?
3. As the Roman governor of Judea, what did Pilate want to know about Jesus? How did he seek to discover the truth? How is Pilate's question in John 18:38 ironic in the setting of a trial?

---

19. These insights are adapted from Kysar, *Maverick Gospel*, 64–66.

4. In your estimation, was there a historical person named Barabbas? How does he function as a character in John's narrative? What do the other gospels say about him?

5. Do you believe John had a chiastic structure in mind in the account of Jesus' trial and crucifixion, or is this most likely a modern scholarly imposition? Explain your answer.

6. If you were to write an account of Jesus' trial, how would you portray Jesus' and Pilate's roles?

7. What to you stands out as the most remarkable detail or aspect in John's account of the crucifixion? Support your answer.

8. How do you view John's appeal to scripture in the trial and crucifixion of Jesus? Do you find direct correlation between Old Testament "prophecy" and New Testament "fulfillment"?

9. In essay 10, which theme or way of understanding the meaning of the cross seems to you most helpful or significant? Why?

CHAPTER 11

Jesus' Resurrection
(John 20:1–31)

Summary: Chapter 20 reports the discovery of the empty tomb and the Easter appearances of Jesus to Mary Magdalene and the disciples. Three recognition scenes are portrayed, including the Beloved Disciple (20:3–10), Mary Magdalene (20:11–18), and Thomas (20:24–29). After Mary witnesses the empty tomb, she informs Peter and the Beloved Disciple, who run to the tomb, finding it empty. Mary then encounters the risen Jesus and informs the disciples of the meeting. That evening Jesus appears to the disciples and bestows on them the promised Holy Spirit. Thomas, absent from this meeting, demands proof, which he receives the following Sunday during another resurrection appearance. The chapter ends with a concluding statement concerning the purpose of the Gospel.

Assignment: Read John 20

Key Passages: John 20:18, 28–29

Central Theme: Jesus is Lord

Key Symbols/Concepts: the empty tomb, the resurrection of Jesus, receiving the Holy Spirit, Thomas as doubter and subsequent confessor of the risen Christ

Learning Objectives

Participants will examine:

1. The post-resurrection appearances of Jesus in John and in the Synoptics
2. The meaning of the empty tomb
3. The role of Mary Magdalene as witness to the resurrection
4. The association of the "first day" of the week with the resurrection
5. The meaning of the actions of Peter and the Beloved Disciple at the empty tomb
6. The role of Thomas as doubter and subsequent confessor of the risen Christ
7. The meaning of the giving of the Holy Spirit in John 20:22
8. The meaning of John 20:30–31 as the Gospel's closing statement
9. The role of women as witnesses in John's Gospel

Outline to John 20:1–31

I. The Empty Tomb 20:1–10

II. The Appearance to Mary Magdalene 20:11–18

III. Jesus' First Appearance to the Gathered Disciples 20:19–29

    A. The Appearance without Thomas 20:19–23

    B. The Appearance with Thomas 20:24–29

IV. Conclusion: The Gospel's Purpose 20:30–31

Five Versions of the Resurrection

First Corinthians provides a synopsis of the Easter proclamation of the early church: Jesus was raised and appeared (15:4–5). These two pillars of tradition are given narrative form in the empty tomb and post-resurrection appearance stories of the gospels. Each gospel begins at a similar place: the early Sunday morning visit to Jesus' tomb, the presence of Mary Magdalene, the stone removed from the tomb's opening, and the appearance of an angel (or angels)—but after these similarities, each gospel goes its own way in recounting resurrection traditions. It might be more accurate to say that as the Easter experience made its literary journey through the gospels, the account grew, became embellished, and changed.

Paul, whose description of the events of Easter was the first to be written, said that the order of resurrection appearances was to Peter first, then to the Twelve, then to five hundred brethren at once, then to James, then to all the apostles, and that he himself was the last (1 Cor. 15:1–6). Mark, the first gospel to be written (in the late 60s or early 70s), makes no mention of an actual appearance of Jesus (keep in mind that the material in Mark 16:9–20 is a late addition, not found in the earliest and best Greek manuscripts, meaning that a lost ending might account for the abrupt ending at verse 8). In addition, women are the only disciples to appear in Mark's account of Easter. In Mark's account the women meet a young man dressed in a white robe, who tells them to inform the disciples that Jesus is alive and will go before them into Galilee (Mark 16:1–8). Matthew, writing in the early 80s, says that the first appearance was not to Peter, but to the women in the garden. Matthew describes a later appearance in Galilee to the eleven, not to the Twelve, but he never relates an appearance to Peter (Matt. 28). Luke, writing in the late 80s, declares Peter the first witness to the resurrection, but second in his listing is an otherwise unknown man named Cleopas, traveling with a companion on the road to Emmaus. Only after this episode, according to Luke, did Jesus appear to the disciples (Luke 24). John, the final gospel to achieve written form, states that the risen Christ appeared first to Mary Magdalene, not to Peter, and only second to the disciples, but not to all twelve, since both Thomas and Judas were absent (John 20). No source in the biblical tradition corroborates Paul's mention of an appearance to five hundred brethren, to James, or even to the apostles, if we assume that this is a group different from the Twelve.

Other details of the resurrection change during the retelling, expanding the tradition. Matthew heightens the miraculous nature of the account by introducing an earthquake into the story of Jesus' crucifixion, adding a strange episode in which the graves of the saints are opened and long-deceased bodies rise from their tombs and enter Jerusalem (Matt. 27:51–53). Matthew also includes an earthquake in his story of the resurrection. A supernatural angelic being is said to appear, replacing Mark's simple messenger. In Matthew, the angel rolls the stone away, solving the mystery of how this might have occurred in Mark's earlier account. Unlike Mark's women, Matthew's women are not afraid but go and tell the disciples, who are not yet present at the tomb. Matthew allows the women to see the risen Christ in the garden and even to grasp him by his feet (Matt. 28:9-10). In Matthew, Jesus appears to the disciples only on one occasion, on a mountain in Galilee, where he commissions them to evangelize the world and from where he presumably ascends to heaven.

Luke, writing after Matthew, adds a second angel to Matthew's account. The empty tomb is described in detail, providing additional proof of the resurrection. Luke mentions no post-resurrection appearances of Jesus in Galilee, however, but confines his account to the environs of Jerusalem, adding that Jesus' ascension took place on the Mount of Olives, on the hill overlooking the Jewish temple. Luke separates the resurrection from the outpouring of the Holy Spirit, which he places fifty days after Easter, on the Day of Pentecost (Acts 2).

In some ways the Fourth Gospel reflects primitive tradition and in other ways adds to the developing tradition. In contrast to Luke, John combines the resurrection and the outpouring of the Holy Spirit and speaks of the ascension only indirectly (20:17), for he collapses the ascension into Jesus' exaltation, his being "lifted up" on the cross, and his resurrection. John's understanding of the ascension is metaphorical rather than physical.[1] In John, Jesus appears first to Mary Magdalene, but unlike in Matthew, where the women cling to his feet, John's Jesus tells Mary not to cling to him. The story of the ascension is not told in John, but is assumed, because on Easter evening, when Jesus appears to the disciples, he appears as the ascended, glorified Lord, now making himself manifest to the disciples, who are free to touch him (20:27). Whereas the Synoptics portray Peter as doubter and betrayer, the Fourth Gospel, while not sparing Peter, creates a new narrative featuring Thomas as the unbeliever. This story, with its Christological confession (20:28), represents later material. Between the first full awareness of Easter's meaning and the writing of the Fourth Gospel there was a gap as long as sixty years. Thomas stands as a representative of those removed by decades from Christianity's foundational events, as indeed he stands for modern Christians (Matthew's motif of disbelief appears in 28:17: "When they saw him, they worshipped him, but some doubted"). Speaking to those for whom John's Gospel was written and to generations yet unborn, Jesus says: "Blessed are those who have not seen and yet have come to believe" (20:29).

John's setting in chapter 20 is Jerusalem, not Galilee (as anticipated in Mark and affirmed in Matthew), joining Luke in emphasizing

---

1. Culpepper, *Anatomy*, 96.

the primacy of the holy city, the liturgical and geographical epicenter of Judaism. The burial of Jesus is treated far more elaborately by John than by any other gospel. John's account includes the role of the Beloved Disciple, adding yet another story about the one he regards as mentor and hero. The Fourth Gospel conflates two Easter traditions, the one involving Mary Magdalene and the other Peter and John at the tomb, by having Mary report to the disciples and then return to the tomb. In John, Mary displays none of the fear shown by the women in the Marcan and Lukan narratives. John's version takes the Synoptic themes of the resurrection, the ascension, and the giving of the Holy Spirit, combining them in unique ways, reflecting a tradition more original yet more primitive.

Analysis of John 20:1–31

The Empty Tomb (Chapter 20:1–10)

The resurrection narratives assert that the first visit to Jesus' tomb occurs very early on the first day of the week, that is, on Sunday morning. In the Synoptics, Mary Magdalene is accompanied by other women, but in John she comes to the tomb alone. While Luke's Gospel identifies Mary as a Galilean woman from whom Jesus had exorcised seven demons (8:2), it is important to distinguish her biblical portrait from the traditions developed about her in later periods, which portrayed her as a "sinful" woman or prostitute. John 20:18 shows her legacy to be the first disciple to proclaim the good news of Easter.

Noticing the absence of the stone that had covered the opening of the tomb, Mary assumes that the grave has been robbed, apparently a common practice in antiquity, especially if the tomb held a wealthy person. Her report brings Peter and the Beloved Disciple on the run, the latter reaching the tomb first. (These disciples are paired frequently by John.) As the Beloved Disciple hesitates, Peter advances into the tomb. Both see the same thing—the linen strips of cloth in one place and the cloth that had wrapped Jesus' head rolled up by itself—a clear sign that no one has removed the body. John declares it to be the second disciple, not Peter, who believes as a result of what he sees, but the Evangelist does not mention *what* he believed. We *are* told that as yet neither disciple understood the scripture that Jesus must rise from the dead. The episode concludes with their return home.

Surprisingly, we are not told that either disciple saw anything supernatural, not even any angels, when they visited the tomb, nor does the event result in behavior that one might expect of persons with Easter faith. Neither disciple goes forth to proclaim the resurrection; they simply go home. As G. R. Beasley-Murray observed, it is likely that if the disciples had understood Jesus' prediction of his resurrection before the post-resurrection appearances, they would have understood this eschatologically, meaning that Jesus would be raised with all the righteous dead as the kingdom dawned.[2] As Matthew 27:52–53 indicates, they would not have been expecting an isolated resurrection in the midst of human history. The Beloved Disciple would have believed, on the basis of the empty tomb, that God had taken Jesus up into heaven bodily, much like the prophet Elijah or Moses. In John's Gospel, there is no hard evidence of Easter faith prior to the appearances of the risen Jesus. That the Beloved Disciple believed more than Mary or Peter at this juncture does not mean an end to his pilgrimage of faith. We should remember that 20:3–10 relates an empty-tomb story, not the story of a resurrection appearance. To say that the Beloved Disciple's faith is complete is to rush the story. His one clear role in John's Gospel is to embody the love and intimacy with Jesus that is the goal of discipleship. The narrator points to the significance of the study of scripture in understanding events such as this (20:9). Only later did believers understand the meaning of events witnessed by the disciples—after they had studied the scriptures, reflected on what Jesus had said, and been enlightened by the Paraclete (2:22; 12:16; 20:9).

The Appearance to Mary Magdalene (Chapter 20:11–18)

It is remarkable that in the rather short narrative on the resurrection, John devotes so much attention to Mary Magdalene's encounter with Jesus. As C. H. Dodd noted, there is nothing quite like this story anywhere else in the gospels. By devoting more space to Mary than to the story of any of the male disciples individually, more attention than even to Jesus' own mother and the Beloved Disciple, there is little doubt that the Evangelist wishes to portray this Mary as integral to the Easter story and its meaning for Jesus' followers. The story of Mary Magdalene as presented

---

2. Beasley-Murray, *John*, 373–74.

in John 20 is "a moving drama of the progress of a soul on the way to full faith in the risen Lord."[3]

After reporting to Peter and the other disciple her discovery of the open tomb, Mary returns to the tomb and weeps there. Finally, she discovers two angels sitting like bookends where the body of Jesus lain. Striking to John's version is the virtual silence of the angels. The point of their inclusion was surely to signal, as angels normally do, that divine activity was involved in the space between them. There is a void, clearly, but it is not devoid of meaning. The angels signal that Jesus' body is no longer in the tomb. They attempt to draw Mary out of her sorrow, away from fixation on the past, and ironically, only when she turns away from the empty tomb does she see Jesus.

John 20:15 Jesus opens the dialogue by repeating the question of the angels: "Woman, why are you weeping?" It is not, however, until Jesus calls her by name that she recognizes him (cf. 10:3-4). The revelation becomes more personal as he progresses from "woman" to "Mary," and it is at this point that she becomes the first witness to the risen Lord. By including the question, "*Whom* are you looking for?" Jesus implies that Mary's focus should be on someone, not on something. She wishes to know where the corpse is, but Jesus responds by speaking about a living person. By focusing on the past and on physical things, Mary mistakes Jesus for the gardener who may have moved the body.

Though Jesus calls Mary by name, her pilgrimage is not over, as indicated by her reply to Jesus, calling him *Rabbouni* (20:16; "my master" in Aramaic); she is still thinking of Jesus in terms of her past relationship with him, as her teacher. Jesus' words "Do not hold on to me" (20:17) imply that Mary is approaching Jesus in a limited (physical) way. Jesus is not interested in renewing past relationships with his disciples, for he is no longer the same Jesus. Though his ascension is not yet complete, he is truly on the way to the Father. The command to Mary, however, applies to this interim period only. After the ascension, the disciples would be united with Christ in a manner that could be described as "holding," to which worship and the sacraments point. The Evangelist focuses on the important theme of witness; Mary completes her faith pilgrimage by journeying to the disciples and bearing witness to the risen Lord (20:18).

That Jesus calls the male disciples his "brothers" in 20:17 indicates the sort of family relationship he wishes for the community of faith (cf.

---

3. Witherington, *John's Wisdom*, 328.

John 19:25–27): "Go and say to *my brothers*, I am ascending to *my Father and your Father*, to *my God and your God*." Something has changed, decisively. A new relationship has sprung to life, welcoming the disciples into a new world, "a world where they can know God the way Jesus knew God, where they can be intimate children with their father. They can be, in other words, true Israelites at last."[4]

Mary's declaration in 20:18, "I have seen the Lord," is crucial. It indicates that she is no longer fixated on the past but rather on the task before her. Ironically, Jesus reestablishes fellowship with his brothers by first reestablishing a relationship with one of his sisters. As we will notice in the Thomas story, Mary, having touched Jesus, does not need to cling to him but rather can be commissioned to undertake an apostolic task. Thomas, by contrast, must be bidden to touch, but is not given an apostolic task. In other words, "this sister comes off better in these stories than either Peter and the Beloved Disciple mentioned before her as examining the empty tomb or the cynical Thomas mentioned after her."[5] Her portrayal shows how far true faith in Jesus can bring a person. Mary Magdalene is featured because John sees in her a model for all Christians. Even so, the modern church has not yet fully grasped what it means for men and women together to confess the risen Lord boldly and proclaim him equally in the world.

Jesus' First Appearance to the Gathered Disciples (Chapter 20:19–29)

In the four gospels the appearances of the risen Lord may be grouped according to location. John is the only gospel to record appearances in both Jerusalem and Galilee. In two scenes John tells the story of Jesus' Jerusalem appearance to the disciples, one without Thomas and, a week later, with Thomas. In the first scene (20:19–23), the risen Jesus appears to the disciples and commissions them on the evening of Easter day. This section has elements in common with Luke 24:36–43: both occur on Sunday evening (thereby validating the Christian practice of worship on the first day of the week); in both sections Jesus greets the disciples with the same words; and in both Jesus displays to the gathered disciples the wounds of his crucifixion. Various differences appear as well, such as in

---

4. Wright, *John*, 2:145.
5. Witherington, *John's Wisdom*, 332.

portrayal of the disciples. The Fourth Evangelist rarely uses the term "the Twelve" to speak of the disciples and never identifies them as "the eleven," so at this crucial juncture they are simply identified with the general term "disciples." This gathering of disciples, as at the farewell meal, probably included the core group, but there is no indication that it was limited to them. For John, the gathering on Easter evening represents the faith community in general, not the apostolic leadership. In Luke's account all the disciples are bidden to touch the Lord, the wounds in the feet taking the place of the uniquely Johannine wound in the side; the Lord is depicted as eating—probably to correct the impression he is a disembodied spirit. Significantly, Luke postpones the gift of the Spirit until the day of Pentecost (Acts 2).

The Fourth Gospel describes the band of disciples as huddled in fear behind locked doors. Jesus comes and suddenly appears in their midst. Although the Fourth Evangelist does not speculate about Jesus' sudden appearance, he clearly portrays Jesus as having different physical properties from those he had before the crucifixion. He is still a human being, but much more, one who can materialize at will, passing through grave clothes or through locked doors without difficulty. As the disciples try to comprehend the meaning of his sudden appearance, Jesus offers the normal Jewish greeting, "Peace be unto you." The gesture is repeated, but only the second time, after Jesus shows his hands and side, do they rejoice and recognize the Lord.

John 20:21 presents the Johannine version of the commissioning of the disciples for mission (a more complete commissioning appears in Matt. 28:18-20). While John's commissioning lacks specific content, the nature of that task had been spelled out earlier, in the farewell discourses (see 17:18). Jesus breathes the Holy Spirit into the disciples (20:22), thereby fulfilling his promise to send the Paraclete to them (14:26; 15:26; 16:7, 13). Verse 22 recalls the story of creation, where God breathed life into Adam (Gen. 2:7; cf. the description of the breath of life in Ezekiel 37:9). This act of commissioning and empowerment represents a new creation, the beginning of a new humanity.

In 20:23 the disciples are tasked with forgiving and retaining sins.[6] The similarities of this saying to those in Matthew 16:19 and 18:18 are frequently noted, but their differences are perhaps more significant. In Matthew the discussion is about church discipline; here the discussion

---

6. At the Council of Trent, the Roman Catholic authorities limited this reference to the sacrament of penance.

centers on the witness of the entire faith community, not just its apostolic leaders. The task of forgiving and retaining sins is not a harsh task of judgment, but a natural component of calling people to repentance and offering forgiveness in Christ. As John's Gospel indicates, those who reject the gospel remain in their sins (8:21; 9:41; 15:22–24), a theological failing, not a moral or behavioral transgression.

The next time Jesus appears to the gathered disciples, Thomas is present. Earlier in the chapter the focus was on Mary, the woman of God who comes to full faith. Here the focus is on Thomas, the representative of those who doubt, even after Easter (although the word "doubt" is forever linked with Thomas in the Christian tradition, the word occurs nowhere in 20:24–29, contrary to its insertion by the NIV and NRSV translators at 20:27). Because Thomas had not been with the other disciples, he refuses to believe until he sees and feels tangible evidence. The underlying theme here is that no secondary evidence would have satisfied some disciples after the shattering event of the crucifixion. Some required and received tangible proof that Jesus rose from the dead.

We need not find inconsistency between Jesus' admonition to Mary not to hold him and his invitation to Thomas to touch him. "In both cases he was inviting each one to do what he or she needed to do to take the next step in faith and understanding."[7] The purpose of this story, at least in part, could be to combat docetic tendencies (viewing matter to be evil, docetists argued that Jesus was solely divine and only appeared to be human) that seem to have plagued the Johannine community shortly after John's Gospel was published (cf. 1 John 1:1; 6:6; 2 John 7).

While Jesus' statement in 20:29 implies that Thomas's faith was weak at this point ("Have you believed because you have seen me? Blessed are those who have not seen and yet have come to believe"), Thomas is not utterly cynical and faithless, as his confession in verse 28 makes clear. That confession, "My Lord and my God!" the last words spoken by a disciple prior to the epilogue, constitutes the climactic confession in John.[8] Only here in John's Gospel (20:27) do we find the words *apistos*

---

7. Culpepper, *Gospel and Letters*, 243.

8. This statement does not imply that Jesus *is* the Father. In confessing Jesus as his Lord and God, Thomas acknowledges the truth of the words that Jesus spoke to him in 14:7: "If you know me, you will know my Father also. From now on you do know him and have seen him"; cf. 14:9: "Whoever has seen me has seen the Father." The language of this confession affirms the central truth with which the Gospel began: "The Word was with God, and the Word was God" (1:1). Thomas sees God fully revealed in Jesus.

(the word means "unbelief," not "doubt," as in the NRSV and NIV) and *pistos* ("faith," "belief"), for we have reached the climax of the many pilgrimages of faith in the Fourth Gospel. Thomas, called upon to show that he does believe, responds outwardly and visibly. Thomas's confession constitutes a Christological high-water mark in John, recapitulating some of the claims about God's Son made in the prologue. Nothing more profound can be said about Jesus. Notice that Thomas confesses Jesus to be *his* Lord and God, a personal and theological reflection of the meaning of "belief" in John's Gospel.

Thomas, whose name is found in every list of the Twelve (Matt. 10:1-4; Mark 3:13-19; Luke 6:12-16; Acts 1:12-14), plays no discernable role in the Synoptic Gospels, but is an important figure in John, where he appears in 11:16 and 14:5, as well as in 20:24-29 and 21:2. The apocryphal *Gospel of Thomas*, a collection of Jesus' sayings, names him as author, calling him Didymus (the Greek word for "twin," much as "Thomas" is the Hebrew word for twin). In tradition incorporated in the third-century *Acts of Thomas*, India is said to have been his special mission field. In that work Thomas is said to have been Jesus' twin brother. The unique prominence of Thomas in John, where he is repeatedly referred to as "the Twin" (11:16; 20:24; 21:2), suggests that John's Gospel emanated from an environment that overlapped the circles in which Thomas was venerated. Elaine Pagels, a leading scholar in early Christianity, argues in *Beyond Belief* that the Fourth Gospel was written to contradict the *Gospel of Thomas* and to denigrate the figure of Thomas by depicting his absence from the commissioning ceremony by the resurrected Christ on Easter evening. For Pagels, the implication of John 20 is that Thomas, "having missed this meeting, is not an apostle, has not received the holy spirit, and lacks the power to forgive sins, which the others received directly from the risen Christ."[9] Whether John's depiction of Thomas is negative or positive is much debated; Pagel's characterization supports the depiction that forever marks him as Doubting Thomas. In the end, however, Thomas believes (20:28-29), uttering the ultimate and most adequate Christological confession in John's Gospel, a confession that led James Charlesworth to identify Thomas as John's Beloved Disciple.[10] The specificity of Thomas's request to examine the side as well as the hands of Jesus (20:25) is perhaps the strongest link in Charlesworth's argument, based

---

9. Pagels, *Beyond Belief*, 71.
10. Charlesworth, *Beloved Disciple*.

on the Beloved Disciple's witness to the crucifixion in 19:35. The Beloved Disciple's presence at the crucifixion, plus the piercing of the side of Jesus (19:34), are unique to John. Despite Charlesworth's argumentation, it is best to view Thomas as the representation of people in later generations who also missed out on the first resurrection appearances, recalling that Thomas's skepticism led to true faith. Perhaps this was John's intention, since 20:29 seems to be directed to a larger audience, including future generations who hear and read his Gospel: "Blessed are those who have not seen and yet have come to believe." Those who do not see and yet believe are more blessed, for their faith is greater.

Conclusion: The Gospel's Purpose (Chapter 20:30–31)

The Gospel concludes by indicating that every word and deed of Jesus is imbued with deeper meaning: "Now Jesus did many other signs in the presence of his disciples, which are not written in this book. But these are written so that you may come to believe that Jesus is the Messiah, the Son of God, and that through believing you may have life in his name" (20:30–31). Most commentators view "many other signs" as a summary statement of Jesus' activity in the Gospel. By introducing the word "other," John is including the events of John 20 as "signs" (in 2:18–20 Jesus pointed to his resurrection as a sign). If we recall the difference in John between miracle and sign, then identifying Jesus' resurrection appearances as signs means that, like Jesus' other signs, the theological truth of the resurrection lies not in the appearances themselves, but in that to which they point. Thus, the resurrection stories cannot be limited to Jesus' miraculous return from death. That is made clear in 20:24–29, where Thomas sees through the physical miracle to that which it points: the full revelation of God in Jesus (20:28). The truth to which the "signs" of Jesus' resurrection appearances point is not his return from death, but the completion of his hour. This is confirmed in the statement of purpose in 20:31: "that you may come to believe that Jesus is the Messiah, the Son of God." Like Thomas and the other disciples, readers are not summoned "merely to believe in the resurrection, but to believe in the revelation of Jesus' identity and relationship with God, of which the resurrection is a sign."[11]

The Evangelist, knowing the early Jewish Wisdom tradition, ends his Gospel (as well as the epilogue; see 21:25) as Ecclesiastes ended: "Of

11. O'Day, *John*, 852.

making many books there is no end" (Eccl. 12:12). The striking difference is that the Evangelist is not worn out by the study of Wisdom but rather is invigorated by Jesus' words and deeds. John's Gospel ends, not merely with a statement that these things are written to engender faith, but that they are written so that those who believe may have life, life in the Johannine sense—abundant life that begins now and transcends death (20:31; cf. 10:10 and 1:4). The Gospel brings us full circle: Christ is the means and the end of life.

Essay 11: Women as Witnesses in John's Gospel

When the issue of women's rights and roles arises, religious people often look to tradition, particularly to scripture, for guidance. Given the limits traditionally placed upon women in monotheistic religions, evident in ongoing patriarchal bias in many Western religious sects and denominations, it behooves us to reexamine the biblical roots, in this case the Johannine perspective, to see whether prejudicial attitudes against women can be sustained.

Two passages in the book of Genesis set the tone for our discussion, Genesis 1:26–28 and 3:15–16. The first passage, attributed to the Priestly writer, establishes "the pattern of creation," affirming sexual equality, and the second passage, attributed to the Yahwist writer, establishes "the pattern of the fall," where women are said to be subject to men. In the first passage, men and women alike are made "in the image of God," together established as stewards over the earth. The second passage, "and [your husband] shall rule over you" (Gen. 3:16), presents a model for patriarchal interpretations. While Israelite society displayed patriarchal patterns, we find examples of female leadership, including Miriam as liturgical leader and prophet (Exod. 15:20), Deborah as judge (Judg. 4:4), Huldah as prophet (2 Kgs. 22:14), and various queens who ruled as co-regents while their sons came of age (see 2 Kgs. 21:1; 22:1). Disparagement of women's character and nature is sometimes asserted in the early Jewish Wisdom literature, most radically in the book of Sirach: "From a woman sin had its beginning, and because of her we all die" (25:24). Likewise, the book of Proverbs depicts foolish women as being contentious, noisy, and indiscreet (9:13; 11:22; 25:24).

New Testament books, particularly letters attributed to Paul, contain passages supporting both Old Testament patterns: the pattern of the fall is evident in 1 Corinthians 11:3; 14:34–35; Ephesians 5:22; and 1 Timothy 2:11–15, while the pattern of creation is illustrated in 1 Corinthians 11:11; Galatians 3:28; and Ephesians 5:21. Other than the 1 Corinthians passages (in 11:2–16 Paul is conserving and breaking with tradition equally; 14:34–35 is a later editorial insertion),[12] passages that depict the pattern of the fall are determined by scholars to be non-Pauline (meaning they were written later by someone attempting to make Paul conform to more acceptable views during the post-Pauline period) or Deutero-Pauline (meaning they were not written by Paul but by a later follower or admirer). In Paul's undisputed letters, as in the early church, women served as evangelists, pastors, teachers, apostles, and prophets. Some served as patrons of churches, allowing congregations to meet in their homes. Some were Paul's coworkers on the mission field. The rationale for this egalitarian treatment may be found in the ministry of Jesus himself, who contravened prevailing Jewish customs and attitudes.

An examination of Jewish social and religious customs in the first century reveals that women were regularly relegated to second-class status.[13] According to Josephus, the learned first-century Jewish historian, "In every respect woman is inferior to man."[14] That view typified the opinion of educated Jews contemporary with Jesus. According to statements taken from the Jewish Talmud and other writings of Jewish antiquity, "Rather should the words of the Torah be burned than entrusted to a woman" (these words are attributed to first-century Rabbi Eleazar).[15] Furthermore, women were not allowed to lead in prayer at mealtime: "Let a curse come upon the man who has his wife or children say grace for him."[16]

Women's social rights were also grossly restricted. For example, women did not count toward the number necessary for a quorum needed to constitute the Minyan prayer service. In addition, at the temple in Jerusalem women were restricted to the courtyard five steps below the men. In the synagogues they were separated from men, if indeed they attended the synagogue service at all. First-century rabbis did not speak with women in public, including wives, sisters, or daughters, regarding it

12. Borg and Crossan, *First Paul*, 56–57.

13. The information on women in Judaism is taken from Swidler, "Jesus Was a Feminist." For a more scholarly approach, including citations of ancient literature, see Swidler, *Women in Judaism*, particularly chapters 3–5.

14. Josephus, *Contra Apionem*, II, 24.

15. pSotah 3.4; cf. bYoma 66b.

16. bBer. 20b.

as actually disreputable. In this respect the Talmud states: "The wise men say, 'who speaks much with a woman draws down misfortune on himself, neglects the words of the Law, and finally earns hell.'"[17] Only rarely were women allowed to bear witness in a court of law. Some contemporaries of Jesus, such as the learned philosopher Philo of Alexandria, thought that women should not even leave the home except to go to the synagogue, and then only at times when most other people would be at home. In home life the woman was under the tutelage of the male, either the husband in the case of a wife or the father in the case of a daughter, and in the case of a widow, the dead man's brother. Rabbinical sayings provide additional insights into attitudes toward women: "It is well for those whose children are male, but ill for those whose children are female. At the birth of a boy all are joyful, but at the birth of a girl all are sad."[18]

The Gospel of John indicates that Jesus deliberately contravened contemporary attitudes and social customs. Unlike the Jewish rule that women were not allowed to bear legal witness, John depicts Jesus as appearing first to a woman after his resurrection (Mary Magdalene), who is asked to bear testimony of this event to the eleven male disciples (John 20:11–18).[19] This account goes squarely against the current view with regard to the credibility of women in bearing witness. By showing himself first to a woman, Jesus was deliberately rejecting the prevailing second-class status of women. The Synoptics agree with this portrayal, emphasizing that the early Christian movement clearly affirmed sexual equality, prompting Thomas Cahill to call the primitive church "the world's first egalitarian society."[20]

With respect to miracles, the raising of Lazarus was done at the request of his sisters Mary and Martha (John 11:17–44). This and related miracles mentioned in the gospels all show Jesus' great interest in the plight of women. The gospels indicate that Jesus had a number of women followers. Luke mentions several of these by name (8:1–3). When one realizes that Jewish women were prohibited from learning the Torah and were discouraged from participating in ordinary synagogue services, the attention that Jesus gives in teaching women is a marked dissociation from current practices. In the intellectual sphere, Luke records an

17. Aboth 1, 5.
18. bNid, 3:1b.
19. In a recent book, *Jesus Was a Feminist*, Swidler views Mary Magdalene as the source for John's Gospel and identifies her as the Beloved Disciple.
20. Cahill, *Desire of the Everlasting Hills*, 148.

interesting account rejecting the stereotype of a woman as fit only for housekeeping duties (10:38–42). While at Mary and Martha's home, Mary took the position of a male pupil, sitting at Jesus' feet, while Martha was distracted with much serving and thinks that her sister is not doing her duty by assisting her in serving. Jesus supports Mary, saying that Mary has chosen the better part, which is not to be taken from her.

In the account of Jesus and the Samaritan woman in John 4, Jesus deliberately violates the prevailing code. His disciples are shocked to find Jesus talking, not just with a Samaritan—that would have been disturbing enough—but with a woman of Samaria. In that same chapter we discover that Jesus chose her— not only a woman but this particular woman—to be the first recipient of his messiahship (4:26). Later in the chapter we find her witnessing of Jesus to her countrymen, and it is on the strength of this testimony that others come to believe in Jesus (4:39). The Fourth Evangelist decides to tell this story—found only in John—in such a way that it reinforces Jesus' stress on the equality of women with men.

The Gospel of John is remarkable for its intentional presentation of women as models of faith. In this Gospel, women appear at all the crucial places: in chapters 2, 4, 11, 12, 19, and 20. Women are found early in the narrative of Jesus' ministry, beginning with his mother's role in his first public act (2:1–11) and followed closely by the story of the Samaritan woman in chapter 4. At the crucial point of the raising of Lazarus, Mary and Martha appear. Martha takes the lead role in chapter 11 and Mary in chapter 12. These chapters are the turning point of the Gospel. Mary's anointing of Jesus (12:1–8) prepares him for his death and opens the chapter that constitutes Jesus' final public appearance before his passion. At the height of his passion, a group of women appear at the foot of the cross, including Jesus' mother, Mary Magdalene, and others (19:25). Their presence is highlighted by the conspicuous absence of all but one of the male followers (the Beloved Disciple). There, at the base of the cross, a new community is formed, with the mother of Jesus as its matriarch. Finally, in the account of the resurrection, the first to discover the empty tomb and meet the risen Christ is a woman, Mary Magdalene. Not even Peter or the Beloved Disciple is so privileged. As Raymond Brown has pointed out, Mary Magdalene is the first apostle—one who witnesses the risen Christ and is sent forth to announce his resurrection. In fact, she is the apostle to the apostles.[21] Women are central to John's narrative, for they are involved in the beginning, the middle, and the conclusion of his story.

The Fourth Evangelist describes the Christian community as a witnessing community. From among the models for the Church's witness to the world, John's Gospel presents three in particular: (1) John the Baptist, whose persistent effort was to point beyond himself to Christ (1:19–34); (2) the Samaritan woman, whose encounter with Christ elicits testimony to others (4:39-42); and (3) Mary Magdalene, the first to greet the risen Christ and to be commissioned by him to share the news of his resurrection (20:17–18). It is not accidental that two of these three models are women.

What is John's subliminal message? First, women are among Jesus' disciples and are the equals of the male disciples. Next, their discipleship is central to the Jesus story. Finally, females are depicted as models of faith. To the extent that Jesus promoted the dignity and equality of women in the midst of a male-dominated society, John's Jesus intentionally contravened social customs that discriminated against women. Followers of Jesus—then and now—cannot do otherwise.

Questions to Ponder

1. In your estimation, what is it that the Beloved Disciple believed when, according to John 20:8–9, he entered the tomb? Was the content of his "belief" primarily Jewish in nature or something uniquely Christian? What does your answer suggest about the disciples' original understanding of the Easter event?

2. Why do you think Jesus appeared to Mary Magdalene before the other (male) disciples?

3. What image or analogy of the church comes to mind when you read Jesus' words to his disciples in John 20:17?

4. What role does Thomas portray in John 20? Was his belief and understanding different from the other disciples?

5. What aspect of John's resurrection account do you find most convincing? Least convincing?

6. What verse or theme stands out for you as the key to John 20? Support your answer.

---

21. Brown, *Community of the Beloved Disciple*, 189-90.

PART VI

New Beginnings

(JOHN 21)

CHAPTER 12

John's Epilogue
(John 21:1–25)

Summary: Chapter 21 is an epilogue that recounts a Galilean post-resurrection appearance. Jesus stands on the shore while seven disciples fish. There is a miraculous catch of fish, whereupon the Beloved Disciple recognizes Jesus. Jesus prepares a meal by the shore, at which time Jesus restores Peter, clarifying the roles of Peter and the Beloved Disciple. John 21:25 provides the formal conclusion of the Gospel.

Assignment: Read John 21

Key Passages: John 21:15, 24

Central Theme: The Disciples are (Re-) Commissioned in Galilee

Key Symbols/Concepts: the seven disciples, one hundred fifty-three fish, feeding lambs/tending sheep

Learning Objectives
Participants will examine:
1. The relation of John 21 to the rest of the Gospel
2. The Galilean post-resurrection appearances in John and in the Synoptics
3. The meaning of the miraculous catch of fish in John 21:4–11
4. The meaning of Peter's commissioning in John 21:15–19
5. The role of the Beloved Disciple in John 21

6. John 21:25 as the formal conclusion of the Gospel

7. Leadership models in John's Gospel

Outline to John 21:1–25

I. Jesus' Appearance to Seven Disciples by the Galilean Sea 21:1–23

   A. The Miraculous Catch of Fish 21:1–14

   B. Peter's Reconciliation and Commissioning as Shepherd 21:15–19

   C. The Beloved Disciple as the True Witness 21:20–24

II. Formal Conclusion of the Gospel 21:25

The Commissioning of the Disciples and the Bestowal of the Spirit: Multiple Stages or Multiple Accounts?

John 20:21 has been called John's Great Commission and 20:22 John's Pentecost story. Such characterizations raise difficult questions about the relationship of this material to John 21 (particularly the symbolic nature of the great catch of fish in 21:11 and the commissioning of Peter in 21:15–19) and to the Pentecost narrative in Acts 2. In light of the general commissioning of the disciples in chapter 20, do the episodes in chapter 21 constitute a recommissioning? Furthermore, did Jesus bestow the Holy Spirit twice, or is Acts 2 an expanded version of the Johannine bestowal in the Upper Room? The differences between these set of events are so dissimilar as to suggest different events.

Modern scholars generally explain the variations as reflecting perspectives of different authors or editors. John's theology of the Holy Spirit and his depiction of discipleship and mission thus constitute one of many distinctions between John and the other Evangelists. Conservative scholars, however, disagree with redactional approaches, finding literary solutions inadequate and contrived. Edwyn Hoskyns, for example, explains the differences between John and Acts as the result of separate historical events. He finds John's account of the bestowal of the Spirit and the commissioning of the disciples as preparatory to Pentecost, since John's account occurs in secret, behind closed doors, whereas in Acts the mission is public. In John 20 Jesus is present, whereas in Acts 2 he is absent when the Spirit falls on the disciples. Such differences seem impossible to reconcile if the stories are the same. Intellectually, literary solutions are appealing, though not always convincing.

Analysis of John 21:1–25

The consensus of modern scholars is that John 21 is a secondary addition to the Fourth Gospel and should be interpreted as a postscript or epilogue to the Gospel. Scholars are divided on whether the material in John 21 was added by the Evangelist himself or by a later redactor, although the latter theory is more widely held. While there is no manuscript evidence that John ever circulated without chapter 21, the secondary status of John 21 is convincing on two basic grounds: (1) John 20:30–31 brings the Gospel to a close, and (2) Jesus' post-resurrection appearances in John 21 introduce a focus that is secondary, contradictory, and anticlimactic to John 20.

In light of the disparities between chapters 20 and 21, John 20:22 does not portray the Johannine Pentecost adequately. If John 20 concluded the Gospel, the Evangelist would have expected the disciples to be out evangelizing the world. Instead John 21 indicates that seven disciples are back in Galilee fishing, as if little had happened in Jerusalem. Furthermore, the epilogue tells us that Jesus' appearance in Galilee is the third post-resurrection appearance (21:14), but the account reads like a first appearance, for the disciples do not immediately recognize Jesus (note the similarity with Mary in John 20 and with the disciples on the Emmaus road in Luke 24). If John 21 belonged to the original plan of the Gospel, as Hoskyns argues, these differences are hard to explain.[1] To this we may add that there are numerous words (some twenty-eight) and phrases in chapter 21 that are not found elsewhere in the Fourth Gospel. For example, here alone we find a reference to the sons of Zebedee. These and other differences suggest that John 21 was originally a free-floating tradition inserted by an editor, probably because the Beloved Disciple died shortly after the Gospel had been compiled from his memoirs. This chapter was added to clear up problems

---

1. N. T. Wright offers an interesting explanation. The futile fishing expedition in John 21:3 should be read as an object lesson to believers, particularly young converts who feel commissioned to work for Jesus. Filled with God's breath, they feel invincible. But if they try to live as they did formerly, in their own way, they will fail. They will toil all night and take nothing. When they fail, the only way forward is "to admit defeat, to listen afresh to Jesus' voice, and to do what he says. Then there is no knowing what they will achieve," *John*, 2:157–58.

caused by the Beloved Disciple's death (21:23), among other things, perhaps shortly before the Gospel was published.[2]

Jesus' Appearance to Seven Disciples by the Galilean Sea (Chapter 21:1–23)

John 21 serves a vital function because it preserves the tradition of a post-resurrection appearance in Galilee, records the restoration of Peter, and clarifies the roles of Peter and the Beloved Disciple. We are not told precisely when these events occurred, but the scene is narrated as one continuous scene. Seven of the disciples have returned to fishing in the Sea of Tiberius (the Sea of Galilee). The group consists of Peter, James and John (called only the sons of Zebedee, a designation known from the Synoptics), Nathanael, Thomas, and two unnamed disciples. As we shall see, one of these seven is the Beloved Disciple, but it is impossible to tell whether he is John the son of Zebedee or one of the others. Since this is not the Twelve, it is unlikely that 21:14 means that this is the third time Jesus had appeared to this particular group.

The Miraculous Catch of Fish (Chapter 21:1–14)

The Evangelist has in this account combined elements from two types of traditions: a story of a miraculous catch of fish (cf. Luke 5:1–11) and a recognition story (cf. Luke 24:30–35). The miraculous catch of fish functions analogously to the miracle at the wedding in Cana (2:1–11); in both stories the miracle is the vehicle for an epiphany. Jesus' first and last revelatory acts in the Gospel narrative are thus both miracles of abundance in Galilee.

Like the introduction to the Cana miracle story (2:1–2), the epilogue establishes the time, location, and characters of this miracle story. While the resurrection appearances in John 20 take place in Jerusalem, the appearance in John 21 takes place in Galilee: "After these things Jesus showed himself again to the disciples by the Sea of Tiberius" (21:1). Matthew also records a Jerusalem resurrection appearance followed by one in Galilee. The verb "to show [oneself]" or "to reveal" in 21:1 is an important verb in John's Gospel. It is associated with the revelatory aspect of Jesus' miracles at 2:11 and 9:3, and it is used to summarize the purpose of Jesus' ministry at 1:31 and 17:6. The repetition of this verb in verse

---

2. Witherington, *John's Wisdom*, 352.

1 underscores that the story that follows is an epiphany and should be interpreted in the light of the revelatory nature of Jesus' ministry.

It is interesting to note that prior to John 21 the Fourth Gospel does not include any material about Peter or others as fishermen. Nor is there any mention of Jesus making them fishers of people (cf. Matt. 4:19; Mark 1:17), though knowledge of such traditions seems to be presupposed here. The story tells us that Peter decides to go fishing at night, supposedly the best time to catch fish. The others join him, but they are unsuccessful. Sunrise comes and they see someone standing on the shore, calling them "children" (21:5). Jesus tells them to cast the net to the right side of the boat, where their catch is so great they can't haul in the net. Yet, unlike the similar tale in Luke 5:1-10, the net doesn't break. The term "children," a term of endearment, is important in view of John's theme of believers as "children of God" (1:12).

The Beloved Disciple, typically, is the first to perceive that the stranger on the shore is Jesus: "That disciple whom Jesus loved said to Peter, 'It is the Lord!'" (21:7). The scene is reminiscent of Peter's conversation with the Beloved Disciple at 13:23-24 and elsewhere in the Gospel. Peter, typically the first to act, puts on some clothes, jumps into the lake, and swims to shore, leaving the other disciples to bring in the boat and the net full of fish. Perhaps in this fragment of the resurrection tradition resides the earliest vestigial remains of Paul's assertion in 1 Corinthians 15:5 that Jesus appeared first to Peter (Cephas). The primacy of this experience also seems to be warranted by Peter's failure to recognize Jesus. If he had seen the risen Christ before, in Jerusalem, his response here in Galilee would be strange indeed.

Arriving on shore, the disciples see that Jesus has started a fire for a meal of bread and fish. This meal should not be given Eucharistic significance, for there is no mention of drinking, breaking bread, or giving thanks. Rather, this is more like a family reunion. While there are parallels in 21:4-14 to the feeding of the five thousand in 6:1-13, there the focus is on bread; here it is on fish. The abundance of the catch is consistent with the abundance of wine at the wedding at Cana and the abundance of food in John 6. When Peter returns to the boat, we are given a description with symbolic overtones that depict the witnessing mission of the early church: the disciples, dragging a net full of fish from the boat to the risen Lord (21:8).

The number of fish in 21:11 (153) has for centuries intrigued interpreters, with numerous suggestions given as to its meaning. Some see here the exact number of the catch; others find the sum of the numbers from 1 to 17, others a sign of the Trinity (using numerical symbolism called gematria), or a number representing what was believed to be the total number of species of fish in the sea. The latter has been used to highlight the missionary task of the church, suggesting converts from all sorts of people. The untorn net (21:11), like the seamless garment (19:23–24), represents symbolic church unity or more likely the fact that Jesus can enable a large catch of disciples without losing any (see 17:12). "In a sense we have two stories here: the former signifies the mission, the latter the ongoing fellowship with Jesus. The latter makes the former possible. It is through union with Christ and being fed by him that disciples are enabled to go out into the world and fish."[3]

Peter's Reconciliation and Commissioning as Shepherd (Chapter 21:15–19)

This section continues the previous scene with only a shift in focus. Whereas the first and longer section of the chapter dealt with the role of the disciples in general, here the Evangelist focuses more particularly on two of the inner circle, Peter and the Beloved Disciple. Peter has been prominent in the Gospel since the opening call narrative (1:40–42), the Beloved Disciple since the farewell meal (13:21–27). While this segment reflects differences between the Petrine and Johannine communities, these differences are not primary. These disciples represent two specific examples of the continuation of Jesus' work: Peter as shepherd of the flock and the Beloved Disciple as teacher of the Christian community.

When Jesus questions Peter three times about his love for the Master, he is providing him with an opportunity to reverse the threefold denial in the courtyard of the high priest (18:15–27). Jesus asks Peter three times if he loves him; three times Peter affirms his love for Jesus, and three times Jesus commissions Peter to feed his sheep. The variations in language, such as using different verbs for "to love" and the terms "lambs/sheep" and "feed/tend," are not significant in themselves but reflect the Evangelist's propensity for synonyms. These verses are regularly interpreted as Peter's pastoral and apostolic commission, following Matthew 16:18–19, but in their Johannine context it is better to see them in the light of Jesus' commandments to his disciples in the Farewell Discourse

3. Ibid., 355.

(a closer Synoptic parallel may be Matthew 25:31-46). This passage does not point to Peter as Jesus' distinctive successor but as embodying what should characterize all disciples: living out one's love of Jesus (13:34-35). The focus of 21:15-17 lies in the relationship between Peter's love for Jesus and the charge to feed Jesus' sheep, not apostolic succession. Christian leadership must be founded on love and on care for the flock.

The name "Simon son of John," repeated three times (21:15, 16, 17), provides an important link with Peter's first appearance in the Gospel, repeating the name Jesus used in 1:42. When Jesus asks Peter if he loves him "more than these" (21:15), the point of the question is probably to see if Peter's love exceeds that of the other disciples, since Peter earlier had falsely boasted about his willingness to lay down his life for Jesus (13:37). Peter's call, like that to every disciple, is to a pastoral role. Ironically, Peter will be a good shepherd in an unforeseeable sense. By the time John 21 was written, Peter had already died a martyr's death (under Nero, in the 60s). Earlier, when Peter had boasted that he would die for Jesus (13:37), Jesus had told him that he was not yet ready, though the Johannine editor knows that Peter would indeed glorify God through his death (21:18-19). Jesus' command to Peter, "Follow me," contains a double meaning. It is a general invitation to discipleship as well as a more specific invitation to martyrdom and death.

The Beloved Disciple as the True Witness (Chapter 21:20–24)

The Beloved Disciple would have a different role. He would not die a martyr's death but would live a long life, bearing faithful witness. John 21:22 ("Jesus said to him, 'If it is my will that he remain until I come, what is that to you? Follow me!'") highlights two forms of discipleship: one to follow unto death, and the other to remain unto faithfulness. These verses underscore the importance of the Beloved Disciple for the community for whom John was written. Rumor spread that the Beloved Disciple would not die but would "remain" (the significant Johannine term *meno* is the Greek word often translated "abide"; cf. John 1:33; 15:4-10) until Jesus came, but the redactor must explain that Jesus had not said this: "So the rumor spread in the community that this disciple would not die. Yet Jesus did not say to him that he would not die, but 'If it is my will that he remain until I come, what is that to you?'" (21:23). The need to correct this misunderstanding may have arisen because the Beloved Disciple had died by the time John 21 was written. John 21:24 makes clear that though the Beloved Disciple does not die a martyr's death, he nonetheless bears witness to Jesus: "This is the disciple who is testifying to these things and has written them, and we know that his testimony is true." The Beloved Disciple's eventual death does not diminish his standing in the community, because his witness remains. "Peter's ministry is marked by his death; the Beloved Disciple's is marked by this Gospel."[4]

In verse 24 the editor identifies the Beloved Disciple as the author of the original edition of the Gospel and the one whose testimony is preserved in the Gospel. He also certifies that the Johannine community ("we"; cf. 1:14–18) knows that his witness is true. As the truthful witness whose words remain, the Beloved Disciple stands as another example of the work and presence of the Paraclete in the community (14:17; 15:26; 16:13).

Formal Conclusion of the Gospel (Chapter 21:25)

The epilogue ends with the direct voice of the narrator, using conventional rhetorical hyperbole common among Greek and Jewish writers in the ancient Mediterranean world. The Gospel concludes in a sapiential fashion, echoing Ecclesiastes 12:12 and John 20:30. John 21:25 is meant as an encouragement to a community that no longer has eyewitnesses to consult: "But there are also many other things that Jesus did; if every one of them were written down, I suppose that the world itself could not contain the books that would be written." The author reassures his audience that the good news of Jesus will continue to flow, through this Gospel and, as we know, through the ongoing witness of the Paraclete.

Essay 12: John's Ecclesiology: Leadership Models in John's Gospel

According to Paul (1 Cor. 12:28), God appointed as leaders "apostles first, prophets second." The term "apostle" in the later Christian tradition came to represent an ecclesiastical system of authority headed by bishops, priests, and deacons. By the fourth century, this position became dominant in western Christianity. Many people are unaware that only sixty years after Jesus' death—and forty years after Paul penned his letters to the Corinthians—the Fourth Evangelist and the religious community he

---

4. O'Day, *John*, 862.

represented modelled an early and very different ecclesiastical system, an egalitarian tradition that was more prophetic than apostolic in nature. In John's Gospel, these two leadership styles appear to be represented by Peter and the Beloved Disciple. Peter and the mysterious Beloved Disciple are explicitly contrasted in five passages in John: in 13:23–26 the Beloved Disciple rests on Jesus' chest, while Peter has to signal to him for information; in 18:15–16 the Beloved Disciple can accompany Jesus into the high priest's palace, while Peter cannot enter without his help; in 20:2–10 the Beloved Disciple outruns Peter to the tomb, and only he is said to believe on the basis of what he sees there; in 21:7 the Beloved Disciple recognizes Jesus standing on the shore of the Sea of Tiberius and tells Peter who it is; in 21:20–23, when Peter jealously inquires about the Beloved Disciple's fate, he is told by Jesus, "Suppose I would like him to remain until I come, how does that concern you?" In a sixth passage (19:26–27), where the Beloved Disciple appears at the foot of the cross, the contrast is implicit: Peter is one of those who have scattered, abandoning Jesus (16:32).

It is clear that John wants us to see in the Beloved Disciple a charismatic figure who exemplifies Christian discipleship and leadership for Johannine believers. What then is Peter's role? Peter is clearly less prominent in John's Gospel than in the Synoptics. In Matthew's Gospel, the only gospel to use the term "church" (16:18; 18:17), the nature and structure of the church is highly important. In Matthew 16:18 the words of Jesus spoken to Peter after his confession ("you are Peter, and on this rock I will build my church") are Matthew's way of establishing the foundation of the church on apostolic authority. This concern is not prominent in John, for the Fourth Evangelist does not seem to have been interested in the institutional structure of the church. Rather, whatever the pattern of leadership, it must be based on mutual love and led by the Paraclete, the Spirit of truth.

In John's Gospel, Peter does not emerge as the leader of the original twelve disciples in the same manner as in the other gospels. Nor does he function as the sort of model disciple that we find in Matthew. Whereas the commissioning of Peter (Matt. 16:13–20; Mark 8:27–30; and Luke 9:18–21) is missing in John (though 6:67–69 may be the Johannine parallel), the story centering on Peter in chapter 21 seems to function as a restoration of Peter after his denial of Jesus. This passage, thought by many scholars to be an editorial addition to the Gospel, has been seen as an attempt to compensate for John's slighting of Peter. While Peter still plays a prime role among the disciples, when paired with the Beloved Disciple, it is always the latter who gets things right. Among the disciples, he is closest to Jesus (13:23), even to the point of taking Peter's place at times. By contrast, Peter's role is diminished in John. In Peter's primary dialogues with Jesus (6:66–71; 13:6–17; 21:15–22), Peter is presented as miscomprehending Jesus at every turn. When paired with the Beloved Disciple, the latter models intimacy with the Lord and faithfulness at the cross.

Does this diminished role of Peter, coupled with the prominence given to the Beloved Disciple, mean that the Fourth Evangelist wished to elevate the prophetic tradition, with its egalitarian elements, over the apostolic tradition, with its hierarchical elements? While the answer to that question cannot be known for sure, the question itself may be misleading. By elevating the Beloved Disciple over Peter, the Evangelist could have been honoring the role and memory of the unnamed disciple upon whose memories the Fourth Gospel was based. Giving prominence to the Beloved Disciple probably had more to do with providing his community with a symbolic ideal than with deliberately depreciating the Petrine model of discipleship and church leadership.

Rather than using the "rock" and "keys" as images of the church, as Matthew does, in John the first image of the church is that of the flock of Jesus, accompanied by the images of sheep and shepherd (10:1–18) and vine and branches (15:1–17). Within this relationship, the intimacy of acquaintance is central. Jesus knows his sheep, they know his voice, and they follow him (10:27). As branches, Jesus' followers are connected to the vine. The mutual abiding of the branch and the vine is both the source of vitality and the way to fruitfulness. In these images the interactive quality of the relationship between Christ and the church is featured. For John, the heart of church vitality is a dynamic relationship with its Lord. As Jesus' will is for his disciples to be fruitful and for their fruit to remain (15:16), such will finally be manifested in their love for one another in the world. To abide in Jesus is to abide in his love and to share in the oneness the Son has known with the Father since the beginning of time (17:18–26).

Ministry in the Fourth Gospel is inclusive in its scope; therefore John's prologue becomes a powerful introduction to the narrative. Its poetic form and stanza-like structure invite others into a participatory mode, connecting with the first-person plural: "*we* have beheld his glory"; "from his fullness *we* have received grace upon grace" (1:14, 16). In addition to Peter's uttering a confession of faith, so do Nathanael (not one of the Twelve) and Martha. At the foot of the cross, John presents his model of the church, a relational and familial image of church authority rather than hierarchical apostleship (19:26–27). In John the risen Lord promises to lead believers by means of the Holy Spirit, who will abide in and with his followers. The accessibility of the Spirit to every believer seems to favor an egalitarian view of church leadership over a structural or hierarchical one. When Peter declares in John 6:68 that Jesus alone has the words of eternal life, is he "returning the keys of the kingdom to Jesus, where, according to the Fourth Evangelist, they belonged all the while?"[5]

The priesthood of believers is more than a mere idea in the Fourth Gospel, where ministry is shared, as from the beginning until the end of Jesus' ministry disciples bring people to Jesus, serving as bridges between others and him. In chapter 1, Jesus invites two of John the Baptist's disciples to "come and see" (1:39), and they in turn bring others to Jesus, also saying "come and see" (1:46; see also 4:29; and 11:34; cf. 12:21). After the resurrection, Mary Magdalene declares to the disciples that she has seen the Lord (20:18); the other disciples witness to Thomas, declaring that they too had seen the Lord (20:25); and in the epilogue, the Beloved Disciple points out the Lord to Peter in the boat (21:7), becoming a personal bridge. Gospel ministry in John is "compassionate in its character, inspired in its empowerment, and inclusive in its scope. Indeed, Martin Luther's primary biblical basis for his doctrine of the priesthood of all believers is built squarely on John 20:21–23."[6]

Because the Beloved Disciple gets things right, he exemplifies the right way to think about discipleship. At the Last Supper, where he reclines against the breast of Jesus (13:23), we learn that authentic discipleship is based on *intimacy* with the Lord; at the cross, alone among the Twelve and in the midst of danger, he exemplifies *courage*; at the tomb, even though he arrives first, he stands aside and allows Peter to enter first (20:1–19), exemplifying *generosity of spirit*; in his final appearance, related to his own death, he serves as the *faithful witness*—an ideal example of leadership for others to follow—all the more powerful because he was a real person, not just a literary device.

As models of discipleship in the Fourth Gospel, the Beloved Disciple and Peter work together; both are indispensable and are meant to work in a kind of healthy tension. Where there is only apostolic authority, there is danger of tyranny; where the prophet alone holds sway, there can

---

5. Anderson, *Riddles*, 41–42.
6. Ibid., 226–27.

be chaos. Through the experience of division and disunity revealed in the letters of John, the Johannine community will learn the importance of structure, but in the Gospel the primary concern is to emphasize the deep mystical intuition of the Beloved Disciple. The clear implication is that administrative leaders in the church should pay attention to the insights of those who are intuitively attuned to the ways of the Spirit.

Lest it be felt that the life of the Spirit is beyond human reach, Jesus emphasizes that God's renewing initiative is forever guiding his church. It is precisely those who open themselves to God's loving presence and grace that the Father actively seeks to draw into transforming worship and encounter (4:23). Because Jesus' Kingdom is one of truth, all who belong to the truth hear his voice (18:37). This includes all who are on the journey of faith—whether in the precritical, critical, or postcritical phase.

John's Gospel is about the revelation of ultimate truth. We are invited to participate in this truth, not simply by hearing about it, but by experiencing the love of the Father and thus becoming one with Jesus: "If you love me, you will keep my commandments. And I will ask the Father, and he will give you another Advocate, to be with you forever. This is the Spirit of truth" (14:15–17). Being Jesus' disciples means trusting his words and striving to love as he did. The Spirit is the ultimate guide, the ultimate model of truth. That Spirit and that freedom, represented in self-giving love, are central. Whether it be apostolic or prophetic models of ministry, Peter's or Paul's style of leadership, or witness modeled by the Samaritan woman or the Beloved Disciple, all styles of leadership working together for good bring God glory. Abiding in the vine, belonging to one flock, that is enough!

Questions to Ponder

1. In your estimation, should John 21 be viewed as written by the same author as the rest of the Gospel, or by a later editor? Explain your answer.

2. Does the story recorded in John 21:1–14 seem like a first post-resurrection appearance of Jesus to his disciples? If so, how does that square with the statement in John 21:14 that this is the third time Jesus has appeared to them?

3. How do you interpret the apparently symbolic nature of the imagery in John 21:11?

4. Why do you think Jesus singles Peter out in John 21:15–19? What is Jesus asking Peter to do in this passage?

5. How do the roles given to Peter and the Beloved Disciple in John 21 square with their roles elsewhere in the Gospel of John? Do these disciples represent a possible rivalry between Petrine and Johannine communities? Explain your answer.

Epilogue

The Gospel of John can be read on several levels: as the story of Jesus himself, as the account of the Johannine community, and as the experience of Christians in every time and place in their individual and communal journey into an ever deeper fellowship with Christ.

Noting that the gospels were written backwards, in the sense that the first stage of gospel formation dealt with the passion story, followed by a selective phase in which the Evangelists chose episodes and sayings of Jesus deemed to be significant in the light of Jesus' death and resurrection, Father Demetrius Dumm wrote a monograph on John's Gospel based on that pattern, beginning with the passion material, followed by the Farewell Discourses, then by stories and sayings of Jesus' public ministry, and concluding with John's prologue.[1] In his investigation, Father Demetrius was influenced by L. William Countryman's contention that the first half of John's Gospel (after the prologue), while appearing to be simply stories from Jesus' public ministry, is organized according to the stages of Christian initiation and growth, beginning with (1) *conversion* (the subject of John 1:19—2:22, including the Cana miracle and the cleansing of the temple, since they also deal with change or conversion), followed by the sacraments of (2) *baptism* (the subject of 3:1—5:47 because water is involved in the story of the Samaritan woman and the healing of the cripple at the pool) and (3) *Eucharist* (the subject of 6:1—7:52, which is about the bread of life and the water that quenches thirst), followed by (4) spiritual *enlightenment* (8:12—9:41, signaled by Jesus' claim to be the "light of the world" and illustrated by the blind man), and ending with (5) the invitation to discover *eternal life* (fullness of life; 10:10), protected by the Good Shepherd and in association with Lazarus, who is raised from the dead (10:1—11:44).

1. Dumm, *Mystical Portrait*.

Although Father Demetrius's procedure reverses the flow of the gospel narrative, it actually follows the process by which the community of John grew toward a deep spiritual awareness of union with Christ, building on the first step, the discovery that in Jesus God had conquered death and given hope to all human beings (John 18—21). The truly revolutionary element in this discovery is the awareness that this victory came through the loving self-sacrifice of Jesus. From the start, early Christians recognized then that the central revelation of Jesus—the ultimate truth—was that unconditional, selfless love is the only means to conquer death.[2]

From that experience of spiritual awakening (conversion) those first Christians deepened their understanding of how the love of Jesus could be realized in their lives. This deeper understanding came through the subtle but powerful influence of the Paraclete sent to them by the risen Lord. The implication of this work of the Spirit is the subject of the Farewell Discourse, where Jesus informs his followers what his death would mean in their daily lives (John 13—17).

Later, in the sixty plus years that separated the death of Jesus from the composition of this Gospel, Johannine Christians began to discover the meaning of Jesus in their lives through the various common means of grace, symbolized by water, bread, light, and wine, not as ends in themselves but as means to spiritual union with God in Christ (John 1—12). It is not surprising that John's Gospel weaves together, as it were, the public ministry of Jesus and one's spiritual journey into eternal life.

The Johannine View of the Spirit

In John the concept of the Holy Spirit is both stunning and revolutionary. The Johannine community's understanding of the Spirit is an essential part of its realized eschatology, because through the Spirit future blessings are already present.[3]

An examination of the Johannine pneumatology (its doctrine of the Spirit) indicates that the term *pneuma* (meaning wind, breath of life, or spirit and generally translated as Spirit or Holy Spirit) appears twenty-four times in John. When the Gospel speaks of *pneuma* in reference to God's presence, it does so in the following ways: (a) the Spirit is the power and the character of God given to the man Jesus (1:32–33; 3:34); (b) the

---

2. Ibid., 90.

3. The material in this segment is adapted from Kysar, *Maverick Gospel*, 126–32.

Spirit is the divine presence given by Jesus that results in the new life of the believer (7:39; 20:22); (c) the *pneuma* life within a believer is said to result from *penuma* birth, through which the Spirit radically reorients a human's life (3:5, 6; 6:63); (d) the Spirit is described as the Paraclete, a uniquely Johannine expression that combines numerous meanings—Advocate, Intercessor, Helper, Comforter—to introduce a revolutionary new concept. Much as the Evangelist takes the word Logos, a term with wide and varied meanings, and applies it to Jesus in a profoundly new way, the word Paraclete catches the imagination by redefining the role of the Spirit. The Evangelist introduces the word Paraclete in chapters 14 through 16 in order to redefine the presence of God for Johannine Christians. Called the "Spirit of truth" in 14:17; 15:26; and 16:13 (you will recall that "truth" in John means "the revelation of God in Christ"), the Paraclete communicates revelation to believers.

With this view of the Paraclete, the Evangelist addresses two basic problems faced by his community in the late first century, (a) the delay of the *parousia* (the expected imminent return of Christ), and (b) the problem of historical distance from the time of the original revelation in the ministry of Jesus. John's solution to the first problem, it seems, is to affirm that Christ had reappeared in the form of the Paraclete. The close identification of the Paraclete and Christ in the Fourth Gospel confirms this view. Reorienting the expectation of the return of Christ from the future to the present experience of the community is part of the eschatology of the Gospel.

The Gospel of John also answered the second question with its doctrine of the Paraclete. We must keep in mind that during the late first century there was as yet no Christian canon of scripture, which would be Christianity's later solution to this problem. The Johannine Christians lived at a time when the eyewitnesses to the historical Jesus were dying. How could they avail themselves of the original revelation if they lived at a later point in history? John's solution stresses that the Paraclete is the medium of divine revelation, the living witness to the revelation of God in Christ (15:26). By virtue of the work of the Paraclete, Christians at all times and places can have as direct access to that revelation as did the original disciples. "Their truth comes from an agent who is nothing less than the alter ego of Christ himself" (20:29).[4]

---

4. Ibid., 131.

By using a new word in a new way, the Fourth Evangelist provided Christians a distinctive way of thinking about the presence of God, answered the nagging question of the delay of the *parousia*, and solved the problem of the growing temporal distance from the original revelation in Jesus. In declaring the Paraclete to be the living presence of Christ, John's Gospel affirms that Christ's presence is ongoing reality for all Christians. For John, the Spirit forever links eternity and history, bringing eternity into the present.

The Johannine View of the Church

The richness of the believers' present is affirmed still further in what John has to say about the Christian community.[5] While the word "church" does not appear in the Fourth Gospel, John expresses an important understanding of the Christian community, a view far different from views found elsewhere in the New Testament. The following concepts summarize John's perspective on the church:

1. *The community is united by its oneness with Christ (17:23).* John's ecclesiology builds on his Christology: as Jesus is one with the Father, so the members of the church are one; as there is identity and individuality between the Father and the Son, so it is with the church. This is not a mystical view of the community, however, if by mystical is meant loss of identity. The distinctive individuality of the community and of its members is maintained in its unity with Christ. The bond within the community of believers is analogous to the modern understanding of marriage. It is a union of two persons ("the two shall become one," Gen. 2:24), nevertheless, the individuality of the spouses is preserved. The relationship can be represented by a figure eight. Viewed one way, the figure is a continuous line unbroken in its unity; viewed another way, it is two circles, each independent yet touching one another. Such an image represents the Johannine concept of the Christian community—unity in diversity.

2. *The community is united in mutual love (13:34).* This theme, best expressed in chapters 13–15, is Christological. God loves the Son and the Son loves the Father. The Son in turn loves the believers, and they are to love one another. The community of believers is to exemplify the kind of love that exists between God and the Son.

---

5. The material in this segment is adapted from Kysar, *Maverick Gospel*, 133–42.

3. *The community is the locus of the manifestation of God (17:22-23).* Again, the approach is Christological. The argument in 17:22-23 progresses as follows: (a) the presence of God is glory; (b) God gives glory to Jesus; (c) Jesus gives that glory to believers; therefore (d) believers manifest the glory of God. This means that the manifestation of God in Jesus has now been transferred to the community of believers. It is among them that God is made known, just as God was made known in the person and work of Jesus. The Paraclete is active among the believers, and it is in their midst that the presence of God is to be found.

4. *The community "democratizes" church order.* Whereas the Fourth Evangelist wrote at a time when church organization was developing rapidly, his Gospel shows little interest in the matter. Indeed, the Evangelist holds a democratic view of church structure and authority. All believers are called to be the kind of disciple represented by the Beloved Disciple. Through the Paraclete all have equal access to the revelation of God in Christ. Based on the prophetic model, all persons have access to the presence of God through their immediate experience. Therefore, all have equal authority. Because eternity is present in the Christian community, there is little need for church structure or authority: all believers are disciples; all are brothers (20:17). This egalitarian way of being the church, this way of knowing and believing, is charismatic, intuitive, and experiential. The clear implication is that leaders in the church should pay attention to those who are mystically attuned to the ways of the Spirit. Or better, they should nourish the mystical side of their own personalities. Perhaps this view of the church and church structure is naïve, given the division and dissension that would develop later, as evidenced in the Johannine letters, though perhaps the image that emerges in the Gospel reflects more what the community of believers could become under the Spirit's guidance, regardless of the circumstances they must face.

5. *The community is sent into the world as Christ's agent* (20:21). In the climactic twentieth chapter of the Gospel, the risen Christ appears to the frightened disciples behind locked doors (20:19). Christ greets his followers, shows them his wounds from the crucifixion, and then speaks words charged with meaning: "As the Father has sent me, so I send you" (20:21). The sending of the disciples actually completes a series of sending in the Gospel, beginning with the sending of Jesus by God (3:16-17; 5:24) and culminating with the sending of the Holy Spirit after Jesus' departure (14:26; 15:26; 16:7). The sending of Christ was motivated by God's love and determination to save the world, the realm of unbelief and

evil opposite from the believing community. Now the disciples are the ones sent. As Christ was the crux of God's redemptive plan for the world, the disciples become empowered by the Spirit to continue that plan. The disciples' place, then, is in the world as Christ's agents. They are agents sent in the same way and for the same reason as was their Lord.

There is much in the Gospel that suggests an insider-outsider dichotomy, a sectarian struggle between "us" and "them." With that sectarian model comes the propensity to withdraw from the world. Now that image must be redrawn. True, the internal life of the community portrayed in the Gospel is strong, but equally as strong is its mission consciousness. The sketch we have drawn of the church moves in two opposite but equal directions. One is inward, consolidating the solidarity and mutual love shared within the community. The other is outward, incarnating God's love in service to the world. Yet these opposite-directed lines are paradoxically conceived as pointing in the same direction, for even the unity of the church is understood to be part of its mission in the wider world, for unity brings the world to belief (17:21). This view of the church is sustained by the fact that the eschatological blessings of the last day are already present in the community. The Johannine view of the community intersects with the view of the Spirit. The Paraclete in the community of faith produces an environment in which believers are empowered for their life together and their mission beyond.

In his final prayer Jesus asks his heavenly Father to sanctify his disciples in the truth (17:17–19). This is the same truth to which Jesus referred in his dialogue with Pilate in the last moments of his life: "For this I was born, and for this I came into the world, to testify to the truth" (18:37). In a word, this truth is the unveiling of the reality of God's unconditional love for "the world," a love revealed in the gift of God's only Son (3:16). To all who receive him, he gives power to become children of God (1:12).

If one asks where God is encountered in the world today, the Fourth Gospel suggests it will be in the lives of persons seeking to follow the Master, and the true evidence of Christian belief is the love that persons display in the world. The goal of every believer is following Jesus—both by embracing his example and by discerning his leading. If that happens, Jesus' followers will know the truth, and the truth will be liberating indeed! Such is the message of the Gospel of John—then and now.

Appendix

The Relation of John's Gospel to the Epistles and to Revelation

The Gospel of John, a book attributed to the apostle John, the son of Zebedee, was written anonymously by a Jewish Christian of the late first century AD who served as theological mentor for a Jewish Christian community called the Johannine community. This community, a cluster of congregations in Asia Minor, was considerably different from other expressions of Christian faith in the first century. Yet even that one stream of early Christianity was not monolithic, but rather exhibited diverse understandings of faith and lifestyle.[1]

In addition to the Gospel, four other books of the New Testament are associated with the name "John": three letters of John and the book of Revelation. Like the Gospel, the three letters are anonymous documents; their attribution to John the apostle derived from the manuscript tradition of the early church. The book of Revelation, by contrast, identifies itself as written by "John" (Rev. 1:1, 4, 9; 22:8), though it is unlikely that this person is the author of the Gospel or the Johannine epistles.

There appears to have been a school of Christian thought near the end of the first century organized around a man known as John the elder, who himself may have been a disciple of John, son of Zebedee, which opens up the possibility that the Johannine literature (the Gospel, the three epistles, and the book of Revelation), are the products of different members of that Johannine school. If that is so, it would account for the similarities found in these works as well as for the obvious differences.

---

1. Kysar, *Maverick Gospel*, 165.

The Johannine Epistles

Although tradition labeled the epistles as having been written by the same author as the Gospel, the internal evidence does not support that conclusion.[2] In 2 and 3 John, the author calls himself "the elder", but 1 John does not indicate the identity of the author. On the basis of internal evidence, the author of 1 John was a person of authority in the church (or churches), for this person presumes to guide the audience in matters of faith and life. While the term "elder" claims some authority, the title may not identify an established office. It may simply refer to an elderly person who by virtue of age and experience is respected by the community. With such scarce evidence, it is not surprising that the church took nearly three centuries to bring these writings together and to attribute them to the same author, the Fourth Evangelist.

The form of 1 John differs markedly from that of 2 and 3 John. The latter two are clearly letters, while 1 John lacks the usual features of a letter. The document appears to be an anthology of loosely related admonitions, possibly sermonic fragments, strung together into written form. Though the structure of 1 John remains obscure, its message revolves around five themes: (1) the fleshly humanity of Christ (4:2); the saving work of Christ (1:7, 9; 2:2; 3:5; 4:10); (3) the understanding of sin (1:8, 10; 3:4, 8, 9; 5:16–17); (4) the importance of moral living (1:7; 2:3, 4, 6, 24; 3:7, 14; 4:5, 6, 16), based upon the commandment to "love one another" (3:11, 23; 4:7, 11–12); and (5) the "last days" (2:18, 28; 3:2; 4:17, 18). Some of these themes appear in 2 and 3 John as well.

While we are limited in our knowledge of the setting out of which and for which 1 John was written, it seems clear that a group once within a church (or churches) has withdrawn, and its members—in the view of the Johannine author—were never full participants nor even authentic Christians (2:19). The differences between the author of 1 John and the separatists seem to center on proper views of Christ, sin, and morality. It appears that 1 John was written to strengthen the confidence of the original Johannine churches. The author wants to solidify the readers into a coherent group around a single understanding of Christian life and belief. The readers have been shaken by trauma in the churches and need reassurance that their understanding of Christianity is true. According to the author, the dissidents do not practice love (2:9–11; 4:20–21); they deny the humanity of Christ (2:22; 4:2–3; 5:5–6); they are allied with forces

---

2. The material below is adapted from Kysar, *Maverick Gospel*, 165–76.

at odds with the faith of the church (2:15–16; 4:5–6); they are weapons of evil (3:8) and even the antichrists of the last days (2:18–23) because they do not maintain the teachings of the community (4:6); they claim to know and love God and to practice their faith but in fact do not (1:6; 2:9); they are thereby guilty of "mortal sin" (5:16), even though they claim to be free of sin (1:6–10; 3:3–6); and they live without moral restrictions (3:4–10).

The author is clearly prejudiced in the assessment of these dissidents, a group that is difficult to characterize but presumably during the second century blended into groups of gnostic Christians. The separatists of 1 and 2 John seem to have been the precursors of gnostic groups that denied the humanity of Jesus in favor of a purely spiritual being and were inclined to think that their Christian faith freed them from traditional morality.

The setting for 1 John is related to that of 2 John, whose author urges the readers to lead moral lives, perhaps in contrast to the dissidents (verses 5–6). These dissenters are propagating their views in nearby congregations, and the "elder" is attempting to defuse their influence. First John also counsels a view of Christ as a fleshly being, against "deceivers" who teach otherwise (verse 7). Such false Christians should be denied hospitality when they arrive (verse 10).

Third John presents a different setting, a power struggle between rivals within a congregation. A certain Diotrephes has proven himself an irritant in the congregation of which Gaius (the recipient of the letter) is a leader. An isolationist who views himself a purist, Diotrephes refuses to recognize the authority of the elder and gossips about his leadership (verse 10). He has driven off those who disagree with him and is refusing even to welcome Christian visitors. The elder in this case tries to win the loyalty of Gaius and thereby strengthen the author's influence in the congregation.

These three documents are important in the New Testament for they present a Christian community struggling to maintain its unity and integrity. The Johannine epistles show us early Christian conflict between doctrinal and ethical purity on the one hand and tolerance on the other. The twin issues of orthodoxy and authority are paramount in the emergence of the church.

The Relationship of the Epistles to the Fourth Gospel

The question of the authorship of the epistles and their relationship to the Gospel of John may never be resolved with certainty. While the traditional attribution of common authorship is no longer widely held, they share similarity of language, style, theology, and morality. The similarities are most frequent in 1 John, including the use of words or phrases such as "life" (3:15), "eternal life" (5:11), "truth" (5:6), "Son" (4:14) and "new commandment" (2:7–8). The similarities with the Fourth Gospel are less frequent in 2 and 3 John, though all are united in the use of the word "truth" (2 John 1–4 and 3 John 1, 3, 4, 8, and 12). However, since 2 and 3 John are very short and are letters, we should not expect many parallels.

First John shares a number of distinctive themes with the Fourth Gospel, often expressing them in exactly the same words. Among the shared themes are (1) the images of light and darkness (1 John 1:5–7; 2:9–11 and John 8:12; 12:46); (2) abiding in Christ (1 John 2:27–28 and John 15:4, 6); (3) the command to love one another (1 John 3:11 and John 13:34–35); (4) being hated by the world (1 John 3:13 and John 15:18–19; 17:13–16); (5) Jesus as "Paraclete" (1 John 2:1 and John 14:16); (6) the "world" as the realm of disbelief or hostility (1 John 2:16; 3:1, 13; 4:5 and John 7:7; 8:23; 15:18, 19; 17:26, 25); (7) Christ "laying down his life" for others (1 John 3:16 and John 10:11, 15, 17–18; 15:12–13); and (8) Christ sent by God into the world out of love (1 John 4:9 and John 3:16). Furthermore, 1 John begins with an echo of the prologue of the Gospel (see the unique title for Jesus "word of life" in 1 John 1:1, a composite of two distinctive concepts associated with John's prologue).

Despite the similarities, there are important differences. For example, the role of the Spirit, so pivotal throughout the Gospel, particularly in John 16:8–11, is missing in 1 John, which is preoccupied with community life. The understanding of sin and atonement (see 1 John 1:7; 2:2; 4:10) is also quite different from that found in the Gospel, though some of these differences can be attributed to a change in the situations addressed by the Gospel and 1 John. Whereas the Gospel is oriented toward the community's conflict with Jewish opponents, the epistles are primarily concerned with intra-church conflicts. Perhaps the most significant difference occurs in eschatological perspective. In 1 John the reader is struck by the emphasis on futuristic eschatology (2:18, 28; 3:2) with little, if any, evidence of the present, realized eschatology that characterizes the Fourth Gospel. In the epistles the delicate balance between the present and the future so effectively achieved by the Fourth Evangelist has tilted toward the future.

It is therefore widely held that the epistles originated within the same faith community that produced the Gospel, but not from the same author or at the same time. In fact, each of the three epistles need not have come from the same hand. Obviously, 2 and 3 John are from one who uses the title "elder." The author of 1 John might well have been another leader in the community. Much of the conflict to which 1 John is addressed seems to be generated by disagreement over the interpretation of the theology contained in the Gospel, including the reality of the incarnation (see 1 John 4:2–3; 5:6). The concerns for proper Christian belief and practice and ecclesiastical authority suggest that the epistles come from a later stage in the community's life than does the Gospel, at which time the community is fractured by theological differences.[3]

When the Gospel was written, the Johannine church may have been concerned with more basic questions, particularly with finding its place in a Roman society unfavorable to Christianity. Its task was to establish its own identity, particularly as related to the messianic confession: Jesus is the Christ. There seems yet to be little or no interest in differing views of Christ within the broader Christian community. Moreover, the Johannine community at this time displayed little interest in the apostolic authority of its leaders. Rather this community conceived of itself as ruled by the authority of the Spirit through charismatically inspired members.

By the time of the writing of the epistles, attention has shifted inward, focusing on concerns such as what kind of messianic confession was proper and true and how members should relate to one another. The sense of the direct guidance of the Spirit has given way to mediated guidance through church officials, though as 3 John suggests, there remain Christians who feel free to challenge the authority of the "elder."

If we must put dates to these writings, it can be argued that the Gospel was written first, perhaps in stages beginning around AD 75 to 85 and concluding no later than 95, with the work of the redactor. The epistles were written between 90 and 95, beginning with 1 John (authored by the redactor of the Gospel, the "elder," or another author) and concluding with 2 and 3 John, written by the "elder."

3. O'Day, *John*, 499.

The Relationship of the Book of Revelation to the Fourth Gospel

Because the author of Revelation identifies himself as "John" (1:1, 4, 9; 22:8), this book is often aligned with the Gospel and the epistles of John. Especially since the authority and value of Revelation was questioned in the early church, the book's attribution to the apostle John was a way of authenticating its place in the Christian canon.

Some commentators have noted similarities between Revelation and the Fourth Gospel, particularly in vocabulary and in doctrine, including (1) "Lamb" for Jesus; the Gospel uses the title twice (1:29, 36), but in Revelation it is the most frequent title for Christ (5:6, 8; 12:11; 13:8; 17:14; 21:9); (2) "Logos" for Jesus, used nowhere else in the New Testament (John 1:1, 14; Rev. 19:13); (3) "truth" (used thirteen times in the Gospel, ten times in Revelation, and only five times elsewhere in the New Testament); (4) "witness," used frequently in both; and (5) the concept of God's dwelling (tabernacling) with his people (John 1:14; Rev. 21:3).

Beneath the apparent similarities, however, lie fundamental differences. John of Patmos (the author of Revelation) recounts no stories or sayings from the ministry of Jesus, though some would have been appropriate for the message he advocates, nor does he give any indication that he had known Jesus during his earthly life. Furthermore, the differences in language, theology, and general point of view make clear that this John is not the same as the author of the Gospel and the epistles of John. While both write in Greek, the Fourth Evangelist's usage is that of a native, whereas the author of Revelation writes in a peculiar and irregular style, the sort of Greek written by one whose native language was Hebrew or Aramaic. Since John of Patmos was acquainted with Palestinian prophetic traditional material, it is likely that he was originally a Palestinian Christian prophet who immigrated to Asia during or shortly after the Jewish war with Rome in AD 66-70.

The differences between the Gospel and Revelation are accentuated when we examine the topic of eschatology. Revelation is a peculiar genre of literature, known as apocalyptic, meaning that its entire perspective is devoted to futuristic eschatology. By contrast, the Gospel of John is careful to temper that kind of futuristic perspective with attention to the present. The emphatic "now" in John 12:31 ("Now is the judgment of this world; now the ruler of this world will be driven out") indicates that the eschatological judgment has already been achieved by the coming of the Son. John Ashton rightly calls the Gospel "an apocalypse in reverse,"[4] for the heavenly mysteries are not to be sought in heavenly visions but in Jesus, the one who has seen the Father (5:37) and makes the Father known. The book of Revelation is the most apocalyptic document in the New Testament, the Gospel of John the least apocalyptic, devoid of the symbolism of cosmic struggle with the powers of darkness familiar to us from Revelation as well as in the Synoptics (reflected in the eschatological discourse of Jesus in Mark 13 and parallel texts and in portents such as the rending of the temple veil or the preternatural darkness that attends Jesus' death). Though the book of Revelation can be interpreted as not entirely oriented toward the future,[5] the genres of Revelation and of the Fourth Gospel are profoundly different, leading to radically dissimilar eschatological perspectives.

Supposing, however, that the book of Revelation did arise from the Johannine community, how might it be related to the history of that community? Two different solutions have been suggested. The first conceives of Revelation as arising early in the history of the community, before the writing of the Gospel and the epistles. Such a hypothesis would require an early date for Revelation, probably during the 60s. The other pattern reverses the order, focusing on the trajectory of eschatology: the Gospel came first, then the epistles, followed by Revelation. Whereas the Gospel focuses on the present, 1 John stresses more firmly the future dimension of God's promises, followed by Revelation's concentrated attention on the future. In this proposed relationship, Revelation would have been written soon after the epistles, during the time Christians were suffering persecution at the hands of Emperor Domitian (or as John anticipated that persecution) around the middle of the last decade of the first century (c. AD 95).

While this proposal has obvious merit, it seems better not to force Revelation into the already speculative construction of the history of the Johannine community (see below). Surely there were numerous "Johns" in the early Christian church. We shall never know with certainty the relation of the Gospel and the Apocalypse. It is best to treat each work on its own merit.

---

4. Cited in Rowland, *Revelation*, 515.
5. See my commentary on the book of Revelation, *Hope Revealed*.

The History of the Johannine Community

Examining not only the Gospel but also the epistles, which reflect a period late in the life of the community, the history of the Johannine community can be divided into five periods:[6]

(1) Origins: An eyewitness to the ministry of Jesus, one known from the Gospel as the Beloved Disciple, gathered traditional words and deeds of Jesus, independent of the Synoptic tradition. This disciple may originally have been a follower of John the Baptist (see John 1:35-40), for the tradition reflects a detailed knowledge of Judea and Jewish festivals and familiarity with the language and dualistic thought of the Dead Sea Scrolls, written by Essenes of the Judean desert near where John the Baptist conducted his ministry;

(2) Early Period: (within the synagogue): During this period the earliest Johannine Christians, forced to leave Judea, went to Antioch or directly to Ephesus. During the Judean or Syrian phase of this early period these Christians may have engaged in mission work among the Samaritans (John clearly devotes attention to the Samaritans; see Acts 8:14 and 25, which connects the apostle John with such a mission, and John 4:39-42; cf. 8:48). At this time Johannine Christians functioned rather comfortably within the Jewish synagogue, living as Jews and thinking of themselves as Jews who had found the Messiah (the discussion in John 1:35-49 suggests that Jews could have regarded Jesus as the fulfillment of messianic expectations drawn from the Hebrew scriptures). The passion narrative, in addition to the signs source, could have been collected at this stage, forming a "gospel of signs";

(3) Middle Period: (formation of the Johannine community): The middle period began with the exclusion of Johannine Christians from the synagogue, a social crisis caused either by their exodus from the synagogue or by the development of a new, higher Christology not based on the royal Davidic pattern. The Logos hymn found in John's prologue, a liturgical piece adapted by the Evangelist, is often assigned to this period. The relaxation of legal and cultic rituals, together with differences over the war of the Jews against Rome (66–70), may also have hardened relations between the two groups. Some Johannine Christians may have elected to remain within the synagogue as "secret Christians" (12:42; the accounts of Nicodemus who came to Jesus secretly in 3:2, and of Joseph of Arimathea in 19:38, reflect such a possibility). Those who were excluded

---

6. Culpepper, *The Gospel and Letters of John*, 55–61.

from the synagogue gathered around the Beloved Disciple, their living link with Jesus and the source of their teaching.

The discourses in the Gospel were formulated during this period, developed from (a) reflection on sayings received from Jesus, (b) preaching and teaching the signs source, and (c) the activity of Christian prophets among the Johannine Christians, who declared words they received from the risen Lord. Eventually the community found it necessary to test prophetic utterances against the norm of the tradition received from the Beloved Disciple. The community began using more dualistic language to describe its faith and its relationship to the surrounding world. The community was persecuted by Pharisaic authorities from the synagogue (15:18–16:2). The writing of the Gospel was in part a response to this persecution, resulting in a move to Ephesus;

(4) Middle Period: (the second generation): During this period the community was shaken by pressures related to Roman imperialism, which appeared to increase under Domitian (81–96), and by the death of the Beloved Disciple. Domitian reinstated the widespread practice of emperor worship and even required his own lieutenants to regard him as "lord and god," which suggests that the confession of Thomas, "My Lord and my God!" (John 20:28) conveys an anti-imperial intention. The final verse of 1 John (5:21) admonishes believers to "stay away from idols," a clear warning against offering sacrifices to the emperor or participating in civic festivals, which sometimes lasted for many days.

Regarding the Beloved Disciple, many in the community believed this individual would not die until the Lord returned (21:23). The death of the Beloved Disciple provoked deeper reflection on the role of the Spirit in the community. This reflection reaffirmed the egalitarian character of the community, since all possessed the Spirit. The chief concern for the emerging second generation was to preserve its unity by loving one another (13:34) and by "abiding" in the words of the risen Lord as preserved by the tradition coming from the Beloved Disciple. These emphases are reflected in discourse material added to the Gospel during this period, especially chapters 15—17.

The relationship between the Johannine community and other Christian groups was becoming an issue, as reflected in the "other sheep" of John 10:16. Evidence of the relationship between these communities can be found in 2 and 3 John. The "elder" sought to maintain a position of leadership with these communities. An inner group (the "Johannine school") closely related to the Beloved Disciple led in worship and in producing the community's written materials. The Johannine community functioned as the center of a network of churches possessing a distinctive Christianity. This entity also faced rival claims coming from churches that regarded Peter as their apostolic authority;

(5) Late Period: (schism): Eventually internal schism destroyed the unity of the Johannine community, causing new groups of believers to emerge such as (a) Gentile Christian leaders, who probably attended civic festivals and perhaps showed tribute to the emperor cult, likely participating in other aspects of Greco-Roman society that Jewish Christians would have opposed, and (b) docetic Christians, who emphasized the divinity of Christ while minimizing the humanity of Jesus (1 John 2:19; 4:2). This group also taught a realized eschatology that led believers to disregard the necessity to resist sin, since they believed that they had already crossed from death into life (1 John 1:8, 10; 3:14). Dissension resulted in schism, and the author of 1 John charged those who had left the community as being false prophets and teachers ("antichrists") who had violated the community ethic of love for one another (1 John 2:19; 3:10; 4:1–6). In response to this crisis, 1 John was written to admonish those who remained to stay faithful. Second John was written to warn a sister community of the dangers schismatics posed. The last we see of the Johannine community, it is torn by dissension and struggling for survival. The elder's group (the "faithful remnant") was probably absorbed by the dominant apostolic churches of the early second century, while the elder's opponents probably found their way into the gnostic communities of the mid-second century.

Bibliography

Anderson, Paul N. *The Riddles of the Fourth Gospel: An Introduction to John*. Minneapolis: Fortress, 2011.
Ashton, John. *Studying John: Approaches to the Fourth Gospel*. Oxford: Clarendon, 1994.
———. *Understanding the Fourth Gospel*. 2nd ed. Oxford: Oxford University Press, 2007.
Barbet, Pierre. *A Doctor at Calvary: The Passion of Our Lord Jesus Christ As Described by a Surgeon*. New York: Image, 1963 (1936).
Barrett, C. K. *The Gospel According to St. John*. 2nd ed. Philadelphia: Westminster, 1978.
Bauckham, Richard. *The Gospel of All Christians: Rethinking the Gospel Audiences*. Grand Rapids: Eerdmans, 1998.
———. *Jesus and the Eyewitnesses*. Grand Rapids: Eerdmans, 2006.
———. *The Testimony of the Beloved Disciple*. Grand Rapids: Baker Academic, 2007.
Beasley-Murray, G. R. *John*. Waco, TX: Word, 1987.
Black, C. Clifton. "The First, Second, and Third Letters of John." In *The New Interpreter's Bible Commentary*, vol. 12, 365–469. Nashville: Abingdon, 1998.
Borg, Marcus J., and John Dominic Crossan. *The First Paul*. New York: HarperOne, 2010.
Brown, Raymond E., S.S. *The Community of the Beloved Disciple*. New York: Paulist, 1979.
———. *The Epistles of John*. The Anchor Bible, vol. 30. Garden City, NY: Doubleday, 1982.
———. *The Gospel According to John*. The Anchor Bible, vols. 29 and 29A. Garden City, NY: Doubleday, 1966, 1970.
Bultmann, Rudolf. *The Gospel of John: A Commentary*. Translated by G. R. Beasley-Murray, R. W. N. Hoare, and J. K. Riches. Philadelphia: Westminster, 1971.
———. *Theology of the New Testament*. 2 vols. Translated by Kendrick Grobel. New York: Scribners, 1951, 1955.
Burridge, R. *What Are the Gospels?* Cambridge: Cambridge University Press, 1991.
Cahill, Thomas. *Desire of the Everlasting Hills*. New York: Anchor, 2001.
Carson, D. A. *The Gospel According to John*. Grand Rapids: Eerdmans, 1991.
Charlesworth, James H. *The Beloved Disciple: Whose Witness Validates the Gospel of John?* Valley Forge, PA: Trinity International, 1995.
Craddock, Frederick B. *John*. Atlanta: John Knox, 1982.
Countryman, L. William. *The Mystical Way in the Fourth Gospel*. 2nd ed. Valley Forge, PA: Trinity, 1994.
Culpepper, R. Alan. *Anatomy of the Fourth Gospel*. Philadelphia: Fortress, 1983.

———. *The Gospel and Letters of John*. Nashville: Abingdon, 1998.
Dodd, C. H. *Historical Tradition in the Fourth Gospel*. Cambridge: Cambridge University Press, 1963.
———. *The Interpretation of the Fourth Gospel*. Cambridge: Cambridge University Press, 1970.
Dumm, Demetrius R., O.S.B. *A Mystical Portrait of Jesus: New Perspectives on John's Gospel*. Collegeville, MN: Liturgical, 2001.
Ehrman, Bart. *A Brief Introduction to the New Testament*. 3rd ed. New York: Oxford University Press, 2013.
Ellis, Earle. *The World of St. John: The Gospel and the Epistles*. Grand Rapids: Eerdmans, 1984.
Harvey, A. E. *Jesus on Trial: A Study of the Fourth Gospel*. London: SPCK, 1976.
Hoskyns, Edwyn Clement and Francis N. Davey. 2nd ed. *The Fourth Gospel*. London: Faber and Faber, 1947.
Keener, Craig. S. *The Gospel of John: A Commentary*. 2 vols. Grand Rapids: Baker Academic, 2010.
Koester, Craig R. *Symbolism in the Fourth Gospel*. 2nd ed. Minneapolis: Fortress, 2003.
———. *The Word of Life: A Theology of John's Gospel*. Grand Rapids, Eerdmans, 2008.
Kysar, Robert. *John: The Maverick Gospel*. 3rd ed. Louisville: Westminster John Knox, 2007.
Lincoln, Andrew. *Truth on Trial: The Lawsuit Motif in the Fourth Gospel*. Grand Rapids: Baker Academic, 2000.
Martyn, J. Louis. *History and Theology in the Fourth Gospel*. 3rd ed. Louisville: Westminster John Knox, 2003.
McGrath, Alister E. *Christian Theology: An Introduction*. 5th ed. Malden: MA: Wiley-Blackwell, 2011.
Miller, Carol J. *That You May Believe: The Gospel of John*. Pittsburgh, PA: Kerygma, 2001.
Morris, Leon. *The Gospel According to John*. New International Commentary on the New Testament, revised edition. Grand Rapids: Eerdmans, 1995.
Newbigin, Lesslie. *The Light Has Come: An Exposition of the Fourth Gospel*. Grand Rapids: Eerdmans, 1982.
O'Day, Gail R. "The Gospel of John." In *The New Interpreter's Bible Commentary*, vol. 9, 493–865. Nashville: Abingdon, 1995.
Pagels, Elaine. *Beyond Belief: The Secret Gospel of Thomas*. New York: Random House, 2003.
Painter, John. *John: Witness and Theologian*. 2nd ed. London: SPCK, 1979.
———. *The Quest for the Messiah*. Edinburgh: T. & T. Clark, 1991.
Rowland, Christopher C. "The Book of Revelation." In *The New Interpreter's Bible Commentary*, vol. 12, 501–736. Nashville: Abingdon, 1998.
Schnackenburg, Rudolph. *The Gospel of St. John*. 3 vols. New York: Crossroads, 1980–1983.
Segovia, Fernando F. *The Farewell of the Word: The Johannine Call to Abide*. Minneapolis: Fortress, 1991.
Sloyan, Gerard. *John*. Interpretation: A Bible Commentary for Teaching and Preaching. Atlanta: John Knox, 1988.
———. *What Are They Saying About John?* New York: Paulist, 1991.

Smith, D. Moody. *John*. Abingdon New Testament Commentary. Nashville: Abingdon, 1999.

———. *The Theology of the Gospel of John*. New York: Cambridge University Press, 1995.

Spong, John Shelby. *The Fourth Gospel: Tales of a Jewish Mystic*. New York: HarperOne, 2013.

———. *Liberating the Gospels: Reading the Bible with Jewish Eyes*. New York: HarperSanFrancisco, 1997.

Swidler, Leonard. "Jesus Was a Feminist." *Catholic World* (Jan. 1971) 171–83. Available online: http://www.godswordtowomen.org/feminist.htm.

———. *Jesus Was a Feminist*. Lanham, MD: Sheed & Ward, 2007.

———. *Women in Judaism: The Status of Women in Formative Judaism*. Metuchen, NJ: Scarecrow, 1976. Available online: http://astro.temple.edu/~swidler/swidlerbooks/womenjudaism.htm.

Tenney, Merrill C. *John: The Gospel of Belief*. Grand Rapids: Eerdmans, 1976.

Valantasis, Richard, et al. *The Gospels and Christian Life in History and Practice*. Lanham, MD: Rowman & Littlefield, 2009.

Vande Kappelle, Robert P. *Hope Revealed: The Message of the Book of Revelation—Then and Now*. Eugene, OR: Wipf & Stock, 2013.

Von Wahlde, Urban C. *The Gospel and Letters of John*. 3 vols. Grand Rapids: Eerdmans, 2010.

Witherington III, Ben. *John's Wisdom: A Commentary on the Fourth Gospel*. Louisville: Westminster John Knox, 1995.

Wright, N. T. *John for Everyone*. 2 vols. Louisville: Westminster John Knox, 2002, 2004.

Subject/Name Index

Anderson, Paul N., xvii
Andrew, 48, 49, 50, 51, 156
Annas (high priest), 216, 218, 219
apocalyptic(ism), 2, 42, 57, 99, 285
aporia, 14
ascension, 245
Asclepius (deity), 3
Ashton, John, xvii
Athanasian Creed, 182

baptism, 73–74, 183–86, 232, 273
Barabbas, 223–24
Barrett, C. K., xvii, 189
Beasley-Murray, G. R., 244
believe, belief, 27–28, 51, 52–53, 67–68, 71, 75–77, 98, 103, 105, 106, 121, 135, 151–53, 158–59, 160, 174, 177, 178, 201, 248–50, 278
    knowing and, 144–45
    paradoxical nature of, 141–45
Beloved Disciple, x, 10–12, 16, 17, 51, 108, 171, 196, 213, 216, 228, 230–31, 232, 243, 244, 246, 254, 259, 261–62, 263, 265–66, 269–70, 277, 287
    and Peter, 171, 218–19, 239, 264, 267, 269–70
    and the Paraclete, 180
    identity of, 15, 38, 49, 50–51, 150, 230, 231, 237, 249–50
Bethel, 53
Bible. *See* scripture
Booths (Tabernacles), feast of, 43, 112, 113, 115–18, 119, 138–41

Brown, Raymond, SS, xvii, 14–15, 78, 80, 229, 254–55
Bultmann, Rudolph, xvii, 13–14, 86n18, 96, 160
Burridge, Richard, 6–7

Cahill, Thomas, 253
Caiaphas (high priest), 11, 153–54, 216, 218, 219
Carson, D. A., xvii
Charlesworth, James, 249–50
chiasm, 33–34, 104, 220
    Jesus' crucifixion and, 227–34
    Jesus' trial and, 220–27
Christology, 13, 29, 30–31, 32, 43, 48, 54–61, 63, 83, 139, 140, 170, 234–35, 242, 249, 276
    adoptionist, 54
    agency, 54, 59, 93–94, 116, 120, 140, 159, 179, 195, 235, 278
    incarnational, 54, 56
    trial of Jesus and, 220
    See also Holy One of God; "I Am" sayings; Logos Christology; Lamb of God; Son of God; Son of Man
church. *See* ecclesiology
Clement of Alexandria, xiii
Countryman, L. William, 189, 273
Culpepper, Alan, xvii, 33, 204–5, 206n13, 208

Dead Sea Scrolls, 42, 119, 157, 176, 286
determinism. *See* free will, determinism and

discipleship, 29, 48–49, 51, 52–53, 54–55, 67–68, 120, 121, 185, 191–92, 207–8, 231, 244, 255, 265
docetism, docetic, 16, 106, 248, 288
Dodd, C. H., xvii, 199, 244
dualistic imagery, 37, 42, 84–88, 110, 123, 206, 287
Dumm, Demetrius, OSB, xvii, 273–74

ecclesiology, 266, 276–78
   apostolic (Pauline/Petrine) model, 3, 114, 266–70, 288
   charismatic (Johannine) model, 3, 266–70
election, 104, 105, 108, 192
Ephesus (city), 3, 17, 58, 286, 287
eschatology, 16, 66, 67, 77, 105, 129, 152, 157, 159–61, 172, 198, 202, 275, 280, 282–83, 285
   realized, 16, 77, 82, 105, 159–61, 175, 274, 282–83, 288
eternal life, xi, 27, 59, 65, 75, 76, 79, 87, 99, 104, 106, 107, 137, 149, 152, 160–61, 184, 200, 273, 282
   See also life
Eucharist (Lord's Supper), 8, 14, 16, 66, 91, 100, 101, 106, 165, 167–72, 183–84, 215, 232, 263, 273
Eusebius, 12
evil, 37, 57, 77, 84–88, 108, 129, 157, 169, 277–78, 281
exaltation, 59, 135, 174, 205, 216, 229, 235–36

faith. *See* belief, believe
Farewell Discourse, xii, 30, 157, 159, 167–68, 172, 173, 179, 190, 191, 192, 196, 197, 198, 203, 264, 274
filioque, 180–81
Fourth Evangelist, x, 7, 9, 14, 15, 17, 19, 179
   identity of, 10, 13
   influences on, 41–44
   paradox and, 60
   perspective of, 55–56, 97, 109, 114, 121, 130–31, 149, 156, 159–61, 167–68, 169, 174–75, 184, 196, 197–99, 203–8, 216, 230, 254–55, 267–70
   technique of, 77, 95, 119–20
   use of irony, 206–8
   See also irony
freedom, 122
free will, 192
   determinism and, 141–45

glory, glorification, 34, 39, 59, 60, 67, 68, 71, 84, 99, 115, 117, 126, 149, 151, 156, 157, 159, 172, 199–200, 202, 205, 225, 235, 236, 242
   Book of, 18, 167
Gnostic(s), 11, 16, 37, 119, 281, 388
Golgotha (Calvary), 228
gospel (genre), 5–7, 35
   as biography, 6–7
   as drama, 7, 32
grace, 40, 43–44, 131, 192

Hanukkah (Dedication), feast of, 43, 113, 119, 123, 128, 138, 155
Harvey, A. E., xvii
hearing, 74, 144
heaven, 174–75
Hebrew poetry, 33
   John's prologue and, 33
Helms, Randel, 15–17
Holy One of God, 108
Holy Spirit, 2, 4, 39, 55, 58, 180–81, 183, 185, 195, 203, 239, 242, 243, 260–61, 269, 274–76, 277, 278, 283, 287
   Paraclete as, 15, 16, 98, 126, 178–80, 187, 195–96, 197, 244, 247, 267
   See also truth, "Spirit of truth"
Hooker, Morna, 30–31
Hoskyns, Edwyn Clement, xvii, 199, 260, 261

"I Am" sayings, xi, 48, 82, 103, 104, 119, 120, 123, 124–27, 136–37, 139, 171, 176, 190, 217
incarnation, xi, 8, 34, 35, 37, 39–41, 54, 103, 129, 131, 177, 185, 194, 198, 223, 283

SUBJECT/NAME INDEX

Irenaeus, 12
irony, 75, 83, 116, 120, 130, 151, 154, 176, 203, 206–8, 223, 225, 227, 231

Jews, "the," 49–50, 95, 99, 101, 105, 108–10, 116, 121, 133, 138, 150, 173, 190, 205, 220–21, 225, 227
Johannine community, 10, 14, 15, 28, 29, 80, 109, 131, 140, 170, 175, 194, 196, 198, 266, 273, 279, 283, 285
  history of, 286–88
John (apostle), 10, 11–12, 15, 50, 262, 279
John, epistles of, xiii, 34, 198, 279–83
John, Gospel of, ix–xiv, 17, 21, 41, 43, 273
  and book of Revelation, 284–85
  and Judaism, 41–44
  and Synoptic Gospels, 7–10, 31, 50, 68, 83, 94, 96, 102, 108, 132, 149, 150, 154, 155, 157, 165, 167, 169, 178, 181, 199, 215–16, 220, 224, 228, 235, 242, 243, 249, 286
  as biography, 6–7
  as drama, 7, 131, 217
  composition of, 13–17
  eschatological perspective, 159–61, 175
  exclusivist claims, 177
  kingship motif in, 102
  outline of, 18
  passion narrative, 215–16, 234–37
  perspective of the church, 266–70, 276–78
  perspective of the Holy Spirit, 274–76
  problems of, 4–5
  prologue, 29–41, 54, 65, 207, 249, 268
  purpose of, 26–29
  study of (guiding principles), 18–20
  trial motif in, 71, 91, 95, 99, 113–14, 120, 134, 153, 219, 221–22, 224, 226
John Mark, 11

John the Baptist, 8, 30, 31, 32, 34, 39, 40–41, 48, 49, 50, 51, 58, 65, 77–79, 99, 141, 183, 255, 269, 286
Joseph of Arimathea, 110, 158, 213, 219, 233, 286
Josephus, 252
Judas, 87, 104, 108, 147, 154, 155, 165, 169, 170, 171–72, 190, 201, 207, 217, 224
Judas (not Iscariot), 181
judgment, 76–77, 99, 115, 129, 130, 132, 135, 157, 160, 172, 195–96
Justin Martyr, 234

Kingdom of God, xii, xiv, 2, 7–8, 16, 66, 73, 125, 160–61, 222
knowing, 26–27, 144–45, 194
Koester, Craig, xvii, 203
kosmos (world), 86–87, 115, 157, 160, 182, 193, 198, 278, 282
Kysar, Robert, xvii, 56, 236

Lamb of God, 29, 48, 50, 57, 78–79, 235, 284
Last Supper. *See* Eucharist
Lazarus, x, 11, 13, 95, 99, 147, 149, 150–55, 156, 175, 204, 253, 273
Leroy, Herbert, 204
life, xii, 20, 27, 37, 41, 57, 65, 67, 84, 87, 98–99, 106, 125, 132, 137, 147, 148–49, 153, 176, 251, 282
  abundant, 137
  word of, 282
  See also eternal life
"lifted up," 59, 75, 121, 159, 216, 221, 229, 235–36, 242
  See also exaltation
light, 27, 34, 36, 37, 38–39, 41, 43, 58, 76–77, 84, 87, 119–20, 125, 129–30, 131–32, 148–49, 177, 217, 282
living water, 81, 112, 207
Logos Christology, 8, 19, 29–31, 32, 34, 36–38, 40–41, 42, 55–57, 122, 177, 284

love of God, 27, 42, 74, 76, 129, 131, 160, 171, 173, 186, 199, 201, 203, 237, 270, 276
Luke, Gospel of, 3, 31, 55, 154, 246, 253–54, 262
    resurrection narrative in, 241–43
Luther, Martin, 269

Mark, Gospel of, 3, 4, 5–6, 31, 154, 215, 216, 218
    resurrection narrative in, 241–43
Martha, 138, 147, 149, 150–53, 204, 253–54, 268
Mary (Magdalene), x, 230, 239, 240, 241, 242, 243, 248, 253, 254, 255, 261, 269
Mary (of Bethany), 147, 149, 150–53, 154, 253–54
Matthew, Gospel of, 3, 31, 55, 124, 154, 178, 247, 262, 264–65, 267, 268
    resurrection narrative in, 241–43, 244
Messiah, xii, 8, 15, 43, 44, 48, 50, 51, 52, 57, 58, 59, 81, 82, 98, 106, 116, 117, 134, 138, 156, 157–58, 205, 227, 234, 286
Miller, Carol J., xvii
miracle(s), 68, 133, 250
Morris, Leon, xvii
Moses, xi, 15, 31, 32, 36, 39, 41, 43, 44, 79, 80, 99, 101, 102, 104, 110, 124, 168, 244

Napoleon, xii
Nathanael, 27, 48, 49, 51–52, 58, 64, 110, 262, 268
New Testament, ix, x, 1, 4, 42, 54, 74, 140, 158, 251
    dualistic thought in, 85, 87
    See also scripture
Nicaea, Council of, 182–83
Nicodemus, x, 53, 63, 65, 70–71, 72–73, 77, 80, 110, 117–18, 158, 204, 205, 213, 233, 286

O'Day, Gail R., xvii
Old Testament (Hebrew Bible), 31, 39, 100, 131, 140

Pagels, Elaine, 249
Painter, John, 101
parable, 136–37
Paraclete, 70, 126, 165, 173, 178–80, 193–94, 195–96, 197, 198, 201, 247, 266, 275, 277, 278, 282
    See also Holy Spirit, Paraclete as
parousia (Second Coming), 16, 179, 196, 275, 276
Passover, 8, 43, 57, 69, 101–2, 113, 154, 167–68, 184, 215, 220, 223, 227, 235, 237
Paul (apostle), ix, 42, 161n8, 198, 234, 235, 241, 251–52, 266
Pentecost, 260
Peter (apostle), 10–11, 17, 50, 51, 107–8, 165, 167, 169–70, 171, 172, 173–74, 205, 207–8, 213, 218, 219, 225, 242–43, 244, 245, 246, 259, 263, 264–65, 267–68
    commissioning of, 260, 264–65
    See also Beloved Disciple, Peter and; ecclesiology, apostolic model
Philip, 51, 52, 102, 156, 177, 205
Philo of Alexandria, 42, 253
Pilate, xii, 201, 207, 213, 215–16, 220–27, 229, 234, 236, 278
predestination, 158, 191
proverb, 136

realized eschatology. *See* eschatology, realized
Renan, Ernst, xii
resurrection, 42, 49, 66, 70, 71, 106, 147, 149, 152, 161, 240–51, 254
revelation, 74–75, 110, 122, 126–27, 177–78, 180, 194, 197
Revelation, book of, xiii, 2, 161, 198
    Gospel of John and, 279, 284–85

Sabbath, 43, 91, 95–98, 99, 113, 116, 132, 133, 134, 227, 232
sacrament(s), 16, 170, 183–86, 232, 273, 274
    See also baptism; Eucharist
Samaria, Samaritans, 14, 78, 79–83, 109, 123, 286

Samaritan woman, x, 53, 63, 79–83, 204, 207, 254, 255, 270, 273
Satan (the devil), 84, 85, 86, 87, 123, 171–72, 182, 196–97
scripture (Bible), ix, 5, 100, 218
    fulfilled in Jesus, 28, 48, 229, 232, 233
    plot of, 19
    reading principles, 20
    three worlds of, 17–18
    witness to Jesus, 99
Second Coming. *See parousia*
seeing, 51, 74, 105, 106, 143
Septuagint, 15, 105, 126
Shroud of Turin, 233
signs source, 13, 15–16, 18, 64–65, 120, 130–31, 135, 226, 280, 282, 288
sin, 120, 130–31, 135, 226, 280, 282, 288
    illness and, 97–98, 132
Sirach (Ecclesiasticus), book of, 2, 36, 199, 251
Sloyan, Gerard S., xvii
Smith, D. Moody, xvii, 177
Socrates, xi
Son of God, 31, 32, 44, 48, 49, 50, 51, 53, 58, 131, 223, 225
Son of Man, 43, 53, 58–59, 74, 99, 107, 121, 124, 130, 131, 172, 183, 207, 225
Spong, John Shelby, x, 224
Suffering Servant, 57
Synoptic Gospels, xiii, xiv, 11, 14, 31, 51, 83, 94, 158, 161, 235, 253
    passion narrative and, 12, 215–16
    Son of Man and, 58
    See also John, Gospel of, and Synoptic Gospels

Talmud, 252
temple, 65, 68–71, 83, 114, 123, 175
"the Jews." *See* Jews, "the"

third day, 49, 66, 71
Thomas (apostle), x, 11, 53, 151, 175–76, 205, 239, 241, 242, 246–50, 262, 269, 287
Thomas, Gospel of, 249
Torah (Law), 36, 39, 42, 43, 44, 100–101, 110, 116, 118, 119, 121, 158, 218
trial of Jesus. *See* John, Gospel of, trial motif in
Trinity, 4, 56, 139, 180–81, 193–94, 264
truth, xi–xii, 26–27, 29, 34, 39, 40, 44, 56, 57–58, 74, 75, 121–22, 125, 135, 141, 176, 201, 202, 222–23, 235, 270, 274, 275, 278, 282, 284
    Spirit of, 178–79, 193, 196, 201–2, 270, 275
Twelve, the, 101, 104, 107, 108, 181, 207, 241, 247, 249, 262, 268
Tyndale, William, 174

unity, 137, 138, 202, 230, 264, 268, 276, 278

Valantasis, Richard, 38
Virgin Birth, 8, 55
Virgin Mary, 12, 53, 66–67, 230–31

Wells, H. G., xii
Wisdom literature, 2, 35, 100–101, 136, 177, 250–51
Wisdom of Solomon, book of, 2, 35, 140
wisdom personified, 35–36, 101, 140, 168
Witherington, Ben, xvii, 35, 97, 135
witness(es), witnessing, 28, 41, 74, 99, 120, 176, 179, 180, 193, 284
    women as, 251–55
world, the. *See* kosmos
Wright, N. T., xvii, 97